Broken Pieces

By Martha Perez

All rights to this book are reserved.

The rights to individual works are owned by the author. No part of this book may be copied or distributed in any printed or electronic form without permission from the publisher. This is a work of fiction. Any names, places, things, events, or incidents are the product of the authors' imaginations and are meant to be used for the sole purpose of entertainment, and any resemblance to actual persons–living or dead is entirely coincidental unless otherwise expressed.

Self-Published by: Martha Perez
ISBN-13: 978-0-9600477-0-3
ISBN-10: 0-9600477-0-0

Distribution Rights US & International

Cover image artist by Gary Karapet

Table of Contents

Authors Note

Chapter 1

Chapter 2

Chapter 3

Chapter 4

Chapter 5

Chapter 6

Chapter 7

Chapter 8

Chapter 9

Chapter 10

Chapter 11

Chapter 12

Chapter 13

Chapter 14

Chapter 15

Chapter 16

Chapter 17

Chapter 18

Chapter 19

Chapter 20

Chapter 21

Chapter 22

Chapter 23

Chapter 24

Chapter 25

Chapter 26

Chapter 27

Chapter 28

Chapter 29

Epilogue

Other Books by Martha Perez

About the Author

Authors Note

Writing this story about Abby's life was great. I always had this story in my heart: something inside of me told me to write and I wrote. I know you will enjoy this story as much as I loved writing it. I want to take this opportunity to say thanks to my daughter Patricia and my son Rudy and my two granddaughters: love you.

'Broken Pieces' is the emotional journey of a young Abby Pena, chronicling her life from childhood to the woman she becomes; it's a story of life, love, loss, struggle, pain, unpredictability, sorrow, healing and the many facets of human relationships that each of us can identify with in our sphere of existence.

Chapter 1

There's no guessing how we got here.

My sister and I were so young and so very happy with Dad. Now, we're just scared of the unknown... of the fact that no one wanted us.

We were living with Dad but because of his drinking problems, his depression and his womanizing ways, he wasn't capable of taking care of us anymore.

Life with him had been far from normal. He took us to bars once or twice a week. His friends were always drunk and seemed to enjoy being around us all the time. You know the type: drunk with touchy hands. So gross. Were it not for my older sister Megan who with good reason watched over me like a hawk and didn't trust anyone, there's no guessing what could've happened.

Dad couldn't take care of us or maybe he didn't want to anymore, so we had to go and live with our paternal grandma, for a while. I knew she really didn't want us either but who could blame her? We were my father's children, not hers. Megan grieved and sobbed all the while. She didn't want to leave our Dad. She was so depressed that she made me shed tears too. Megan hated to see me cry.

One time, she saw me weeping and startled me when she yelled, "Stop weeping, Abby! Just stop! God."

That made me stop. I'd never seen Megan so furious with me! I couldn't believe she was yelling, and I didn't know why. I realize now, that it may have been because she was so young, and yet, had so much responsibilities.

I slowly glanced up to face Megan and saw the pain in her big, cheerless, blue eyes. We were both weeping at that point. We knew with Mom passing away, our life would never be the same. Dad never talked about her. Megan remembered her, but I didn't. Or maybe I didn't want to. I was too young when she passed away. I'd blocked out a lot of things, but sometimes, bits and pieces of memories came back to me. They seemed like dreams, but when I shared them with Megan, she said they really happened. We embraced each other so tight; we didn't want to let go ever.

Megan was beautiful; rosy cheeks, fair skin, light brown hair that was silky smooth and fell over her face in slight waves. Her big blue eyes were in sharp contrast to her pale skin and thin pink lips. On the other hand, people said I was cute, and not that beautiful like Megan... but cute. I had dark brown hair with lots of tight natural curls. Though my eyes were hazel, I shared the same pale fair skin with Megan. I had what some would say, full cherubic lips that seemed like they had bitten into a whole bunch of cherries.

About a month later, after we were shipped off to live with my Grandma, we found out that Dad had got married. Well, Dad had mentioned to us that he was going to Mexico to find us a mother. So, we weren't that surprised. We both told him we didn't want a new mother, and that he was all we needed. But it seemed he went ahead anyway. We just wanted our Dad. So, we stayed with our

Grandma for a while, and he went to find that mother we didn't want. Megan cried for days.

I was five then and Megan was eight. Who at that age would understand what was going on?

Grandma's house was no better, and we knew she didn't want us there. But we had no choice in the matter.

What will happen to us now? How will we survive? What will Maria, Dad's new wife, think of us?

Only time would give us the answers to these questions.

Our nightmares had just begun. We always thought we would stay at Grandma's forever, not that her house was any better.

———

It all started on a stormy winter day. It was a Saturday afternoon in October 1966, when Dad picked us up from Grandma's house in Highland Park, California. Dad's apartment was just South on Figueroa St. which wasn't too far by car.

Dad smiled at Megan and me when he arrived; we didn't have a care in the world–we both were just really happy to see him. He said that he missed both of us so very much, that we both looked pretty and asked if we were wearing new dresses?

Megan smiled and said, "Yes, Daddy." She got a big huge squeeze from him. She loved Dad so much—don't get me wrong, I love him too. "Grandma made our dresses, Daddy."

"How about you, Abby? You look beautiful, just like your mother. Do you like your dress?"

I simply nodded, having always been the quiet one. Anyway, I didn't even remember what my mother looked like.

Grandma had gone all out with our dresses. Megan's was red velvet with white lace trimming. Mine was green velvet with white lace trim. Our hair was softly curled down to the length of our shoulder, with a silver barrette keeping them in place. We truly looked like dolls.

Dad held both our hands. "Ready to meet your new mommy?"

Megan pulled her hand away from him in anger. "She's not our Mom! She will never be my Mom, ever, never, ever. Why are you doing this, Daddy? I don't want to meet her." She started sobbing.

"You really have to stop acting like that! Megan, you are scaring Abby! Go get your jacket, both of you"— now Dad was yelling at us–"And stop crying like a baby. Maria is nice and is waiting to meet you both." He said thanks to Grandma for taking care of us.

She smiled, "You better take care of those girls, son."

Dad hugged her and said his goodbye.

We walked to his car, and he opened the door for us. No one said a word. The gloom of the heavy rain fitted everyone's mood. Dad had never yelled at us or spanked us before. He always said he loved us more than life itself. So why was he doing this to us? We couldn't understand. Why? Things were changing and not for the good.

Megan just stared out the window at the pouring rain and never said a word throughout the whole drive back home. I just played with my fingers, not comprehending but knowing that something was wrong. I was just playing with my fingers—I was a nervous little girl.

Finally, we got to the apartment and Dad opened the car door for us. Megan took my hand and whispered in my ear, "It will be fine, Abby. She will never be our mother."

I smiled at her, trusting her and feeling much better, because, Megan was truly like my Mom, friend, and big sister all rolled in one. Looking back, that must have been rough for her, since she had been so young herself. We could only wish for the best when it came to our Dad.

Dad lived in the bottom apartment, way in the back, so we had to pass all the four apartments in the front. It was still raining hard, so we ran as fast as we could so that we wouldn't get wet. And there she was, standing with the door open, with a fake smile. Dad smiled back and told her something in Spanish.

Megan had a look of disgust on her face and she whispered to me, "OMG, she doesn't even speak English! I can't believe this! Can you believe that, Abby? She doesn't speak English! It can't get any worse than this, could it?"

Well, that's what we thought. We were so wrong.

Dad pulled us both closer to meet his new wife. Megan frowned and then smirked. Maria had short brown hair, huge brown eyes, and a big black mole on her right cheek. Kind of on the heavy side, she wore a black pencil skirt and a white blouse. She had slippers on, so we guessed we were staying in for the evening. Megan continued to look her up and down.

Our Dad was a handsome man. He had hazel eyes, thin and tall, with a nice tan; he had full lips that often turned into a wry smile and jet black hair that was always trimmed short. He wore nice suits. Don't know what he saw in her. She was not pretty at all. Megan was not warming up to her... not one bit. And maybe it was because Maria's smile did not make us feel welcome. If looks could kill, she would be dead from Megan's stare. I noticed that Maria never looked at Megan; her eyes were only on me. I kept my eyes down, because to tell you the truth, she was kind of scary. And she kept staring at me.

Dad said, "This is Megan Lisa Pena, the oldest."

Maria replied, "Migin," and nodded her head."

Megan got so angry. "My Name is Megan, not Migin." Dad glared at her, then looks at both of us with a frown. "She doesn't speak English," Megan says to Dad. "It's not my fault! You always told me to correct people if they're saying it wrong, so I'm correcting her."

Dad did not look happy, but he took my hand and introduced me next. "Maria, this is Abigail Marie Pena."

Shyly looking up at her, I whispered to Dad, "Tell her to call me Abby."

Maria nodded again and said, "Abe."

Megan laughed so loud it made Dad more upset, but he continued, "Abby looks just like her mother."

Maria looked at me and frowned.

We didn't know how to talk to her. We didn't know how to speak Spanish.

Finally, with the introductions over, Maria told Dad that she made dinner.

Megan whispered, "Guess we're not going out to dinner. We have to eat her food." She rolled her eyes.

Maria pointed to the table and we followed with heavy steps.

The apartment was not that large, just two bedrooms. Of course, Dad and Maria had the master bedroom. The walls were the color of ivory. There was a full-size bed, a wooden dresser, two nightstands with plain lamps, and some pictures of Megan and me with Dad.

We were happy with him before he got married. Okay, he had a problem drinking. He was not perfect. But still, it had been better when we were alone with him. He had kid's books in one of the nightstands; he would read to us sometimes when we got scared at night. Yeah, he drank a lot but we were together. And that's all that mattered to us. Things felt different now and it was.

The kitchen was really small and simple. It was painted white. There was just enough room for a fridge and a stove. There was also a dining room with a wooden table with four chairs next to the living room. A brown recliner with a couch to match along with a black and white television completed the room.

We all sat down to eat dinner. Afterwards, we all complimented her on the food. She did know how to cook.

Dad had started to get restless. It was time for his drink. He wanted to drink. We knew all too well that he would be leaving soon. He sent us to bed early and Megan asked him if could tuck us in bed.

Daddy said, "Not tonight baby girls."

I frowned. Megan got enraged again. "You're leaving us alone with her? Don't leave, Daddy, please don't."

"Okay! Okay!" Dad gave in. "Okay, I'll tuck you in."

"Thank you, Daddy." Megan replied with a gigantic smile.

We jumped to our beds, and he kissed us both on our cheeks. Dad didn't read to us, but he sang a lullaby until we fell asleep. Then he left the room, and the house, to get some beer.

The next morning, we woke up to a loud thumping sound. We jumped out of bed, confused. Maria had entered the room, looking furious. She rushed to Megan and pushed her roughly as she told her to get dressed. Although we couldn't understand her, her message had been quite clear. Maria continued to push her towards the closet.

"Where is Daddy?" I asked.

Maria strode towards me next, and I had to step back. She pushed me so firmly I stumbled to the floor.

Megan came out of the room, "Hey, don't touch Abby like that." Megan shouted.

Since she didn't speak English, I was sure no one understood what the other was saying. But that didn't matter. Maria didn't care, and we knew that.

Maria grabbed Megan's arm and tossed her in the closet. Then, she grabbed me by the hair and kicked the side of my small leg. I could feel it burn and she then pushed me onto the bed.

She could hear Megan sobbing inside the closet. "No, don't hit Abby, please! Don't! Not her."

She told me to get dressed and threw some clothes on the bed. I tried to get dressed really fast before Maria got any angrier. I was trembling so heavily, but I made an effort to be quiet. I cried silent tears. Where's Daddy? I wondered... or maybe, prayed. We never got hit or pushed around like that before.

Maria finally calmed down. With gestures, I knew she was telling Megan to get out of the closet, and was herding us out of the room to eat breakfast. I didn't really want to eat. My leg was hurting so much. I lifted my dress and saw a huge bruise.

Megan came to me and whispered, "Abby, you've got to eat or she'll hurt you again."

My tears continued to fall slowly down my cheeks.

Megan gently held my arm and gave it a squeeze to reassure me, then she hugged me tight. "It will be fine, Abby!"

I didn't believe it, but I nodded at her through my tears, "Love you."

She looked at me with sad eyes. "Love you too, Abby."

We waited for Dad. A day passed, and another, but Dad was a no-show. Maria was in a bad mood all that time, hated he was gone and took it out on us. It had been two days since he left to get some beer.

One time, I was sitting in my bed and when I glanced up, Maria was staring at me, with her middle finger flexing for me to go to her. Just a few minutes ago, she had told Megan to take a bath, but Megan wouldn't. I knew Maria was calling me over to take it out on me.

As I approached, she grabbed me by my hair so roughly, I cried out, "Stop it, you're hurting me. I want my Daddy." She dragged me across the room and was saying something to me in Spanish... I don't know what! All I knew was it sounded bad and it couldn't mean anything good. I couldn't fight her. I was only five. So, I let her smack me as long as she wanted. What else could I do? I was too small.

I never mentioned it to Megan. I didn't want to worry her. I had bruises on my legs, arms, and stomach. My whole body was in pain.

Maria told me to go to bed. Megan was asleep already. She didn't let me take a bath that night or eat.

I heard Dad come home late that night, falling, and bumping on the walls. I could hear Maria telling him many things in Spanish, and then there was only silence.

Dad opened our door, and came in quietly towards us. I didn't want him to know I was still awake. He kissed Megan's forehead, then turned to me and kissed me on my cheek. Then he walked out of the room.

I cried myself to sleep that night, wondering why this was happening to us.

It was Monday morning, and Dad came to our room to wake us up. Megan was so happy to see him she hugged him as soon as she woke up. She was cuddling in his arms. We had to go to a new school but he still had to register us. He would be late for work so we got dressed as quickly as we could.

When I came out of the room, Dad saw me from the door and frowned. He said, "Come here, Abby," and hugged me and asked, "What happened to your leg and arm?"

I just told him that I fell hard playing outside. I didn't want to cause more trouble and I was afraid of Maria. If he only knew we didn't even get to go outside.

"Baby, be more careful, ok?" he said as he gave me a huge kiss on my cheek.

That's what I loved about Dad; he gives the biggest kisses and hugs. But what happened while he was gone will be forever remembered.

Dad took us to school, and thank God, Maria didn't come with us.

In the car, Megan looked at me and frowned. "Are you okay, Abby?" She was always worried about me.

"Yes, I'm fine."

She held my hand and didn't let go.

I really didn't feel like going to school. I was in pain and confused, but I realized that anywhere away from Maria would be better.

"Ok, Mr. Pena."

Dad smiled mischievously at the lady at the front desk. He told her to call him Andres. He could be such a flirt and it always worked.

She smiled. "Nice to meet you, Andres. I'm Candy Taylor."

Dad told her she had a beautiful name and the lady's face lit up with delight at the compliment.

Behind him, Megan was rolling her eyes. She tugged on Daddy's hand. She looked like she was going to gag and mumbled, Oh God. "Come on, it's getting late, Daddy."

He frowned at Megan and she rolled her eyes again. Dad just stared at us and continued his conversation with Ms. Candy.

Finally, we were enrolled and he said goodbye. "Have a nice day, baby girls, Love you both." He didn't forget to give us a kiss before he left. He said Maria will be picking us up. We both frowned at that, but he didn't notice and left in a hurry.

Being the new girls in school didn't go very well for us. Megan hit a girl because she kept making fun of her shoes while I was getting bullied by a boy named Jimmy. He constantly pushed me around, took my pencils away, laughing while he did it. I don't remember much of our first day in school. It was horrible anyway.

I got out of my class earlier than Megan, so I waited outside. I was expecting Maria to be there already, but she wasn't. Two hours later, Megan came out and saw me waiting for her.

"What are you still doing here, Abby?"

I looked down at the ground.

"She didn't come for you? That ugly bitch." She grabbed my hand and started to walk home fast.

It felt like we were walking forever, but that was okay. It was nice to just be with Megan. She was making me laugh, like she always did. So I could forget what was going on. But you can't just forget when people who were supposed to protect you, treat you badly, and become so mean; it was hard to understand why things were the way they were. But at that moment, everything was ok. We held hands and protected each other like we always did.

We finally made it to the apartment, and Maria was waiting for us. She looked furious again! So, we just ignored her the way we knew best and tried not to get in her way. Maria didn't even care how we came home. I sometimes wondered how Dad would feel if he knew how she treated us.

She told Megan to go and clean the bathroom. Of course, Megan told her she had homework to do. Well, she didn't care. She dragged Megan towards the bathroom so hard that after that, we just did what she told us to do.

Maria came up to me next and pushed me towards the kitchen. With the language barrier, pushing seemed to be her favorite way of communicating with us. I guessed she wanted me to wash the dishes. I got a chair so I could reach the sink. Maria waited for me to stand on top of the chair, and then for no reason at all, she pushed me. I fell, my head hitting the cabinet. As I lay on the floor, she kicked me on my leg. Again! I tried to get away from her, but I was too dizzy. So, I just laid there and let her kick me–all I could do was cry.

Megan and I didn't eat dinner that night. Dad came home late all week, having fun with his drinking buddies, going to bars. We waited each night for him, but he arrived late and went straight to bed.

The more time passed, the angrier Maria became. Lately, her hatred seemed to be coming out of her pores in full force. At least she wasn't hitting us too much, just pushing or pulling our hair.

Weeks went by, and finally, Christmas season arrived. We were so excited. We had a small but beautiful tree. Dad bought it for us the other night when he came home. Maybe he was trying to make up for his absence or felt guilty. So he brought the tree and some gifts. Grandma had also sent us some dresses she made. They were very pretty, made of red velvet with white trimming. Dad bought us shoes and ribbons for our hair, so we could wear it for Christmas.

We were having a grand time, but then, Dad got a phone call.

Megan stared at me and said, "I know he's going to leave, Abby. I can't believe he's going to leave."

She was right. He told Maria he was leaving but that he'll be back in a couple of hours. I could sense Maria's anger. She shouted at him and pointed at us. I knew she was telling him to take us with him. She didn't want to care for us anymore. That we weren't her daughters. It was quite obvious from her face and gestures.

"No!" my Dad said.

Maria was furious.

He said goodbye to us, and we were both sobbing as we clung to him. We didn't want him to leave. We just knew what would happen when he was gone.

"Abby and Megan, I'll be right back. Don't worry, you'll be alright! I won't miss Christmas with my baby girls"

"Megan, grab his arm, please! Don't leave! Please, don't leave!" Megan pleaded.

I hugged him tight, but Dad pried us off him gently and assured us he'd be back, and he left us sobbing. Maria glowered as she stood there in silence, looking at us like we were prey. We were terrified to even look at her.

As soon as Dad left and we were alone again, she started slapping Megan in the face for no apparent reason, all along, mumbling in Spanish. She caught Megan by her hair and threw her in the room. All I could hear was Megan crying. Maria then turned to face me.

She grabbed me by my hair and it hurt, but I didn't cry out loud. As young as I was, I sensed that my crying caused her satisfaction and made her hit me more. When she finished releasing her anger at me, she pushed me in the closet where I stayed the night.

I don't know why, but I had felt safe there, in the darkness, where I could not see Maria. Other kids would have been scared of being in the dark, but not me. The closet had become my safe haven. All I could do was cry. Leaning my head on the door, I sat for hours wishing I was elsewhere, dreaming of better days.

Then, I heard a soft knock at the door. It was Megan with two gifts in her hands. She smiled at me and told me the bitch was finally asleep. Then, she looked at me with a puckered brow.

"Are you okay?"

I hugged her and started crying. "No, I'm not okay. Where's our real mom? Why won't Daddy stay home with us?

Megan hugged me tight. "Our real mom is in heaven, and we'll see her one day, okay? It'll be fine, Abby, you'll see. Now, open your gift."

So, we both opened the gifts our Dad bought for us. We both got a pretty doll, and we played for a while, then greeted each other

Merry Christmas, and fell asleep in the miniature closet; our arms around each other, woeful that this was happening to us, but thankful we always had each other.

We woke up early that morning, and Megan and I rushed to our bedroom before Maria arose. I started to get dressed, wondering how our day would be. Then, I heard our Dad talking to Maria, who acted like nothing happened when Dad was around.

Dad called Megan and me to the living room. We ran to him, hugging him with all the love we felt for him. He swooped us both in his arms and gave us a big hug. He didn't even realize that we slept in the closet, and we never told him either. He tells us he loves both of us. We never looked at or spoke to Maria.

We opened the rest of our gifts. Spending the day with our Dad was wonderful. For the first time since he brought us home to Maria, we got a chance to play outside. It was a happy time for us. It was probably killing Maria to see us so carefree in those moments, but we didn't care. It had been nice to feel the breeze blowing on our faces. That was the best gift we received that season. We missed Dad. He had his faults, but he had tried his best to take care of us.

He wanted to take Maria out and he took us to Grandma for the night. We didn't understand why it had to be on that day. It was supposed to be Family Day. Although I knew Dad loved us, I couldn't help but notice how much he was changing. It didn't surprise us anymore. He had stopped singing to us, and seldom spent quality time with us anymore. Well, he was hardly home.

We were not excited to go to Grandma's house since all they did there was drink, play cards, and smoke. It smelled like a bar. But we were happy not to be with Maria, even if it was for just one night.

Grandma had made us a very nice dinner. She was a great cook, and we loved her cooking. Everything was homemade–the whole turkey dinner. Grandma had seven children; three girls' and four boys. Her daughters' names were Marissa, Teresa and Victoria, and her sons were Mario, Lorenzo, Dad, and Paul. They were all there, except for our Dad, and they all enjoyed drinking. Paul, one of our cousins was there. He was Megan's age—eight. We loved Paul. He was fun to be around and was always getting in trouble. He would get hit a lot, just like me, so he and I had a lot in common. Not Megan though. She fought with him a lot.

Paul was very cute. He was tall for his age; light brown eyes, dark brown, messy hair, but it was his huge smile that made everyone notice him. He also was a protector. I noticed that he didn't smile very often, always looking so serious even at a young age. Paul was our cousin but to me, he was more like a big brother.

Since they were all busy drinking and playing cards, Paul called us aside and said, "We're going to the park."

Megan told him it's too dark.

"So? Come on, stop being scared. Let's go." Paul tried to convince Megan until she said okay. "It's time to have some fun!" he shouted.

We ran on the sidewalk on the way to the park. God, it had felt so good not to have someone pushing us around, or hitting us, or being scared to wake up not knowing if she'd finally decide to kill us that day. With Maria, we just didn't know, she had so many mood swings.

Megan and I enjoyed the feel of the breeze on our faces. We were all holding each other's hands. We all felt so carefree. It was cold, but we didn't care. We started to push each other's shoulder as we played around, laughing so hard at Paul's jokes that it hurt, but in such a good way. That was freedom. We wished everyday was Christmas. That day held happy memories that we didn't have much of.

When it was time to go home after that fun day in the park, Megan and I felt sad about going home... to lose that freedom. Without knowing it, I craved it as a child, even dreamt about it. But we both had to live with Maria's resentment. At least we had that memory in the park. I would wait for that freedom again. All my life, I would wait to feel that kind of freedom again.

Megan woke me out of my thoughts.

"Abby are you listening to me or not? Are you daydreaming again? Because if you are you'd better tell me about it! No secrets, Abby!" So, promise me that you'll tell me everything okay!"

I couldn't help but smile at Megan. I nodded my head. "I don't have any secrets."

"Ok, then tell me."

I frowned. "I was just thinking of the park."

We both smiled at the memory, something we didn't do much of.

As we heard Maria calling us, we returned to reality, and boy, we ran as fast as we could. But we weren't fast enough to please her.

It had always been and would always be that way. Maria hated us. Megan mumbled what a bitch she was. Megan had learned fast how to say bad words, although she knew that it wasn't right to curse.

Maria was never warm even when Dad was around, and as soon as he left, she would unleash all her anger and resentment out on us. Maria was the wicked stepmother, and it was the worst year of our life.

Dad was not aware of the abuse we went through. We kept it from him. I don't know why.

Months passed, and the situation didn't change. Dad continued drinking and not coming home until the time came when Maria had decided she had enough of us.

Saturday, early in the morning, she packed all our clothes and put them in trash bags. Then, she shoved us out of the door, shooing us like flies. Once outside, she came out with our belongings and gestured for us to follow her to the corner by a crosswalk. She motioned for us to stay put, and we stood there with our bags beside us, not knowing what would happen next.

The tears started to flow down our cheeks. I don't know how long we stood there, and to make matters worse, it began to thunder really loud, and the rain came down hard. It was terrifying–Megan hugged me and said it would be alright. I was cold and had a runny nose, and my body was shivering.

Maria told us to wait on the street corner. That's what we did. We had no place else to go. We kept looking for Grandma or one of our uncles to come for us. But nobody came. We were all alone–two little girls standing in the pouring rain–broken into pieces. That day, it was like Megan, and I had died. We were buried six-feet down–and no mourners came around. Then a car pulled up, and a man rolled down his window and said, "What are you two little girls doing out here in the pouring rain? It's a big storm coming; you see how dark the sky is? He opens the back door, "Get in the car."

Megan looked at me. We both knew that Dad always told us never to get in the car with strangers, but we were going to die if we stayed out here in this storm. I was already cold and shaking, and it was thundering, and a loud roaring sound like a tornado was coming.

"Where's daddy, Megan?" my voice crackling.

"Come on, Abby get in…"

"No, I don't want to."

She grabbed my hand, "We can't stay out here. Abby, get in the car."

"Yes, get in the car, Abby," the strange man with the creepy voice said to me.

I reluctantly got in the car… and Megan hugged me to keep me warm. The man turned to face us in the backseat.

"You girls look like you're hungry?" We didn't say anything. "I'll take you to my house, and my wife will cook you some breakfast and get you some dry clothes." That sounded good, but what if the man didn't have a wife or any dry clothes? What if we never saw our daddy or grandma ever again? I whispered in

Megan's ear, "I'm scared, Daddy said never get in the car with a stranger." She didn't say anything. I could see the fright in Megan's eyes.

The man said, "Hey girls, I'm going to pull in the service station here and get some gas. Do you want some candy or something to drink?

"No sir, thank you," Megan said.

"Well you both get out of the car and come with me inside the store."

He opens the door and we get out of the car. He grabs my arm, I said, "Please, don't touch me."

Then Megan pushes the man against the pump, "Leave her alone!" The man stumbles and falls to the ground.

"Run! Abby!!! Run Abby Run!!!"

Abby grabs my arm and we start running. "Run Abby!!!! Run faster! Keep Running Abby!!" Megan was almost dragging me on the ground. Then she sees a telephone booth and calls the operator and gave her grandma's number. We were so scared, looking around to make sure that creepy man wasn't following us. Megan spoke to Grandma crying, to come get us. I could hear Grandma screaming, "Oh God!!! My babies, what happened, where are you girls?" Megan was smart she knew what to say I had no idea where we were.

"We are at the Piggly Wiggly store."

One hour later my uncle brought grandma and we ran into her arms. We were safe.

Chapter 2

Here we go again, back and forth. Hopefully we stay here a little longer. Spending a year with Dad and Maria was a nightmare. We didn't hear from Dad, so we didn't know for sure what Dad did about Maria kicking us out like two little puppies in the street. Now we live with Grandma in a big yellow house— six bedrooms, three bathrooms, and a fence around the house. There was also a small back yard with a little house in the back. Grandpa had beautiful flowers in the front yard that made the house look nice.

Although we were happy to be there, we felt uncomfortable. We knew that no one wanted us. Grandma reminded us every day that we were lucky to be here, that we could have been in foster care. At this point, we couldn't care less about where we lived; we knew it would be the same. We wouldn't get those hugs, kisses and love that you need as a child. At least we got them sometimes from Dad, but reality kicked in; no more Dad or love, just sadness and emptiness. Megan was miserable, missing Dad the most. I did too, but it is what it is, we just can't change anything. He will always put his drinking before Megan and me. We had to accept that because it was our reality. It's hard enough without him. We will miss him an awful lot. I'm strong and that's what counts right now, we truly have to suck it up, or we will not survive.

We were staring at the living room, our hearts felt empty. Holding our bags with trembling hands we look around. Grandma had good taste. The house was beautiful. Everything was clean. Well it was spotless: light ivory walls, everything matching, even the couches in the front room matched and the dining room a large wooden table which could easily seat eight people. Well, we were looking over everything even though we stayed here before. We really didn't notice a lot here earlier, but we had a feeling we will be here for a while and call it home.

I glanced up to look at Megan and noticed how sad she had looked, when Paul, our uncle, calls out, "AB!" He always called me that for short. I like that nick name from him. "Hey, AB!" He holds my arm and turns me around and around in circles. "God! AB you're lucky that I live here," and with a huge smile Megan rolls her eyes.

"Really! You really think it's going to be peachy because you're here?" Give me a break will you, Paul. You're just trouble that's what you are."

Paul rolls his eyes back at her. "Who cares if I'm bad or not: AB is happy to see me. Right Abigail Marie?" Me grinning at him, he gives me his great huge smile again. I really love that smile. To me, it was a feeling of comfort and protection, and I always felt safe with him. Paul always made Megan have more angry outbursts than anyone I've ever known, but that was Paul.

Funny, he showed he cared in so many different ways. Sometimes he's funny or pushing our shoulder in a gentle sort of way telling jokes. I was happy being around him: we just got along. Paul asks Megan, "So what happened? The witch from the west kick you both out? That's what I heard?"

Megan frowned. "If you already know why ask?"

He scowled. "Just wanted to know!"

"Ok," Megan says, "Well stop rubbing it in okay! It's not funny; that bitch didn't want us."

In no time at all Grandma told us to put our stuff away. The house had two floors so we went upstairs. That day was passed without any major hiccups. I and Megan felt oddly out of place, but really there was nothing much we could do. This was our new reality and we were grateful to have a new start; even if that meant we had to start at a different school once again. Basically, change after change. Once again, we knew life would be tough.

Grandma was making our clothes for school. "Your Dad didn't give me money for you both, so you are going to wear what I make. Also, we have rules in this house. You will listen very closely. You both will go to school.

After school, Megan will clean the restrooms, all three of them." Megan starts to roll her eyes. Grandma stops with a scowl, looks at both of us and says, "Don't ever roll your eyes again because I'll hit both of you very hard. So as I was saying, then you'll wash dishes and Abby will help. And make sure to teach Abby everything, do you hear me Megan?"

"Yes, I hear you Grandma."

"Okay then, I don't like repeating myself and don't call me Grandma anymore. Call me Ma. Since I'll be taking care of you both, I will be like your mother so people won't ask too many questions."

The moving around, and the many changes we were going through was taking a toll on us. It's a cold and cloudy Monday in December. I and Megan and are getting ready to join our new school. Ma bought us some underwear. They have a print that says Monday through Sunday. "So I guess I'll wear my Monday underwear." Megan start to giggle. We have new socks. Ma made our dresses, and skirts and white blouses–she also bought us new shoes. Ma tells us to take good care of our clothes because she doesn't have money to be buying us stuff all the time, so it's up to us to take care of our things. We're nodding as she talks; all we could say is ok.

We are starting school two weeks before Christmas, and then will have two weeks off; I'm quietly hoping we don't have a Christmas like last year when we were staying with Dad and Maria. Dad never even called us. I know it's been a couple of days. We are hoping he will come to see us on Christmas. Ma always has a huge party for Christmas Eve. I realized I was getting nervous about the new school. I was scared of being bullied like it was in the last school Megan and I attended. Fingers crossed that it's better than that school At least I will be in first grade. I just turned six and we'll all be in the same school at least for another two years. Megan and Paul, they are nine.

Ma calls all of us to come down to eat breakfast when we step in the kitchen and look at Ma. Megan remarked, "Oh my God she's not going dress like that is she?"

Paul laughs. "Yep! Oh yeah she is."

Ma had no makeup, and she had a dirty dress that had flour all over the front because she made flour tortillas this morning—well, every morning, and that's a fact. Ma had slippers on; her hair had a bad perm. All messy, she is a pretty lady with bronze colored skin. She had big features: huge hazel eyes, full red lips. When she wears makeup, she looks beautiful. So, anyway we go to school. Megan is mumbling something. Ma is getting angry and tells her to be quiet! Paul is laughing at this point, making me giggle, but I tell him to stop giggling else Ma won't like it.

Ma didn't change clothes so we were absolutely embarrassed when we saw the lady at the front desk where Ma registered us.

Paul goes to his class; Megan was told classroom number ten. Mrs. Smith, the lady at the front desk then turned to me and said, "You're class number six." Ma told us to walk after school together. We say bye and she left.

I walk to quietly to my classroom. Of course, everyone is staring at me like some alien walked in. There were some kids that laughed at me like I just came from the circus. I looked around looking to see if there was anyone who could be a new friend. That's when my eyes settled on this one boy who kept a steady gaze at me. He was smiling sweetly when I felt the gaze of someone behind me. It was Mr. William, my class teacher.

Mr. William smiles. "Hello Abigail." And welcomed me into class.

I give him the papers that Mrs. Smith provided for me and he reads it. "Well Abigail Marie Pena, take a seat please! Next to Ricky right in that corner on the left."

I do as told and take a seat, and of course Ricky is continuing to give me a wide, gleeful smile.

I see Megan at lunch. She is not a happy camper at all. If looks could kill they would. She calls out to me, "Come here!"

I glanced up at her: she has a scratch on her face, and made a face when I asked her, "What happened?"

"Don't worry about it!"

Paul sees us and joins us. "What going on? AB you like your class? I heard your teacher is Mr. William. He's a good teacher AB." Giggling a little because he's tickling me at my side, then he looks up to ask Megan, "How do you like your class Megan?" Then Paul stops in his tracks. "What happened to you? First day in school and you're already fighting."

"I have problems," Megan tells him. "Shut up!" Megan shouts irritated.

"Alright, just saying," Paul laughs.

I hate this school! I hate everything right now! Megan pushes Paul away and starts weeping out of frustration. I can't watch Megan cry like this, I've seen her being strong and she was crumbling before my eyes. Paul gets my hand. "Come on AB; I'll walk you to your class." Paul knows how sad I get, all nervous biting my bottom lip. "Don't worry about

Meg AB! Okay? Everything is going to be fine."

How much more do I have to hear that! Everything will be fine when it's clearly not. I stare down to the ground rubbing my shoe on the concrete. "You don't want to be late AB. Your teacher is nice, you don't want to make him upset."

I'm five minutes early so I take my seat at my desk. I'm just thinking about Megan when I notice Ricky just smiling at me again. He leans over me so close that I could almost feel his breathing on my neck. Ricky is asking if I ever played marbles.

I said, "No!" puzzled at the strange question.

"I could teach you Abigail." He said.

"Call me Abby."

"Okay Abby, do you want to learn?"

"Umm, no that's for boys."

He frowns like if I just made him taste sour lemons or made him feel bad! I just try to ignore him. My ignoring him doesn't help change anything because he just keeps on staring at me not knowing what else to do or say. I was nervously biting my bottom lip, hesitant to talk to him, but finally said, "Ricky maybe you could teach me, you know how to play the marble game sometime."

I could see he was very pleased with this request as his eyes twinkled with child-like glee. He says, "Give me your hand Abby."

Well, I don't like anyone touching me, not that he would know this. Unfolding my hand, he slips the most beautiful red shining marble I had ever seen. "Here, that's for you, so when I teach you tomorrow at recess, you can use that, okay?"

I'm nodding my head and hoping he would just stop bothering me for once; at the same time, he's a very sweet boy. I know Ricky is being nice. Mr. Williams asks Ricky Owen, "Past papers please!"

That's when I really take a good look at Rick. He's really sweet and cute. He has clear blue eyes which look like the color of the ocean. His hair is messy, light brown with a tint of blonde. His skin is pale like mine. He's wearing a blue sweater and blue pants that make his blue eyes stand out.

School finishes and as I walk out of class, I see Paul waiting for me and Megan to walk home together just as Ma had said. However, I don't see Megan around. I think to myself that she may have had a problem again and had gone home alone without us. My stomach is in knots again just thinking about it.

Chapter 3

I walked home hurriedly with thoughts of Megan clouding my mind; I wondered where she was and hoped I'd find her home safe and sound. Finally, Home sweet home! I go running up the stairs to find Megan cleaning the house. I changed clothes trying my best to hurry. I didn't want Meg to be alone doing all this work alone.

"Okay Megan! I'm here to help!"

"I want to be alone Abby!"

"But I have to help you; Ma will get angry at me."

Megan gets really irritated and screams at me. "Get out of here! Told you, I want to be alone, so listen!"

Startled by Meg's behavior, I was sure that something was bothering her. I decide to leave her and finish my homework.

One hour later, Ma calls me downstairs. Ma looks furious because she thinks I didn't help Megan. She didn't know I offered to help and

Megan wanted me to leave her alone. She's asking why I didn't help Megan. I'm ready to tell her when she gets the belt. She even wets it and whips it right on my leg. It stung so bad that I found myself crying out of pain, tears were running down my cheeks like a waterfall. I didn't know why I was getting punished when all I tried to do was help Megan. Well it doesn't matter now, as I look at the bruises on my upper thigh. At least I didn't have to go from one house to the other for the same treatment. And the bruise will stay covered under my clothes.

Ma issues a dire warning, saying, "The next time you don't listen, it will be worse. We have rules in this house."

I didn't have a chance to find out what happened to Megan at school that made her so upset. She was still upstairs, as I'm trying to smooth over the stinging sensation on my bruised thigh.

Paul came into Megan and my room. "Hey! AB I heard you got hit because of Megan?" Paul looked concerned.

I wince in pain and tell him. "Don't tell Megan, Paul please?"

"Don't tell?" he says. "Why? AB it wasn't your fault!"

"So just don't tell her k?"

"Oh! AB you are so feisty for a little thing." I stare at Paul my eyes pooling up with tears. He holds me to reassure me and says, "OK! AB I won't tell!" Relieved, I hug him and grin from ear to ear. "I'm sorry you got hit AB. You have to follow the rules even if Megan says no!"

"I know."

The next day we all go to school. I'm sitting at my desk. Megan hasn't spoken yet about what transpired at school yesterday. I try to push thoughts about what happened as I try to concentrate in class.

Mr. William says we have a treat today. "We are making Christmas tree cards for art today, so chose someone for your partner to work with. Help each other."

In no time, Ricky is by my side. Emily's face is turning green with jealousy; even though I'm not quite sure why. Betty walks straight to us. She smacks her fist on top of our desk. Ricky looks up. "What do you want Betty? Or are you just being your own mean self again? Well?"

"I'm waiting."

"Well! What do you want?"

"Shut up Ricky."

At this point she is staring at me from her head to toe. Ricky appears flustered and pleads, "Why can't you leave us alone? Finally, she walked away with a huff. So now, there was Betty & Emily to contend with in class because of Ricky. I was however captivated by the art of making the Christmas card because it's art. And I always loved making art.

I heard we have art class every Wednesday and that was something to look forward to. Of course, it didn't help that Ricky was copying my work for whatever the reason who knows.

I made all my ornaments gold, red and blue. It looked so pretty! We glued it together to make a Christmas card. Doing art is so much fun; it makes me think of the good things and helps me to forget the bad. Even if it was just for a little time, making the artwork made me happy.

Ricky asks, "Who is that card for?"

God. I roll my eyes like Megan so often does and wish he would just leave me alone.

"It's for my Ma." I said.

"Is that your mother?"

"Yes, she is," I bit my lip knowing full well I was lying but I didn't want to go into all the details with Ricky. And she really is our mother because she takes care of us.

"So who did you make yours for?" I ask to break his train of thought surrounding my lie.

"You!" He gazes intently at my face and says, "For you Abby! Made it for you."

"Why?"

"Because I like you, I want to be friends that's why."

It's the first time I felt someone really wanted to be my friend. Feeling shy, I looked up at Ricky, "Okay we could be friends. Anyway, you are going to be my marble game buddy," I said with a grin.

Mr. Williams says, "Okay, lunch time." We break for recess.

Rick and I walk down the hall. He has a lunch box with him. I never bring lunch because Ma never gives me money. I just don't eat. I could see from the corner of my eyes that Ricky just kept staring at me. "Hey! Abby, before we play, I have two delicious peanut butter jelly sandwiches if you want…"

I don't even let him finish, saying "No!" right away because I don't want him to feel sorry for me.

"Hey come on Abby! Eat with me."

I don't like this feeling, just wish he would leave me alone. I know he's being sweet in sharing his lunch box with me and he'll keep insisting till I take a bite, so I reluctantly agree. He gives me a huge smile. We eat lunch together. My stomach growls. I hadn't realized how hungry I really was till I took a bite of that yummy sandwich. It felt like heaven.

Ricky is going to teach me the marble game and I'm ready for it. "OK put your thumb next to your finger and flick it, so you could hit the other marble of your choice."

I tried a couple of times, guessing that it takes practice. It is not as easy as it seemed. Ricky was sure having fun seeing me missing all the shots I took. It was lots of fun playing with him; and though I couldn't hit a single marble, I was already looking forward to playing with him again. I thank him for lunch and for playing with me. I was pleased with how school went today.

As I finished class, I see Megan waiting for me. I join her and we both start walking home. For a while, we both were quiet and then she said she missed Dad. I knew that but there wasn't much to do than to wait for Dad to come and visit us. It was months now since we last saw him. I tell her that the best we can do is to obey Ma and finish school properly.

On our way home, I was glad that Megan finally spoke something! Her silence was unbearable. I go quickly into our room to change and get my homework done but along the way I wonder where Paul is. I haven't seen him yet. So I go to his room looking for him.

I open the door just a bit, forgetting to knock. I see him lying in his bed face down. He sensed someone was in his room so he turned to see who's at the door. His body is full of bruises. "Go away AB, just go away."

I don't say anything to him. I walk closer to his bed and seat myself beside him. He was badly bruised; I knew how it stung as I remembered the bruising on my upper thigh. I hold his hands because there was nothing I could do to stop his sobbing.

Ma must have hit him for some reason and she hits really bad. She uses belts and shoes and cords; they really hurt. I sit with him for some time and then go back to my room, feeling sad but I don't want Ma to find out that I was in his room. She tells us that we're not allowed in any rooms; they're only to be used for sleeping. Those are the rules. I finish my homework and this time Megan doesn't tell me to leave her alone when I try to help her. We go about quietly with our chores at home. All along, I was thinking of Paul, who's in his room, pretending to sleep but no doubt wincing in pain like I was a couple of days earlier. I'm just relieved I wasn't around at home to see him getting beat up. It's too painful and he looked terrible. Megan didn't know he got beat and neither did she know about Ma beating me that day. It's better that way. I don't want her to get sadder and more miserable than she was already from missing Dad.

It's Friday and it's just one week more to Christmas Eve but it's been far better than our previous school here. And I think it's because of Rick. I call him Rick while everyone else calls him Ricky. Being in school and having a friend like him makes all the bad thoughts go away. For some reason, he makes me forget and things seem like they're normal, even it's for just a little while.

I make two sandwiches and hide my lunch bag. We aren't allowed rummaging in the kitchen, not even for lunch for school. I get so hungry by lunchtime that I can't help but eat what Rick offers from his lunch. He always makes sure I eat something so this time I'll bring a bag of lunch to share.

School has been so much fun. I am getting better at the marble game, and Rick seems pleased with the progress I've made. What I like about Rick: he's not a sore loser. Kind of did feel badly for him at lunch though. The sandwich it was—well let's just say it didn't taste good, but he ate it. Poor guy, we were both laughing so much when we made faces eating it. We enjoyed the friendship we shared. This wasn't looked upon too nicely by Emily and Betty. They tried to bully me whenever they got the chance. As I was heading back to class from lunch, Betty kicked me really hard in the hallway. Returning to class after lunch, Betty kicked me again.

"Hey! Stop it!" As soon as I say that, Rick is in front of me and tells the mean girls, "Don't even get close to Abby or else."

Emily and Betty's eyes bulge out in surprise seeing Rick defending me, but they leave, not before turning around and giving me a dirty look. We get back to class and get on with our lessons. All the while, I was looking at Betty & Emily from the corner of my eyes and could feel that they were talking behind my back. I wonder what their problem was; after all I didn't do anything to hurt them.

Betty Cox looked lovely. She had long, wavy blond hair with small but striking emerald green eyes. She was paler than I and Megan were which made her look deathly white at times, unless she got tanned in the sun.

On the other hand, Emily Johnson was a pretty brunette with golden brown eyes and a rich caramel-chocolate skin. Her skin looked like cocoa butter and was always glowing. Now, if only their looks matched their behavior because that was far from being lovely. The whole school knew they were mean and rude, always trying to stir up trouble.

Knowing how they were in the first few days of school itself, I knew it'd be better to stay away from them. I had enough trouble to deal already. If Rick is the reason why they're kicking me around, they should know that it's not me who asked Rick to be friends with me. He always followed me right from the beginning. He's my best friend now and a sweet boy.

I make a quick run after seeing Paul and Megan waiting for me. They are both smiling. Paul says, "What's up AB?"

I don't speak, just smile at him. We are all holding hands to walk home. Megan asks Paul, "When does Ma get a Christmas tree?"

"This weekend."

Wow! We're excited because it's our first Christmas with Ma and Paul at home. I catch Megan smiling at me, all three of us happy at the prospect of decorating the tree. Christmas will be here soon! Yay!

We will surely have a nice weekend. Saturday morning, Ma kicks the door open with a moan. I think it's around seven am. She yells at us to get up, that we have to clean the whole house, and then we could go later to get the tree, so we better do what she says. Paul, Megan and I are so excited; Ma lets us decorate the big beautiful Christmas tree. It's been freshly cut and is a deep green. We even made some of our own ornaments. I made an ornament for Rick. It's a snowflake sprinkled with, blue and silver glitter, it also has a little bell with blue and white ribbons to hang it from his tree. I don't have the money to buy him anything so this is like my small Christmas present for him.

Paul tells us that Ma is leaving and won't come back until late. "So you know what that means AB, we are going to the park."

Megan doesn't look very pleased with Paul's idea and says, "Not me, I won't get in trouble for no one."

"Well," Paul says, "In that case, stay home."

Then Megan tells me, "You aren't going Abby. You're going to get in trouble. Don't go."

"Paul says, she's going with me, so get ready for some fun Abby. Yeah! Let's go Megan."

She rolled her eyes. "Okay, go. But come back before Ma comes home." So we walk down the little hill then make a right turn. Paul is still holding my hand. He tells me, "You know the name of this park?"

"No."

Paul smiles at me. "You don't talk much, do you AB?"

I just smile back at him. In my mind there is really nothing to talk about. I was wondering how we were going to sneak back in before Ma came home, Megan's words were ringing in my ears. We'll be in a whole lot of trouble if Ma found out that we were outside.

Paul interrupts my thoughts. He's telling me the name of the park is Montecito Heights Park. We are running faster and faster. It's a sunny day but kind of windy. There's a chill in the air but I don't care, feeling free. "Come on, AB! Let's go to the hills." There is a small hill we're going to climb up and then down. "You are going to like this AB. Ok! Let's go."

We spend the day laughing going up and over and down the hill again. Paul was right, I loved it.

Though I fell a few times, I couldn't care less. The freedom of running through the hills and feeling the wind on my face was exhilarating. I thought about Megan and how she missed out on this. I knew she was missing Dad sorely. When it came time for us to go home, I felt sad because this was so much fun. I could do this every day!

Dad never came to see us, so Megan just stays home and gets grumpy. I and Paul hurry back home after our little outing over the hills and thankfully we get back home before Ma came.

 Of course, Megan's angry so we go to the bedroom. She tells me Dad called and that he said he loves us. I don't get excited or happy anymore. She doesn't look happy giving me that message. "You should have been here Abby, you could have talked to him."

Monday morning, I can't wait to go to school. We are all eating breakfast thinking about going to assembly because on Friday, we are all supposed to be singing "Jingle Bells" in the auditorium. I ask Ma if she's going to come and watch us sing. Right away she says no. There was no surprise there: I knew she wouldn't come to watch us sing. Megan seemed happier today. She's been feeling better since Dad called. I hardly know what's going on with her these days except that she misses Dad and longs to see him.

It's Friday. We are going to sing at the auditorium at school. I feel great about it, even if Ma or Dad will not be there, I guess it's ok. I'm getting used to the idea of their absence for these events. Megan's the one who gets sad and grumpy about Dad not being here.

Anyway, Mr. William has the whole class in a straight-line walking down the hall. Ma made me a new skirt—it had thin red, green and gold stripes, like the colors of a decorated Christmas tree. She made me a white button blouse that I wore with a deep red sweater and knee-high white colored socks.

My hair is in a ponytail, tied with gold satin ribbons. I was pleased with my dress and could see Rick just grinning at me. He looks cute today. Rick usually wears his hair messy, but today it's on the side. It looks greasy. He's wearing a white shirt, a green vest, black pants, and a black bow tie. I really think his Mom made him wear that. He looks really uncomfortable but it didn't stop him from being his happy self. On the other hand, I see Betty and Emily giving both of us a dirty look. Betty and Emily, pretty as always, were wearing red dresses as if they were sisters. Both of their hair was knotted into a small bun and wore similar green barrettes: too bad they're the mean girls from school else I'd have walked up to them and said they actually looked pretty. They were back to their well-known bullying antics even today as they tried to make me fall. Rick is holding my shoulder from the back; he stood right behind me in the line. The whole class is lined up for the recital in three rows.

The auditorium is decorated so beautifully and the parents of all the children were present. I glanced around and then closed my eyes trying to imagine Dad being present there; he'd be so proud of us if he were here to see us today.

Rick snaps me out of my dream to reality. "Quick," he asks Abby, "Are you okay?"

"I'm ok."

"Good. I thought you were feeling sick."

"No, I'm okay!"

So we all started to sing, "Jingle bells, jingle all the way," as loudly as we could. I and Rick amused and snorted so loudly. I suddenly wanted to pee but I couldn't run to the restroom in the middle of this singing. After our class finishes the recital, all of us gather to watch the other classes. I quickly go to the restroom and get back because I didn't want to miss out on Megan and Paul's singing.

Watching Paul and Megan, of course they weren't singing, just moving their lips. But it's okay: I loved seeing them.

After all the classes finished singing, I and Rick were walking back to class when Rick whispered in my ear that he had a small gift for me. He said he'll miss me during the two-week long Christmas holiday and I knew I'd miss him too though I didn't tell him that.

I told him that if I got the chance, I'll go to the park during the holidays because I loved being there. I told him that we could meet there. He readily agreed. As we begin leaving to go home, Rick hands me my present. It's all wrapped up so pretty, "Open it!" he says, waiting for me to tear open the ribbons and packing. I open it excitedly and see it's a little bag of colorful marbles.

I smile at Rick, pleased at his choice and give him a little peck on the cheek saying, "Thank you."

"You really like them, Abby?"

"Of course. They're beautiful." Unfortunately, I don't have a great gift to give him back except the ornament I had carefully made and packed for him in a little blue and white paper box. I say reluctantly, unsure if he'd like it.

"Rick, I made you an ornament." He smiles and starts removing the simple paper wrap and takes out the glittery, silver blue snowflake.

"Everything on it was handmade." I say, casting my eyes down to the floor below me, praying he likes it.

He looks at me with a grin and says, "This is very pretty Abby, can't believe you made it!"

He takes my hand and kisses the palm of my hand. I blush away a beet red and say, "Thanks."

"Bye see you at the park," and I started blushing again.

School closed down for holidays and it was finally Christmas Eve. We didn't know if Dad would come but if he was, Maria his wife would come also.

Not really looking forward to that monster. Megan is sobbing: She is missing Dad so much. I for one don't blame her, he was with us first but we can't force him to be a Dad, that's the way it is. The house smells of tamales and our aunt and uncles are coming through the door. Teresa is walking in, she's the oldest. She is the one that loves money. She's married a man with wealth, I heard he drinks too much. She is really pretty, short black hair, brown eyes, she makes her makeup perfect. She dresses like she has money. Then comes Marissa. She is looking for a man to love her and take care of her, but still hasn't found him yet! She is beautiful. She has long dark brown hair, hazel eyes, blush pink cheeks, and a very natural tan skin like my Dad.

Victoria is just noisy. She is in everybody's business. She has brown eyes, and light brown hair. She's thinner than her sisters and Lorenzo. He's married, but never brings his wife, he's always bringing a different woman every time he visits. It's gross. He has dark tan skin, dark black hair, and green eyes. Tall and thin, he's dressed nicely in a black suit, white shirt, and black tie. He dresses much like our Dad and has a sarcastic grin. He's already at his drinking game. They're all enjoying a round of Poker and the drinks are flowing freely. Who plays poker at Christmas?! They do.

Uncle Mario came next. He has green eyes. Tall and lean, he came dressed up in black slacks, and a black sweater. His hair was black and, messy. He was the sweeter one among the lot, seeing me and Megan, he walked up to us and asked, "Abby where is your Dad and his wife?" I frowned at the question.

Paul just says, "He's not here yet."

"I thought he would be here by now?"

Megan, upset by the question, decides to go upstairs and excuses herself. Paul grips my arm. "Come on, AB. Let's go eat."

We had five tamales each. We love Ma's food. They were so good.

Megan finally came down after a while. Sitting on the last step by the front door, she just kept waiting for our Dad. It was already 10.00. Everyone was opening the gifts. I and Megan were waiting for our turn to open our gifts.

Ma looks at us and says curtly, "Well I didn't buy you any gifts because your father didn't give me any money."

Meg and I, surprised at this rude gesture, started to shed silent tears wondering if this situation in our life would ever change.

Grandma tells us to go to bed quietly without making a scene...

We go upstairs quietly. I could hear Uncle Mario being very upset apparently because of Dad's absence. "Why is Andres not here? Christmas is for kids! Those poor girls." He remarked to everyone present there.

Grandma tells him, "They'll be all right."

We are in bed. Dad never came. There were no gifts. We felt like orphans even in our own grandmother's house. However, it was slightly better than the previous last Christmas we had. It was a nightmare last Christmas; we were kicked, locked and hit at by that monster

Maria. We never felt so helpless and small. At least no one's doing that here except for the occasional belt whipping for not doing something Ma told us to do. As Megan drifted off to sleep, I could hear the drunken singing coming from downstairs. That's their idea of celebrating Christmas. I knew deep down Megan and I were sad and maybe it was part of our lives to be crying on any given occasion but there was a small part that whispered a prayer of gratitude. We were alive and together. Though our tears flowed down our cheeks and onto our pillows, our hearts and spirits were one through all the bad stuff; nothing else mattered.

Chapter 4

It's Christmas day. Everyone stayed overnight. The house was a huge mess. There are bottles everywhere. It smells gross, like a bar, and we should know, right? Dad has taken us to bars plenty of times before, to meet up with his drinking buddies. Poor Megan tried hard to take care of me and protect us from gaze of unruly, drunk men. She should have been more like a kid, but we both had to deal with the selfishness of our parents. Even though we don't know what happened with our Mom and how it was between Dad and her, we grew up being close to our Dad because he's all we had. That was until Maria came into the picture.

Megan snaps her fingers at me from across the bedroom walks towards me asking "Are you daydreaming again? Answer me when I talk to you Abby."

"What!"

"Go downstairs and eat, then come help me. We have to clean the house."

"Why? We didn't dirty it. We didn't even get a gift."

"So what?! That's beside the point. Just do it!"

"God, OK!"

So I'm going down the stairs when I hear one of my aunts whispering to Grandma that Dad couldn't come because Maria was feeling sick. She's having a baby. I run up the stairs two at a time shouting, "Megan, Megan!"

"What?!"

"Did you already eat?"

"No."

So I told her the news, that Dad didn't come because Maria was feeling sick, and that Maria is having a baby.

Megan is in shock. "She's pregnant? I can't believe it! Abby, he will never want us anymore."

We both started to shed tears; that's all we needed. "What a horrible Christmas gift!"

The next day we were miserable about the news, Maria with a child. Grandma was going somewhere and I couldn't wait to be free for a little bit. Paul went with his friend next door. As soon as Grandma left, I told Megan where I was going: to the park. She just nodded. "Don't come late, okay?" I ran out of the door going down the hill to get to the park. The feeling of bliss and happiness can't even explain it; the sadness of our Dad being a father again when he can't even be a father to us. I was heartbroken and happy at the same time, if that's even possible. I'm walking around the park. Not many people are here and I am so grateful of being alone. Then my eyes fell on a boy sitting on a swing. He looked familiar and I started walking closer, I saw it was Rick! I run seeing him, I was so happy but when I finally get to where he's sitting, I see he has a black eye.

He says, "Hi!" and gives me a happy smile. I don't want to ask why he's hurt because if he wants to tell me, he will when he's good and ready, or maybe he won't and that's ok with me. Anyway, I never tell him about Megan and my Christmas. So we leave that topic behind.

"Come on Abby, let's run up the hill." We are laughing so much as we ran around in circles. This park has a little hill and if you're not careful you could get hurt. We are running up and down the hill. I'm not that good yet, like Rick, so we are running down. I suddenly slip and roll downhill.

I see Rick's face as I tumble and he runs quickly towards me.

"Abby! Are you okay? I'm sorry!"

Getting up, I say, "I'm okay," brushing off the dirt from my knees.

Rick speaks with a grimace. "No you're not!"

"I'm ok!"

"You have cuts on your knees and scraps on your arms."

"I got to go, because Ma will be home soon!"

Sneaking around can get very exhausting, but this was fun. Rick agrees, and he smiles reluctantly, not very happy that I was hurt and I had to leave early.

"We will do it again but will be more careful next time."

"I won't let you fall again."

I kind of felt sorry for Rick: he's so sweet. "Okay, don't feel bad that I got knocked down okay? It's nobody's fault, when I get a chance I'll come back."

I ran home as fast as my body would allow. Ma was not home so I went straight to take a bath. There were cuts here and there but it was worth it, we did have so much fun. I was lucky to have such a good friend.

It's the Sunday after Christmas. We have to go to church. We all walk together. It's really far, but we do this every Sunday, so we are used to it by now.

The pastor preached hard. I can't tell you what the sermon was about but it sounded good anyway. We walk back after the service. I've always liked going to church.

Megan, Paul and I hold hands walking home. Ma is in front of us. We have one week more: after New Year's we go back to school. I can't wait. School seems better than being at home for holidays; I didn't like being home. Ma makes us dinner. We never eat out so we don't know what that's like. We eat and clean up. Ma tells me to sit next to her and I do. Megan is upstairs. And Paul goes to play with his friend. I'm watching Ma knit when she slaps me just out of nowhere on my mouth. My hands are trembling, and with her fingers she gently touches her lip and she sees blood on her fingers. Ma tells me don't ever stare at her, ever, when I sit next to her. "You just look down. Do you hear me Abby?"

With tears flowing down my face, I just nodded, "Yes, Ma." I do what is expected of me. So staring down the rest of the evening even if your neck is all twisted, guessing that's part of the rules too.

The week goes by fast. New Years was the worst; they all got drunk again and played poker all night. There was the smell of cigars and smoke like it became a bar overnight, but this time they started to fight as well. Megan was frowning, "Why do they come here? Just to drink and fight." She holds my hand and I'm relieved because I couldn't sleep. "I really miss Dad, Abby! He's never coming to see us again." I was really tempted to roll my eyes at her, but she was staring at me with those big blue eyes. I just love my sister very much and she was hurting.

I began to let go of Dad slowly and didn't show much feeling. I was scared of being hurt over and over. Megan was different though, she was so attached to Dad and couldn't let go, despite knowing that his chances of visiting us is even less now that Maria is having his baby.

Three years passed by very fast. We saw our Dad maybe three times, once year. He had a family now—two healthy kids—but he never came with Maria or his kids.

I was nine now. I look older than most girls my age. My body is almost formed with a little waist. Even my breasts are growing. My body was firm and shapely because I was always busy cleaning up the house every day with Megan. Every chance I got I ran fast out the door to the park, sometimes with Rick or Paul, never with Megan. I always kept myself busy.

We had adapted to our new life with Ma, Grandpa and Paul. Because Ma didn't drive, we would always take chances to walk around the neighborhood. We didn't see our grandpa much, age had taken a toll on him; he walked slowly and didn't drive much either.

All these years made both of us resilient. Megan learned how to make Ma happy. She always made her coffee and served it to her in bed, and that was a plus for Megan. Megan was always trying to teach me how to make coffee. I wouldn't, though, just say no because I'm not a kiss-ass. I'm so stubborn; she always did what was told of her so she never got beaten, but she looked angry all the time.

I started to watch people's faces when they weren't looking. I would notice, like Paul hiding sometimes in his room. It wasn't like him. Maybe he was doing something he didn't want me to know about? We got in trouble all the time, Paul and me. We're both very stubborn though we didn't care about getting hit: we were used to the abuse. I think that's why we got along so well.

It's summer. I help Megan clean the house. Ma and Pa are leaving for Mexico and boy I'm happy as hell that they will be gone for a month. My Uncle Mario is taking care of us. He's the nice one.

After I finished all my chores all I could think about is Rick. He's my best friend in the whole wide world. All these years he has been next to me like glue stuck to paper. We had learned not to talk about our home or how we lived. I knew he'd get beaten a lot and he had two older brothers. I only saw them when they picked him up from school. I have got to say; the Owen brothers are very cute. They really looked like brothers. They all have beautiful blue eyes, and light brown hair, with a hint of blonde, but I know Rick was the sweetest person among the three. Always beside me, we basically were inseparable. Betty and Emily always talked about us till this day. They just grew meaner and ruder; the best bullies around!

All the boys made fun of Rick because of me. We just didn't care: we always played together. We played in the monkey bars four squares, and I'd gotten so good at the marble game that I've beaten Rick at his on game. We would play for money—when no one was looking. I would use the money to buy lunch and if I didn't win, Rick would always share his lunch with me.

Saturday morning Ma and Pa said their goodbyes, telling us that to be on our best behavior while they were gone and not give Uncle Mario a hard time.

He tells us if we want to go to the park, we could go which is always an excellent idea. Uncle Mario was making breakfast. He tells us if we want to go to the park, we could go which is always an excellent idea. Uncle Mario was a teacher so he was on vacation. Of course, I loved him. He was always nice to us.

Megan and Paul were in a happy mood because Ma wouldn't be there for a whole month! I felt the freedom in my heart and it feels great! Without wasting much time, we all walk down the hill to the park. I see Rick is playing basketball with some boys. He doesn't see me yet! So I just stare at him playing for a bit. He was wearing shorts and a blue t-shirt. I and Megan were wearing Levi's shorts. Paul gave us some Levi's to cut so we did. They were really short. We had Paul's old t-shirts on.

I'm so excited to play. I'm more of a tomboy while Megan was more feminine. Uncle Mario tells us we need more players and as we're discussing who should join, I catch Rick glancing up and grinning at me.

"Hello! Glad you're here Abby."

Shyly I say, "Hi!" He is staring at me from my face to my tennis shoes and now I am feeling my cheeks blush and I become a little bit nervous. Rick has never seen me with really short shorts or any short clothes for that matter. We decide to play softball. I feel my cheeks getting warm and flushed as we start running around. I have got that bad habit of rolling my eyes and Rick smirks. He makes my stomach erupt with butterflies and my knees weak. I have no idea why! Since we have known each other for three years and have grown a lot closer. I find myself at peace with him; we spent time together whenever we could. We played all day, got some cuts, dirt, and scratches all over us. We decided to rest on the wet grass, feeling the cool breeze on our faces. Paul and Megan seem so happy. I feel so content looking at everyone smiling and in good spirits that I wish this day would never end. Rick sits next to me he tries to hold my hand. Paul is looking at him. "Hey! Don't touch her!" I turn to look at him with my eyes bulging out. "Paul stop it!! He's my best friend. Don't talk to him like that!"

"AB, you don't have to get annoyed."

"Well stop saying things like that!" I could feel Rick getting away from me. "Would you like me to walk you home Abby?"

"Sure, just let me go tell my uncle." I go to tell Uncle Mario. Of course, he always says yes.

Rick and I are now holding hands and begin walking home. He looks at me with this sheepish smile and says. "You know Abby? You're my best friend, right?"

I say, without a doubt, "Yes, you're my best friend as well."

Staring in his eyes, he has the most beautiful blue eyes I've ever seen. Knowing Rick, the way I do, I know he wants to tell me something. "You are so pretty you know that?" I feel my face getting red.

He continues, "The first time I saw you Abby," he gets the palm of my hand and kisses it so gently. That gesture to me is the nicest sweetest thing anybody has ever done. It wasn't the first time Rick did, but it still felt very nice. I know he wants to kiss me and I'm getting nervous again, thinking back last year. Ma always let people from Mexico stay in our house. I assume they were from our extended family. When I was sleeping, one of the guys who were drinking came to my room. Megan was babysitting at our aunt's house so I was alone. He woke me up. He was sticking his tongue in my mouth. He stole my first kiss from me. I was only 8 years old. I always thought it would be with someone I cared about. Rick nudges me gently from my distant thoughts. "Abby what's the matter?"

"Nothing!" I exclaimed as I looked away because there was no way in the world I'd tell him about that episode. He is watching me very seriously.

He says, "Could I kiss you Abby?"

My face is getting redder now a shade of beet red and I'm blushing with delight. I glance up at Rick. His hand goes to my cheek. At this point, my body is trembling lightly as he cups my face in his hands. He gently kisses my lip. He's so sweet, I want to hug him so badly. I'd never really grown up knowing as much affection and this kiss and the way he held me, felt like a piece of heaven. He was the sweetest boy. Rick kisses me again and this time, it was even longer. It's like he could read my mind. He pulls away and smiles at me and gives me a huge bear hug. We stay like that for a while and then we start walking home again, quietly treasuring our first kiss.

It has been two weeks and I hadn't seen Rick. I missed him and his sweet kisses and bear hugs. Who wouldn't? Uncle Mario makes sure we have fun. We go to the lake, to the park, we go swimming at the pool, and all I could think of is Rick: what is he doing? Is he thinking of me? Paul grabs me from behind, wraps his arms around me, and snickers. "Daydreaming again AB?"

Laughing out loud, I go get a water balloon to throw at him. He gets all wet. He says, "You are going to get it now AB, so you better start running really fast."

I'm hiding and when Paul comes from behind he has a pan full of cold water and wets my whole body. I look at him in shock. That water was so cold and we started laughing so loud. "What's so funny AB?" now he's tickling me so firmly. "Okay, I give up, really!"

He says, "Nope, until you fart AB."

I couldn't stop laughing. "You are such a pig, you know that?"

Now Paul and I were rolling all over the yard. He's making me giggle so much it hurts. "Okay stop! I said stop!" We look at each other. Megan sits next to us. We are happy campers. Paul taps me on the arm, "Rick is here Abby."

Glancing up, I noticed he looks miserable, I ask him, "What's up?"

"Can we walk?"

"Sure."

We start to walk to the park. I'm still so wet, but it's really humid today. "God, Abby I miss you so much."

"Me too, is there something wrong?"

"Same stuff. "

"What do you mean same stuff?"

"It's my Mom again."

"Oh!" We are having some problems. "What about you Abby?"

"Been great. Ma is coming next week so you won't be coming to my house. She would kill me." I am giggling at him, then he gets my hand.

"I really missed you," and he kisses the palm of my hand.

I start telling him, "You know you could talk to me about it?"

He says, "I know." So we sit down by the shade in the park by a huge tree. He's still holding my hand. Rick really doesn't talk about his problems at home, so I wait until he's ready to talk. "It's my Mom." He paused, so I squeezed his hand to continue. "Abby, she drinks a lot. She beats all of us." That's when I noticed his bruises on his arms and the side of his cheek. I was heartbroken because I had known all too well what it felt like being abused and beaten black and blue.

"I'm so sorry Rick."

"Yeah! I know, everyone is always sorry."

"What about your Dad?"

"He's never there Abby! Never! Dad works all the time, my Mom just wants to drink a lot, it's really horrible."

"Well, if it makes you feel any better, my Dad drinks all the time. He has never beaten us, but we have a step-Mom that hates us, so he's never around. Dad has another family now." I stare at the grass feeling sick: that life really sucks if you ask me. Rick puts his arm around me, lifts my chin with his fingers and gives me the sweetest kiss ever. We both hold each other tight for a while. "You do have me Abby. Before I forget Abby, I wanted to give you something."

Rick, still holding my hand and with the other hand, pulls out something–from his front pocket. It's a chain with a heart that has R+A engraved on it. He looks to see if I like it; my tears start rolling down my cheeks. No one has ever done this for me. I know I'm just nine but feel older: we were just growing up so fast. He leans in to my lips and kisses me tenderly. He wipes my tears away. "You like it Abby?"

"Yes! Rick, it's beautiful. Thank you, I'll treasure it."

"Please put it on." It doesn't take much to make me happy. "Let me see it on you, perfect!" I'm so blushing at this point. Rick says that he loves my hair as he twists a strand with his finger. All those curls, and you're so sweet Abby. Thinking about what he said made me happy.

I'm home, looking in the mirror trying to see what Rick sees in me. The necklace is so pretty. It is silver and it shines. It makes me think of him and how poorly it's been for him and his brothers. I really know he's my best friend and what we have is like puppy love. I can't wear the chain with that beautiful heart at home because Ma will see it and take it away from me. So, I hide it in my dresser drawer. It's funny that Rick never asks me why I never called him Ricky, because I'm different than any person. I already feel like I'm damaged; don't feel like a little girl should feel, or maybe because Betty and all the kids at school call him Ricky. We all are growing up so fast and I wonder if Rick feels the same way. Ma and Pa will be back home in a few days. I've had the best time ever and so many beautiful memories.

Megan and I decide that it's time to clean up before Ma arrives from their Mexican trip. Megan wants the home to look clean and neat because that's the only way to keep Ma happy.is cleaning.

Paul finds me and Megan cleaning up in the kitchen when he calls out to me.

"AB want some sweets?" I tell him there are no cookies. I wonder what he's going to whip up now.

"Give me some corn tortillas and jelly and let me show you how it's done." He chimes with a grin. I nod 'OK' and begin to warm up the tortillas while he brings some jelly and spreads it on the tortillas.

It was our version of a quick dessert. We lick our fingers and clean up our plates; we look like kindergarten kids with jelly all over our mouths. We couldn't be happier and treasured these last few days of freedom before Ma arrived.

Chapter 5

Ma and Pa are home from Mexico. They brought two family members with them. One guy seems to be in his late twenties and a girl who's also around the same age. Ma helps them find jobs. I'm guessing the girl cleans houses while the man will work in a factory close by. I dislike it when Ma brings strangers home. Megan and Paul also hate it. Once Ma is home, the whole family comes together every weekend. They would drink, eat and play cards, while we have to clean the mess they've made.

We begin to feel depressed because we had an awesome month and now it's over. I'm missing Rick and longing to go to the park and spend some time with him. Ma and Pa would go to the horse races often and I was hoping they'd go to one of their races soon so that I could go to the park. They always go because they like to gamble. They used to take us when we were younger. Thank God they don't take us anymore. We have a month to go back to school and I want to make the best of it.

Paul asks AB, "Want to come to the store with me?"

"We can't just go!"

"Not right now, but Ma and Pa are leaving. They are dropping that girl with our aunt."

I say, "Okay! I'll go with you. We have to wait till they go." He was acting kind of funny or maybe I'm over-thinking. Who knows? Everything we do is bad anyway. Megan ask us, "What's up?"

Paul is just staring at her. "We are going to the store."

"For what?"

"For something okay! Let's go."

So we all walk down the hill to the supermarket. Paul gets a cart and starts to put all kinds of toys in it. Megan grabs his arm. "What are you doing? And where did you get the money Paul?" Of course, he is grinning from ear to ear. "I found, it all right?"

"Where?"

"In the street, where else?"

"Come on you guys, stop worrying alright? Let's have fun, come on!" So we pick our toys. Paul had a lot of money. He bought plenty of toys. We are walking back home. We go to Paul's room and put all the toys in his bed. Megan and Paul are looking at what he bought. I tell them I'm going to the park. They really didn't care at that moment where I went. So, I make a quick run in the direction of the park because I needed to get back before Ma was back. I sit on my favorite swing in the park just thinking where Paul would have found all that money from. My thoughts were interrupted by Rick's voice. I would know that voice anywhere. "Hi Abby!" Of course blushing is my thing these days, or more like getting red, or both again. I get up, he gives me a bear hug. So sweet. He kisses my cheek. Boy, he's getting taller. "I really miss you Abby!"

"I really miss you too Rick."

"It really sucks that your Ma is back, your uncle was cool."

"Yeah but I could only stay for a while." He holds my hand. Staring up at him, I'm frowning. "What happened to your eye?"

"It's Mom again. She's drinking a lot, so we all try to make her happy. But she never is Abby!"

"Oh I'm sorry Rick."

"Don't feel sorry for me Abby!"

"I'm not; just know what you're going through."

"Abby you are the only person I could talk too". I kiss his eye and he laughs out loud. "Feel better?"

"You are so funny Abby."

"I am?"

"Yes, you are!"

"Well, I try," and we both start to chuckle.

Rick tells me that his Dad is coming home, and they are going camping for two weeks.

"I'll miss you Abby! I mean, really miss you a lot."

"Me too!" He hugs me so tight. Rick didn't want to go because we'd miss seeing each other.

"I know. Okay Rick, have fun with your dad and mom. Maybe she won't drink."

"That's a big maybe Abby!"

"Just try to have fun with your brothers. Got to go: Ma will be back soon!"

"Ok, I don't want to get you in trouble Abby." Rick gives me that last kiss and I'm hugging him so tight, it feels like I'm never going to see him again. I run home thanking my lucky stars that Ma's not home yet! I get home to find Megan cleaning up and I help her, though my heart was still with Rick. Megan and I are in the room when we hear some yelling—Ma and Paul, Oh My God! Ma is beating him, no! Megan stops and grabs me roughly by my arm, so I don't go to him. "Stay here Abby! Or do you want to get hit too? He must have done something." Megan said in a firm voice.

I started to sob badly because I could hear the way she's beating him with the belt she wets. I should know because Ma has hit me like that many times. Megan never got beaten because she is smart, and a straight shooter. She's also very diplomatic and won't get involved unnecessarily. Not me and Paul, we were cut of the same cloth. We were too stubborn for our own good, so we get spanked or beaten a lot. I cover my ears holding to block out the awful sound of Paul's body getting lashed by the belt.

"I don't want to hear it please!!! Make it stop please!!!" I cry and Megan holds me really tight. I can hear Paul's muffled cry and he's trying hard to not break down. I close my eyes and go to sleep and the last thing I hear Megan saying, "Life fucken sucks."

We wake up the next morning feeling horrible as hell. This was hell! I was so scared to see Paul. Ma had beaten him for so long that minutes felt like hours. I knew Ma wouldn't beat someone for hours because people would die, but I was concerned for Paul's life and wondered what he could have possibly done to get beaten that way. But then it only takes a little thing to get Ma angry.

I'm taking a shower I start sobbing like a baby. My heart hurts for Paul. I get dressed and go to see him though I am really scared. I decide against it because Ma doesn't allow anyone to go to his room, rules!

I do everything in my power to do what needs to be done: the cleaning; even helping Megan so Ma won't get angry again. We eat breakfast and there is no Paul. I'm guessing I wouldn't want to eat either, just waiting for the right time to see him again. I don't care how long it takes; I have to see him! I wait it out when Megan tells me about Ma going for one of her horse races. That's my chance to go see Paul.

I knock at Paul's door, ever so lightly. He doesn't answer, so I open the door slowly. He looks up at me. "Don't want to talk AB."

"I know." I decide to sit next to him on his bed. His room is so messy, with clothes everywhere. Ma hit him so badly that there are marks all over his hands, legs and his face. My heart's breaking within seeing him like this. I take his hand and place it carefully in mine, taking extra care to not touch his painful bruises. I cry silent tears and my teardrops fall over his hands.

He looks up swipes them away with his thumb. "Don't you dare cry for me AB? I'm okay."

I bite down on my bottom lip trying not to shed any more tears as I squeeze my eyes shut. He sees how pained I was to see him like this and says "Abby, don't shed tears for me, I'm not worth it"

I get mad hearing this and hold his hand tight. "Who said you're not worth it?! You mean the world to me Paul, stop saying stupid things like that."

"Come on baby girl, no one cares what we feel..."

I look straight in his light brown eyes. "I care Paul! I do! So you don't get to talk that way okay?"

Paul finally gets out of his room and eats a meal. Megan asks Paul why Ma hit him. He told us he stole that money for the toys from Ma; he found it in her closet in one of her coats. I and Megan say at the same time, "Why? Why did you take it?"

"Because I can that's why!"

Megan rolled her eyes. "You will never learn Paul. You just can't take things that aren't yours."

It's been a week since that happened. Megan went to our aunt's house. Ma and Pa went to the horse races again, Paul went with his friend next door. I was happy to be myself. I was dressed in a white blouse and a pair of those Levi shorts Paul gave me and Megan. I was sprawled across my bed drawing pictures. The sun's getting low; I decide to tip toe downstairs and get something to eat. The house was so quiet. I go to the kitchen and get a bowl of corn flakes and treat myself to some jelly. That's the only sweet we have in our house. As I was going to take my first bite of cornflakes and jelly, I suddenly hear footsteps. I thought I was by myself. I'm feeling kind of nervous. Biting my bottom lip, I started to turn very slowly to the direction of the footsteps. To my shock, it's the guy that Ma brought from Mexico. Yeah! I forgot about him. His name is … God, I don't even know his name. I never see him much around, as he's always working, but the way he's staring at me right now makes me feel very vulnerable and uncomfortable. This guy is in his late twenties and he's tall. He is telling me something in Spanish. Within seconds he takes a hold of me and throws me on the floor. I hit my head on the floor and feel like I'm going to faint, but my mind is fighting it and saying you can't. I know I have to scream. But no one is home and I'm feeling dizzy, and my head hurts. I am trying to shout out loud for help but he slaps me hard on my cheek. I scream at him to stop while weeping in pain from the fall I took. I'm trying my best to break away from his hold, but his weight holds me down. I'm not strong enough to fight this guy but I kick and scream as much as I can. He's so strong—he puts his hand on my mouth pressing it down so I won't scream, and with the other hand he's feeling my breasts. I'm trying to tell him to please stop but no words come out. It really sounds like I'm mumbling for words. "Let me, go please!" But this is just making him angrier. He puts his mouth on mine, forcing his tongue inside my mouth. Now I'm struggling to move my head side to side, saying "NO!" All I smell is his breath on me and the taste of cigarette and beer so I'm really fighting him to get off me. He's unbuttoning my shorts and putting his hand down my shorts. Now I am panicking. Oh my God!!!!! Please help me!!!!!!! I'm really scared when I hear someone say, "WHAT THE FUCK!" I look up: it's Paul. Thank God, because this guy just wouldn't get off me. Paul is very strong and with lot of force, he comes straight at this guy immediately pushes him off me, taking him by surprise. Then he punches his face so hard, that I squeezed my eyes shut. I moved away and I could see drops of blood escape the Mexican guy who's name I barely know or recollect.

Then the guy falls on the floor and Paul says, "Get up! Get up Fucker." Paul is kicking him really brutally in his stomach, maybe next to his ribs and I can't even move because I'm so scared. Paul tries to pick him up. He struggles at first and then he opens the front door, kicks him out. Then he runs toward me, and asks, "AB are you okay?"

I can't even speak, this happened so fast. Paul looks me over; I know why he is staring at my shorts. "AB did he touch you?" I can only nod my head because I'm so shaken up. He holds me so tight. "Sorry baby girl." Paul's holds me so tight. And rest my head on his chest. "Come on AB, go take a bath or shower." All I could do is move my head up and down. He nudges gently directing me to my room. All I could do is nod my head my head and agree.

He helps me up and we both walk up the stairs. "AB you're not alone, don't worry! I won't leave; I'll clean the mess." He's trying to comfort me, but I just nodded like I'm an empty shell. Paul really saved me. Paul is young but he's strong. If he didn't come home early tonight, who could predict what would've happened? I scrubbed myself as thoroughly as I could in the shower; I felt so dirty by this man's touch that I just wanted to feel cleansed and purified. After taking a bath, I take a good look in the mirror. I see bruises on my arm and face, and my head hurts.

I had no idea what I'd say to Ma or Megan about this. But later that night, Paul waited for Ma and explained what happened. Ma was furious and the guy was sent back packing to Mexico the very next day. I was grateful that Paul stayed close to me over the next few days, like a protective older sibling. He knew I was badly frightened since the incident and even had nightmares. Megan didn't know yet because she was at Aunt's place and would be coming soon. Paul was my consolation, I always felt safe with him around.

Megan came home days later. Finding me in our room, she asked, "Abby are you okay?"

"Of course." I roll my eyes knowing she means well, I just don't want to talk about it—was that so hard to ask for? But I know she'll be asking until I tell her.

Days went by. I still haven't seen Rick, and I am hoping he's doing well. It's the first time I had smiled in days when I felt a pair of strong arms wrap around me and someone kisses my head. It's Paul, trying to make me feel better. He holds me for a while. He's sweet. "Let's play a game Abby?"

"No, don't want too!"

"Come on AB. You know you want to beat me in checkers okay. I'm red, ok baby girl?"

"Whatever you want." I just smile at him. Of course, he lets me win, then he made me some warm corn tortillas with jelly. He knows how to make me happy–just serve up a platter of sweets and I'd be the happiest girl in the world.

Chapter 6

It is the last week of summer and I can't wait to get back to school. I'm playing outside. There are kids throwing around rocks; not only can that hurt someone, its plain dangerous. It annoys me to see how careless they can be, so I pick one up and throw it at them, in the hope that they'd stop. And as my luck would have it, the rock hits one of the boys right on his head. He whimpers, his hand touching the part of his head where he's hit. He gives me a look that translated as 'you're going to pay for this' and it was sealed in his face with a scowl. Predictably, his mother decides go tell Ma what I did; it's like all hell's going to break loose on me. I could smell trouble in the air. I got home and seeing Ma's livid face confirmed my worst fears. Her weapon of choice is not the belt this time but her own strong hands which begin tearing my hair apart, as she pulls my head like it was a ragged old doll. Then she slaps me firmly on the face when I feel someone's strong hands pull me away from her grasp. Glancing up to my complete surprise, it's Dad! But the feeling of whatever little delight was there seeing Dad was soon replaced with a frown when my eyes settled on monstrous Maria and her two kids. Dad tells Ma, "Don't ever touch Abby ever; I have never hit my daughters."

"She was throwing rocks at the boys next door," Ma says.

Dad is so angry. "So? Never lay a hand on my daughter like that again!"

"You don't want me to touch your daughter then take her! I don't want to take care of her any longer."

Dad took a deep long breath and sighed. Then he said "Go get your clothes, all your stuff, whatever you have Abby! Go get them; you're going to live with me from now on!" I go upstairs to pack my stuff. I don't know how it's going to be, but I don't care because I miss my Dad. Megan will be furious; she's not here and will be worried because she doesn't trust Maria.

I couldn't believe Ma didn't want me here, not in the beginning or now. Anyway, Megan always told me we were lucky—so lucky, yeah! I used to get outraged because I never felt lucky or understood why nobody wanted us, just going back and forth between houses that seldom became homes.

My heart's aching and tears start streaming down my face when I think all these people I'm leaving behind... and Rick! I wish I had the chance to say good-bye–Megan, Paul and Rick. The thought of being with Dad comforted me and I knew it came with the price of being tortured by Maria, if old things are anything to go by as an indication of my future there.

I tuck away my heart necklace that Rick gave me because I know if Maria sees it, she'll take it from me and that would be the last thing I would want to happen. I'm only taking a little bag, I don't have much. Walking to the car, Ma doesn't say goodbye, I don't know why I expected as much from someone who took every opportunity to hit me. Ma must be thinking 'Good riddance' in her head, positively pleased with herself. That hurt me because despite everything, I still thought of her as 'Ma'. I remember the first time when Megan and I got here; she told us about the rules of the house and then asked us to call her 'Ma'. It did come with a certain amount of affection. I won't forget the dresses she made us or the dinners she cooked. I'm mindful of the few good things she's done for us. I choose to remember that instead of the times I've been hit, battered and bruised left, right and center.

As I walk to my Dad's car my heart hurts really badly. I fight my tears, knowing that I can't turn back. I'm heartbroken for the hundredth time, but who's counting right? I set my small bag with the insignificant belongings I have to my name, in the back of the car. I glance up to see Maria eyeing me as if the lion just found its prey. She hates me so much, and I know she'll make me pay for this in ways I cannot comprehend right now.

The drive to Dad's apartment was uneventful. No words were exchanged and the only sound that came was from Maria's two children who hadn't a care in the world about what was going on. I was grateful for the silence that had engulfed us in the car because all I wanted was to escape from this bitter sweet reality. I get to be with Dad but there's a price to pay and at this point, I'm unsure which way Maria's invisible fangs are going to sink in.

When we get to Dad's apartment building, he says our apartment number is 13 and it's on the fourth floor. It looks and feel's different than the last one I and Megan stayed at. This had long hallways and lot of apartments, almost like a hotel complex.

I hate it already. It is kind of scary and lonely once we get inside the building; there's nasty dirty carpet lined along the hallways. I was caught off guard by the putrid smell in the air once we'd stepped into the building. It didn't feel welcoming at all, to say the least. We walk inside. It doesn't seem so bad inside. There were two bedrooms. The walls are white, everything is always white. There are pictures on the walls of Dad, Maria and the kids. There is not one single picture of Megan and me, but that doesn't surprise me one bit—

Maria always hated us. They have their own family and I'm the outsider. It feels wrong. What am I doing here? I shouldn't be here. What's wrong with me? Do I even want to be here? No, I don't.

My focus veers back to observing the little details of my new unwelcome home. The bedrooms were small but neat; the living room on the other hand was relatively cozy and spacious enough to accommodate two brown couches, a lamp, and a small black & white television, a wooden 4-seater table along with a small kitchen area that housed a stove and a refrigerator. Adjacent to this, was a small bathroom.

I am still holding onto my little bag, unsure of where I should put it. Dad notices my discomfort and tells me to put it in the kid's room. Maria says "NO!" so loudly that Dad and I just stare at her and each other helplessly.

Dad presses his lips together before he launches into a rage with Maria, in Spanish! They are yelling at each other at the top of their lungs and the kids scoot off to their room knowing that it isn't their place to be. And so, it all goes down predictably. It makes me feel miserable because I knew Maria would manipulate Dad and get away with what she wants. Now that she's a Mom, she'd easily use the kids as bait and make her job that much easier. She sure won the last time and she'll win again. Maria told Dad she didn't want me anywhere near the kids in no uncertain terms. I'm not allowed to sleep in their room. She makes Dad bring a ragged old, ugly couch from their balcony for my sleeping couch.

The days that followed were a blur; I didn't want to provoke Maria unnecessarily for anything. I knew my best bet would be to stay quiet and to keep to myself. The kids didn't absorb Maria's hatred for me though, innocent and unaware as they are of their mother's monstrous side.

A week had passed by and though I didn't have much of a routine yet, I was preoccupied thinking about joining a new school. Tomorrow would be my first day. I didn't look forward to it; it's too much of a change coming at me from all directions. I wasn't sure how I was going to cope without Megan, Paul or Rick. They seemed far removed from this new world I was in. Let's see how that works out though deep inside, I was both nervous & lonely.

My train of thought was broken by Dad's voice gently asking "Ready for bed Abby?"

"Yes." I say, looking up to see his face, his mouth slightly curved in a half smile. It's Sunday night and he wanted me to go to bed early so that I'd have an early start for school tomorrow. Dad gave me a new blanket replacing the old tattered one Maria so generously gave me with her trademark scowl. He caressed my face and threw his hands around me to give me big a hug. And for once, I felt like I was loved and safe. I could hold onto this feeling forever if I could. This is what I was missing: the love, that feeling of being close to someone that truly loves you. I said 'goodnight', grateful for these precious moments in an otherwise lifeless house.

I'm tossing and turning on my couch, feeling bugs crawl all over my body. The couch smells and its cold. I end up struggling to sleep and stay half-awake throughout the night. When I wake up, I see a small note folded and tucked under a vase at a corner table next to my couch. I knew it was for me and I opened it to see Dad's familiar handwriting. The note read, *"Abby, Maria will take you to school so do what she says. I'll see you at dinner time. Love you baby, so good luck in your new school. Love Dad."*

I fold back the note, grimacing at the prospect of Maria dropping me off to school. Knowing that there wasn't much to do in this situation, I decide to clean up and get ready for school. I scout around for breakfast when I see Maria's eyes scan me over like an x-ray machine. She's getting the kids ready for school and her face is set in a scowl whenever she looks at me. Once she finishes with the kids, she walks in my direction and punches me in my stomach and drags me to the kitchen counter to eat breakfast or whatever scraps were left after feeding her kids. I'm taken aback by the suddenness of all this and my body's still in a state of shock over the stomach punch. I can barely eat the small bowl of oatmeal set before me. She's ranting off in Spanish and then trails off a few words in English.

Trying to catch my breath I am eating my oatmeal with shaking hands. I manage to finish a few spoons and begin dressing for school. My hands still shaking, I hold the comb as firmly as I can to brush my hair. I'm combing my hair. It's long past my shoulder now. Maria yanks the brush away from me, saying that I need a haircut. She yanks my hair and jostles me toward the bathroom. She tells me that my hair is too tangled and begins to cut it with some scissors. I start crying. I don't want her to cut my hair. She takes hold of my thick curly hair. She pulls my head down. Facing the floor, my hair is flowing, knowing what she's going to do and I really wanted to shed more tears. Who cuts hair this way? Facing the floor all I could hear … 'snip' 'snip.' I watch clumps of my hair fall on the floor. It's was painful to watch. I knew I was going to look like a freak at the end of this.

She was cutting it too short and she was doing it on purpose. My hatred for her was increasing with every inch of the hair she cut but I felt helpless.

Staring at myself in the mirror, I stare at the girl staring back at me for a moment. I'm ugly, my hair is cut uneven, like a boy, so short. I hate it! Absolutely hate it! My eyes are bloodshot red like fire balls, as if I had been sobbing forever. Maria took every ounce of pleasure at my reaction to what I saw in the mirror. She motioned with her hands snapped at me to get ready for school. She didn't have the patience to deal with me and hurried me along.

She and I are walking to school. She tells me to pay attention because I have to walk back by myself after school even though Dad told her to pick me up and it's far, almost an hour walk. She throws out a dime at me for some orange juice and no money for lunch. There's no Rick in this class to save me or share a lunch with, how I missed him.

My birthday is next week and things would've been so different with Megan, Paul and Rick around. But right now, as I'm finding a place to sit in this class surrounded by kids making fun of me, I wasn't in the slightest bit inclined to think about a non-existent birthday. All that mattered was to get through this ordeal in one piece.

Mrs. Jones is my new teacher and when she walks in, everyone goes quiet. She notices that I'm new and that I haven't found a place to sit yet. She smiles at me; her kind face puts me at ease. She says, "Have a seat Abby," motioning to an empty seat in the front row. As I make my way to the seat I could hear some of the kids let out a muffled laugh, trying to contain their amusement. She smiles, "Have a seat Abby."

One boy says, "You're way too ugly for a girl." I just didn't care, I grew up immune to these nasty comments and have been through this more than a dozen times. I blocked him out. The rest of the day, I was alone at my seat and no one wanted to be friends with the new girl who oddly looked like a boy. I was waiting for the school bell to ring and get out of here. I had to get back home alone and the route wasn't yet clear in my head but I made it a point to be more observant on the way back. I make it home without much difficulty. I stand in front of the apartment door ready and ring the bell reluctantly, unsure of what more is waiting for me courtesy Maria. She opens the door and welcomes me with a frown, which I'm beginning to get used to.

I've barely caught my breath from the hour long walk back from school and she hurries me along to clean up a rug.

I do what she asks and I remembered dad's morning note; I had no strength to fight this witch especially after all that happened before I went to school. I didn't enjoy the prospect of being beaten black and blue.

The kids are a pleasant distraction and are a year apart. They are still quite little; I'd have been grateful to spend some time with them but Maria wouldn't have it. I kept my distance just as she had wanted it to be.

Dad came home from work exhausted. He calls for me and I run to his arms. I needed a long hug after what I had been through today. When he observes my new haircut, I could see he's getting angry. "What happened to your hair Abby?" I look sideways to see Maria come with a smile, drying her hand with a towel from the kitchen. She knew I'd tell him the truth but before I could utter a word, she reverses the whole narrative and tells him that I'm the one that wanted my hair cut. Dad stares at me in disbelief. "Is that true Abby?" I just nodded my head. I knew he'd believe Maria anyway.

It's been a month since I have been living with Dad. It's been really difficult living here with his family. I truly miss Megan and Paul, Rick, and sometimes even Ma and Pa. My birthday was coming up so Dad gave Maria some money to buy me new clothes and a jacket. Maria goes and buys a boy's jacket and shirts instead of a dress, just to make things worse for me at school. Thankfully, I still had a few skirts that Ma had made for me, so I could manage. It's not like I was making friends by the dozen that I felt remotely compelled to dress well for school. They were going to make fun of me anyway. However, that morning I had something direr to take care of aside from a tattered and unflattering wardrobe. I'd woken up itching and there was a rash all over my body. It made my pale skin taken on a shade of red. I try putting on some knee highs in a futile attempt to cover some visible areas of the rash; on closer inspection, they looked more like blisters than a rash. And it was itchy and sore. To make things more difficult, I had no idea how to fix this uneven, poky hair that'd stick out no matter which direction I combed it in. I manage to get ready, irritated to the core by the rash and the hair. Today Maria puts my dime for orange juice on top of the shelf and tells me to get it. It's really quite high for me to reach, so I get on the chair to reach for this hidden treasure of one dime. If I thought things were bad already, nothing could've prepared me for what came next. Maria pushes me off of the chair and I fall back first onto the hard floor. I try and get up, when I feel a pain up my back. Maria is laughing out heartily, taking it every ounce of pleasure, she gets from hurting me. I just walk out the door to school: no dime, no orange juice, and no lunch. I'm walking, tears running down my face, wondering why she's so cruel and so uncaring. I thought motherhood would've changed her, but apparently not. It's a relief to step out and take in the warm but welcoming fresh air. Closing my eyes, I feel the breeze caress my face just like I used to feel in the park. It feels good and is enough to fuel my body to make the long walk to school. I walk into class five minutes late today and Mrs. Jones is already in class. She's happy to see me and says "Hi Abby!" and then she frowned and looked at me with concern. "Abby, what happened to your legs?" I told her that I got a rash when I woke up today. "You have got to call your mother Abby."

I yelled out loud, "NO!! She is not my mother."

"What about your Dad?"

"Yeah! Call him."

"Have a seat Abby." Mrs. Jones makes the call to Dad and he promptly comes to pick me up. He looks at my leg and has the same look of concern Mrs. Jones had expressed earlier. Dad takes me to the doctor and predictably the doctor's assessment is "It was that dirty couch," I roll my eyes like whatever; I knew this would be the reason even before the doctor concluded his diagnosis. I looked at Dad was in deep thought, wondering perhaps that Maria's proposed solution for my sleep arrangement is the sole reason for this visit to the doctor. I was just glad to be alone with Dad. I didn't get much time with him as much as I'd like to. When we step out of the clinic, he gives me a hug as if to make up for the guilt that was gnawing at him. It feels so nice when we're not with Maria. Dad takes me out to go and eat in a restaurant. I haven't done that in a very, very long time. We ate tacos, and they were delicious. We went back to the apartment, happy to have had the time together but we also knew the happiness was short lived. Maria was waiting for us with her bull dog face. She wasn't an attractive woman and I often wondered what Dad saw in her. It was too late to ask. She's fuming. I wanted to snort out a laugh but I kept my head down to be on the safer side of whatever was going to ensue. Dad was so sweet; he was still holding my hand. Dad didn't even look at Maria, he just went straight to that ugly couch, and threw it away. The rest of the evening, Dad played with his son Timothy and his daughter Emma. They were really adorable but since I wasn't allowed to be close to them, I just smiled, hoping that their innocence is preserved.

Chapter 7

It is now the third month living with Dad. admit, it's been much harder than I had imagined it to be. Maria's resentment and hatred were an everyday exercise in making my life miserable in a million small ways she'd find. Hurting me was her favorite hobby. Dad always remarked to Maria that I looked much like my Mom which ticked her off even more. I had my own hatred and resentment with the way things were in the past and how things were shaping up to be here. Dad was the only consolation.

I was worried because with each passing day, I was getting more angry, depressed and frustrated.

The little time I had with Dad made it worth the slaps, kicks and fist punches on my stomach. I almost welcome the pain. In some twisted way, I enjoyed the pain as a reminder that I was still alive and felt emotions; imagine feeling lifeless and numb! Though it often felt like I was living a nightmare. Dad never knew what she was doing or what she was capable of doing. I miss my sister Paul and Rick so much and going to the park with them and running free.

I felt like I was suffocating at Dad's place. Maria never let me go outside to play. My only outing was the walk to school and back. Thank God for that.

Well, it's Saturday, and Dad says, "Let's go to the park." I think he read my mind. I was grateful for the chance to step out of the apartment. Maria is making a face but then she acts like a monster. We go to a park with a pond. They have ducks in there and I'm happy to see them. Dad gives me bread to feed the ducks. I feel a gentle breeze kiss my face. My mind immediately rushes back to the days I spent at the park with Megan, Paul and Rick. Dad holds my hand and wakes me up from my daydream. I notice him drinking but not as much as he used to. We return home, happy for the little break from the confines of the apartment. Something as simple as feeding a bunch of ducks was so refreshing and relaxing.

Maria was livid when we walked in but didn't say anything. Was she always going to be this miserable or was it that she reserved this behavior just for me? I could never understand how someone could hate a kid when she was herself a mother. She was so bitter that even dad's love couldn't transform her.

The weekends were always great because Dad was home, and Maria never hit me when he was around. During the weekends, she was normal, acting like a doting mother to her two kids and attempting to be a caring wife. But as soon as the weekend was over, her monstrous side came out from its hiding place. I sensed those vibes getting stronger as the weekends drew to a close. But I also got immune to her threats and constant bickering in Spanish and broken English.

Time flew by and Christmas seemed like it was just around the corner. The last few months went by as expected; Maria's anger had only grown and it reflected in her increasingly creative ways of punishing me and hitting me. I prayed at night for the strength to endure it and sometimes I'd break down just begging the Lord to make it stop altogether. She wasn't doing a very good job being a mom either; she'd be a monster to the kids too if they cried or annoyed her in some way.

Sometimes I stared at her out of curiosity, wondering what she was made of. The idea that she could kill me someday wasn't an exaggeration because she was fully capable of doing something like that. So that meant, every day I had to tread carefully when it came to Maria. It was like walking on egg shells, waiting for the moment when she'd lose her last ounce of control.

Anyway, that night Dad came home early from work. He helped me with my homework. He played with the kids, and I looked on. There was something incredibly tender and loving about seeing dad play with Timothy and Emma. I saw myself and Megan in their place and envied the love and attention he was showering on them. While I took pleasure in watching this playtime unfold in front of me, Maria just stared at me with cold, lifeless eyes. Dad tells her to give me some milk and a cupcake. While Dad took a shower, she had me in the kitchen. Instead of pouring milk in a glass, she gave me a cup of coffee that she knew I hated. It kept me up at night. My love for peanut butter & jelly sandwiches hadn't diminished and Maria knew those were my favorite. But instead, she'd serve me the most tasteless meals she could muster from the kitchen. It wasn't like she didn't know how to cook good meals, but she preferred handing out the worst of everything to me. I didn't care, I was just tired of it all. Dad was either blissfully unaware of what she did or turned a blind eye to what he knew. This wasn't the first night I had gone to sleep with tears flowing down my cheeks. I thought about Megan, Paul and Rick. I hadn't heard anything of them and wondered if I even figured on their minds. When will I see them again? I was missing them so much.

Getting ready for school, I take a good look at the mirror. I look like a ghost of my former self. My short hair was impossible to tame, there were dark circles around my eyes from a lack of proper sleep and it was prominent contrast against my pale skin. I had lost a lot of weight and walking an hour each to and from school had not helped. I didn't want to linger longer seeing this reflection. It was embarrassing and hopeless.

The December chill has set in and walking to school today, I notice how cold it is today. I never ate lunch, and the sole dime I get for orange juice cost me bruises on my body. It wasn't worth it.

I'm in school. Mrs. Jones proves to be a good teacher but I've not opened up to her. I don't trust people like that. I miss having friends. I miss my old school and even miss the petty and bitchy mean girls Betty and Emily. But most of all, I missed Rick. The missing had turned into a form of numbness which also became my body's way of response to any negativity. It's funny how it felt but I had gotten so used to it now.

I walked home alone, lost in my thoughts. When I get home, Maria is always there to abuse me in some new way. Today she grabs my head, her hands unable to hold onto my short hair. At that point my stomach starts to ache hurt so badly, that I vomit all over the floor. Maria is really furious now! Still holding her grip, she pulls my hair harder, and I end up falling on my knees. I feel dizzy, but Maria outdid herself this time as far as torture creativity was concerned. She stirs her hand in my vomit and smears it all over my whole face like I was getting a beauty facial. I had no idea what I did to her to merit this new treatment but I continue to vomit, feeling sick in my stomach. Maria threw towels at me and told me to clean it up before Dad came home. I cried quietly, drenched in my own vomit and feeling sick to death, rushing to finish cleaning the mess before Maria hits me again.

I take a shower and muffle out my cries with the running water. I had no appetite for dinner and I'm glad Maria didn't force me to eat. I go to bed, exhausted and sick. There was no strength in my body to stay up and wait for Dad. I sleep off like a dead log. A few hours later, I was woken up by a hand that nudged at my shoulders; it was Dad and he looked concerned. I didn't want him to worry about me so when he asked me how I did, I lied and said I was doing okay. What I really wanted to tell Dad was that I wanted to go home to Meg, Paul and Rick. They were the only family to me than the abuse I had to endure here. I loved Dad and he was my world but living here had become impossible. I just didn't know how to tell him and seeing his concern on his face I didn't want to disappoint him. I could feel an appalling sense of dread regarding Maria. Though I couldn't put my finger on it, my gut was telling me that something terrible is going to happen in the coming days.

Christmas is a bitter sweet time for me. Given the past record of Christmas's in my life, I have no high expectations of it, especially not when you're living under the same roof as Maria. She was worse than Christmas Grinch. Maria was like a time bomb waiting to explode, so all I could do was wait in anticipation and prepare for the storm. She's been watching me even more closely now the last few days; with those evil eyes like a hawk. It's Christmas Eve finally arrives and I'm really hoping that Dad comes home early today from work. Maria's outburst in the morning, a few hours earlier seemed like the first eruption of a bigger volcano of hatred she's going to spew through the Christmas holidays. I've tried my best to hold on but I've had enough of her. I plan to tell Dad to take me to Ma's house. I don't want to be here any longer. At least I'll have Megan, Paul and Rick there for company. I have no one here or any friends in school. Dad put up a small tree and Maria has bought gifts for the kids and placed it under the tree but she makes it a point not to give me any gifts whether it's Christmas or my birthday. Even if Dad gave her money to buy something for me, she still wouldn't give me any. Just thinking of a Christmas with Maria around gets me knotted in my stomach. I get up to go to the bathroom. My stomach it's twisted in knots.

My mind wanders to Dad, my only source of comfort. Where is he? Please, come home soon Daddy! Well I better go out before Maria gets curious or irritated.

Walking out of the restroom, I'm startled by Maria's sudden presence. She stares at me with a scowl. Then she comes at me with both her hands, firmly gripping the back of my neck and dragging me across the hall to the front door. Maria is kicking me out! She pushes me down hard in the hallway, and I fall face first. I'm about to stand when I see her coming at me again, this time with full force as if she's going to kill me. She punches me on the face with her folded fists and then kicks me in the head. I felt something crack; I'm sure my skull is fractured, everything is going around in circles, and there's ringing in my ears. The pain is unbearable. Then she kicks me in my stomach, I'm unable to breathe and feel like I'm dying. I can see her getting ready to kick me again, and this time she doesn't spare my chest. My whole body winces out in pain, and I scream as loud as I can. Oh God!!! Please help me! I'm unable to feel anything, and a numbing sensation is taking over.

I could feel her hands grab my throat, squeezing my neck, trying with every ounce of strength to choke me to death. She shakes me violently with the full intent to kill me right here and right now. It felt like a horror movie being played out in slow motion. All I wanted was for Maria to finish the job! Just finish me off please, I cried out. I had no strength or inclination to live this life any longer than I already have. I open my eyes slightly and see a shadow lurking down the hallway. An unknown lady is quietly watching this nightmare unfold. Maria continues to beat me black and blue. Why is this lady not coming forward to help me? I found it harder to breathe. The sickly pungency of my own blood that was all over the carpet underneath me, was suffocating me; I closed my eyes, knowing that death would soon lay its icy hands on me. Maria takes her hands off my throat seeing that I lay motionless on the floor. When she lets go, I cough hard and feel an intense pain stinging my neck. There's pain coming out every pore in my body. I turn my body sideways and I see Maria walk to the apartment. She slams the door behind her hard, leaving me to die in the hallway. I felt like the final moments of my life were passing before me. My spirit feels detached from my body because I can't feel anything. I closed my eyes, thinking my time to leave this world had come. Then I feel someone holding me. I pry open my eyes to see it's the lady I saw at the stairwell. I could make out that she was trying to talk to me but I couldn't make out any words and I passed out.

After what seemed to have been like an eternal sleep, I slowly open my eyes and feel the soft bedding underneath my body. I could see light and smelled flowers. I thought, maybe this was heaven. I felt safe. It seemed surreal. I turn my head slowly sideways and see the woman whose been watching me from a distance bending over me, frantically saying something to me in broken English/Spanish.

" Little Girl Estás bien. Are you alright? No Speaky English. You need ambulancia Little girl policía. Yes?! What's your name?"

I answered in a whisper, "No police and no ambulance. Abby, my name is Abby. I want my Dad."

By that time, my dad walks up and see the lady standing over me.

"What happened to my daughter, Abby! Abby! Who did this to you? What happened? What happened?!

"I think your wife beat her up because she came out of your apartment. It looked like she wanted to kill her. That poor girl."

I said, "Maria, did it Daddy. She beat me and choked me. She tried to kill me Daddy."

He picked me up and carried me into the apartment and laid me in the bed. Dad shouted, "Maria, where the fuck, are you?" She came into the room and he grabbed her by the hair and started shaking the hell out of her. "Tell me what the fuck happened!" Maria lied and said I was disobedient, that she asked me to do the dishes and I said no, do them yourself and she tried to spank me, and I hit her in the face & she threw me out in the hallway. She's such a liar! Dad hollered, don't you ever touch my daughter again. Do you fucking hear me?! Dad didn't want to call the police because Maria would go to jail and he wouldn't have anyone to take care of me and his two kids. So, he swept this whole thing under the rug.

Chapter 8

Dad knew that it wasn't safe for me to stay here. Let's go for a ride. I knew he was thinking about taking me to Ma. We're sitting in the car and I can hear the pitter-pater of raindrops fall on top of the car. It was Christmas Eve, I'm depressed by the thought of it. Life is going to be tough without Dad, another change in my life. I won't be able to see Dad because he has to stay with Maria on account of the kids. He loves them too. Dad apologizes to me saying he came home late because he went to buy me a Christmas gift. He was so angry that he had given Maria money to buy me a gift when he noticed there was nothing for me under the tree.

Hearing this, I start crying softly, knowing that he meant well and that it wasn't his fault that Maria was a monster. While I listen to him, he lifts my chin up so he could look into my eyes. He starts weeping from the guilt he's been carrying all these years of not being able to be the kind of father Megan and I needed him to be.

It was heartbreaking to watch him cry. I needed to speak up and tell him that I've been miserable here since day one. But when I was beginning to speak, he interrupts. "Do you want to stay Abby?" Is he serious? "Or do you want to go home with Ma?"

I look into his kind hazel eyes and then look away and out to the window. After a brief pause, "I want to go home."

I start sobbing in his arms and I didn't want to let him go. He held me close to his chest and I can feel his tears streaming down his cheeks and down his neck. I reach out my hand to wipe his tears. He looks at me with such sadness that it breaks my heart. Then he reaches out to the back of the car and picks up a black box tied off with a silver satin bow; it's the Christmas gift he handpicked for me. I didn't open it though because it didn't feel like the right time to do it. Dad gives me a peck on the cheek and finally starts to drive home to Ma. I'm not the feeling the same anymore. I was so broken and crushed from my stay with Maria that I don't think anything worse could happen staying with Ma. I could endure that with Megan, Paul and Rick around. I could care less about what could happen from here on. Walking into Ma's house was a sweet relief. It was like getting home from a warzone. Ma is waiting for me in the living room. I walk slowly towards her, unsure of what to expect. I look at her face and see her smile at me! She opened her arms out wide for me. I could hardly believe it! I run to her, holding onto her for dear life. It felt like a miracle because it was the first time she did that! We both say nothing; we didn't have too. I belong with Ma; she loves me in her own way and truthfully, I could live with that.

Paul runs down the stairs at first delighted that I came and then the delight was replaced with concern and then a scowl. "What in the world happened to you Abby?" he says swooping me into his arms. How I have missed him. Knowing the way he's staring at me, I knew I must look horrible enough to play a ghost in a movie. Ma tells him to leave me alone, that now is not the time to be asking questions. "I've missed you so much AB, so much." He says as he holds me tighter.

He doesn't know how much I've missed all of them. All we do is hold each other. I was like a broken record, too exhausted to say anything.

Ma serves me a warm meal she cooked and tucks me into bed. She tells me to rest. Megan was with my Aunt and she'll probably be here tomorrow morning. I drift into sleep, relieved to be here. I'd rather be here all my life than be anywhere else.

I was woken up by Megan as expected, the next morning. She caresses my face with her hands and runs her fingers through my short hair. "Why did you go to live with Dad Abby? Why? What did that monster do to you, why did you let her cut your hair? she asked in a concerned voice.

"Megan, please stop! I don't want to talk about it."

"Okay well, Abby you sure don't have luck when it comes to Christmas." Rolling my eyes at her highly inappropriate and untimely comment, I just hope she will just leave me alone for some time. I missed her and love her; and I'm absolutely relived to be back but I don't have the strength to answer all her questions or tell her about all the things that happened. Yes, maybe I didn't have any luck for Christmas but she didn't realize that this Christmas bought me the best present I could've ever asked. I was released from a hell hole and am back with people I love. It's all that mattered. My body was still sore but I had all the love in my heart for Megan, I had missed her so much. We just hold each other tight. Days passed by. I kept having nightmares and sleep didn't come easily. The bruises were painful and my body ached. I wasn't bed ridden but it wasn't easy to move around either. Paul says that Rick asked for me like a dozen times. The last time he was hurt and angry, which made me feel gloomy, but what else could I do? Ma and Pa went to see a family member. Megan and Paul stayed with me at the house and of course they tried to find out what Maria really did to me but I wouldn't talk about that nightmare.

Dad went back to his family. I heard that Dad beat Maria the same way she beat me. Maria was a very cruel evil bitch for what she did to me. Helping Megan clean the house, Paul gets a hold of my hand. "Come on AB, let's go to the park. Let's go have some fun." Knitting my brow and saying no, he ignores me and drags my hand anyway, and out the door we go. Forgetting what it felt like being free, it's so cold but I don't care: I welcome it with every fiber of my being. I and Paul run down the hill but I have to slow down. My body still hurts so much from all the soreness and the discomfort of it all. So we watch some boys play basketball instead. Sadness overcomes me because Rick wasn't there. I can't believe I was gone for three months. Megan and Paul were not the same either. Something is off but I didn't question it.

A week passed by. I was feeling better, still a little sore though. Not being able to see Dad everyday was a terrible feeling—the sadness about that! And that he chooses that monster over his own daughters; well, can't do much about that either. I missed Rick very much. I was getting quieter too and it was beginning to bother Megan and Paul. Ma never talks about my stay with Dad and I'm thankful for that. It was worth the pain to live with Dad even if it was just for three months. Maria took something from me. She broke my spirit. I just feel empty and heartbroken. I no longer feel normal.

Two weeks passes by real quick. Ma is taking me to school and my tummy is in knots again. I'm nervous looking at myself in the mirror. I was still thin; my hair was growing but it was still short; there were uneven black circles under my eyes. The bruises began to fade away. There's a silver lining however in the midst of all this. Megan is watching me from the bathroom door. "I'll fix your hair Abby." She tries to fix it and does not do a very good job. Ma made me a nice pink skirt so I could wear my pink sweater, Rose the woman that helped me had given me. I love that pretty sweater: it reminds me of that horrible day. That sweater means a lot to me. Ma has to register me in school again; it's taking a toll on me going back and forth. I'm in the office hoping that I'll be in the same room as Rick. God my upset stomach isn't helping. The lady at the front desk tells me that my classroom number is four, and says my teacher is Mr. Dawson. "It's just around the corner by the restroom on your right." She gives me a paper to give to the teacher. I say bye to Ma, and walk to the class. I'm so scared. Turning the knob slowly, I take a deep breath. I'm so nervous walking in. Everyone is quiet. I walk to give the paper to Mr. Dawson. He's a tall man with dark and gray hair, brown eyes and a thick mustache. He has huge black glasses on. He looks up. "Well good morning Abby?" I'm looking down at the floor because I don't want to look at anyone but I know very well that everyone's eyes are on me. "Okay Abby have a seat in the back chair that's empty." Walking in the back of the room someone moved their foot in front of mine and I stumble down. Peeking up, I'm not surprised to see who it is: Betty Cox, just my luck! And I'm surprised by who is sitting next to her—Rick and Emily right behind him. Everyone starts to laugh, making fun of me. Trying to walk fast to my seat, I take my pencil and papers out; I stare down just trying not to hear Betty saying, "Abby's back and she looks ugly."

I have no money for lunch like it usually is, but I am really not hungry. I've gotten so used to not eating. Betty gets right in front of my face. She's become really pretty I roll her my eyes at her and ask, "What do you want Betty?" She stares straight at me, puts her hand on her hip and chews a huge piece of bubble gum while twirling strands of her hair on her manicured fingers. So again, I ask her, "What do you want?"

"God you're so hideous, Abby what happened to you?"

"What do you care Betty? Get out of my way."

Emily laughs. I could see from the corner of my eyes that Rick just staring at me with anger. He looks hurt, so Betty goes and gets his hand. She tells him, "Let's go to lunch. She's not worth it, she's so ugly." My eyes are tearing up so I run away from them. The last thing I needed was for them to see what I'd become. I found a bench and sat quietly, remembering how much I had missed Rick. Now, seeing him hold Betty's hands all that missing was quickly replaced with regret. I leave for three months and Rick goes running to the mean girls. I'm really distraught about the whole thing. Oh, well Rick is not my best friend anymore. Walking home, I feel this was one of the shoddiest days of my life. Walking through the front door, I half expected to see Megan or Paul or even Ma, but no one seemed to be around. I went upstairs to my room and plopped myself on the bed. Paul comes in asks, "How was school AB?"

"Don't want to talk about it, Paul."

"Why, what happened? You saw Rick?"

"Yeah!"

"So what did he do Abby? Because if he hurt you I'm going to fuck him up."

"You are not going to touch him."

"Then tell me AB." Sitting on the edge of the bed, I told Paul that Rick was holding Betty's hand and they all made fun of me, but not Rick: he just seemed hurt, but he is no longer my best friend; he just stood there letting them call me names. Paul wraps his arm around me. "It's okay baby girl, you're alright."

"I don't feel alright."

"Well can't cry over spilled milk, right?" We both smirk at each other. Paul goes to help Megan with cleaning and then goes to his room. Paul is thirteen and so is Megan. They look different now and they're growing up fast. Paul is taller and more handsome, and we all think Megan is just beautiful. Looking out the window, I am watching some people moving in across the street. I see a lady and a man, with two boys. One is her age, the other one is Megan's age and they are cute. Then we see a small little girl running to whom I assume is her Dad. I can't help myself from smile and thinking how my Dad could've been or was. Dad used to open his arms out to me and Megan. Megan is staring at the boy her age. "He's cute." Of course she would notice. "Got to find out his name Abby?" She has a huge wide smile on her face & then she winks. She won't have a problem; all the boys stare at her all the time.

I found a way to make my hair flat down with Paul's beanie when I sleep at night. It actually worked, it didn't look so ghastly. Wearing my blue skirt and white blouse with a blue sweater I put a cute band on my hair, looking somewhat presentable for once. I started to walk to school—of course walking by myself because I no longer have a best friend. I'm starting to get depressed just thinking about it. I walk in to class. I don't make any eye contact with anyone since I could feel everyone's eyes on me anyway. So I go to my seat as fast I can before Betty tries to trip me again. Looking up, I see Rick is just staring at me. It's making me nervous, so looking down at my paper with a pencil acting like I'm about to write something, the new boy I had seen from across the street walks into the class. Wow, he's cute: he as gray blue eyes, jet black hair and light skin. His dress can be best described as sloppy though. Mr. Dawson says, "Good morning Josh Maxwell. You could have a seat in the back. Where is Abby?

Please raise your hand Abby, so Josh will sit next to you on the empty chair. Thank you." My pencil falls to the floor I'm ready to get up when Josh is already picking it up for me.

"Here butter fingers. Hi, my name is Josh." I just nod. "You don't talk much do you?"

Rolling my eyes, I say, "Thank you for getting my pencil."

"You are welcome. Glad you do talk." Josh is just grinning to ear to ear and I could see Rick's face as he frowns, staring at us. Don't know why he's so irritated: Rick is not my best friend anymore and Betty keeps on staring at Josh and trying to hold hands with Rick. Boy I really wanted to roll my eyes.

Mr. Dawson says, "Abby read page seven, the first paragraph, please."

I started to read, and the words looked all jumbled up, so I stopped.

"Abby, please continue reading."

I shook my head and said, "No!"

"I want you to stay after school, Abby." I stare down at my book as if I was writing something then I noticed I couldn't write either. Everyone was staring and laughing at me. I was so embarrassed that I ran out of the classroom. I sat in the hallway until someone came to get me.

I stayed after school as Mr. Dawson requested.

"What happened, Abby? You love to read and write stories."

"I'm sorry, Mr. Dawson, I can't read or write anymore."

I started crying, and he hugged me and said, "Tell me what happened."

I didn't want to get Maria in trouble because my Dad needs her to take care of his kids, so I lied and said that I fell out of a tree and hurt my head.

Mr. Dawson held special classes after school to help me learn how to read and write again. But I was never the same. I have to read slow and sometimes the same line two or three times to understand. I get migraines often from the trauma to my head, and nobody ever took me to the doctor to see what damage Maria caused to my brain.

Chapter 9

"Wake up Abby!"

I'm yelling, "No!" Jerking my head back and forth pushing him away from me. Paul is trying to wake me up! I tried to open my eyes. Tears are flowing down my face.

Paul is holding me tight "It's just a nightmare Abby, that's all. You are safe." That night with Maria changed me in ways I cannot even describe. I felt empty, lonely and broken. The nightmares never stopped.

I was glad it was the weakened, I didn't have to deal with school with all these kids treating me mean and Rick always around them. Josh never spoke to me ever since that day, but it still was a great battle dealing with Betty and those mean kids. Ma's leaving with Pa to the horse races so I'm going to the park. It's cold out there but I don't care. I put on my jean shorts with Paul's oversize sweat-shirt. I tell Megan that I'm going to the park. She says, "Okay, Abby don't come late."

I am wondering what's up with Megan: she's not arguing with me. Running down that hill makes me so happy! I see some boys playing baseball so I walk to sit at the benches and watch them play. It is so nice to feel free again breathing the fresh air deeply even if it's for a little while. The game finishes. Getting up I lose my balance and almost fall off the bench when someone holds my arm tight. I am almost scared to peek up. I am surprised at who it is. "You always were clumsy Abby."

"What do you want Rick?" He is still holding my arm tight. "Let go of me," I say as I am trying to yank my arm from him.

"Why did you cut your hair? Why didn't you tell me you were leaving?"

Rolling my eyes, I asked, "What do you care? You're not my best friend anymore." Still he's holding my arm with an expression of hurt and sadness. I try to pull my arm away but he tightens it more. He is starting to hurt me when I hear a voice. "Get your fuckin' hand off her." We both glance up: to my surprise it's Josh glaring at Rick.

"This is none of your business." Josh has a cap on low but I could see his eyes and he's getting angry. Rick turns to face me. "I just wanted to talk to you Abby!"

"If you want to talk to her let go of her arm," Josh says. Rick lets go at this point. My arm hurts and I start rubbing it. Rick just walks away. Then I yell after at him, "Go talk to Betty since you like her better." I felt my anger and bitterness swell; I was so depressed, sad and frustrated at the same time. Josh just stares at me. I blush a bit when I catch him eyeing me. So telling him thanks, I begin to walk away when he tells me, "Wait! Abby, I'll walk you home since I live across from you." So we walk the long way. He doesn't ask about what happened with Rick, and I don't say anything else, just walk in silence, and there went my day at the park.

I get ready for school, and there was a time when I looked forward to going to school when I was friends with Rick. But now I'm just a wreck. Walking to the corner as I begin to cross the street, I find Josh. "Hi! Abby." He called out, smiling at me. I smile back at him, and we just start walking. Josh really doesn't talk much and I don't either. He was wearing a white t-shirt with Levi's. It's quite chilly outside.

We both walk in the classroom. Betty says real loud, "I can't believe Josh is even walking with Abby: she's so ugly."

Josh gets so annoyed that he walks up to Betty and Emily telling them both, "Why don't you shut up and leave Abby alone?"

Mr. Dawson says, "Ok, Josh please have a seat. Betty start reading page one."

Rick walks in late. His shirt is all wrinkled and he looks awful. "Sorry Mr. Dawson I'm late."

"Do you have a note?" Ricky nods. "Have a seat." The day went by with no more drama, Thank God. Walking home by myself, I see Megan: she's with Josh's brother and they are making out. I can't believe what I'm seeing. She didn't waste any time. Walking in the front door, going up the stairs to put my stuff away and I get undressed. Going back downstairs I hear Dad's voice. I run down as fast as I can. "Dad!"

"Hi Abby!" Running to his arms, his smile has a sadness that makes me feel something's wrong. "Wanted to talk to you Abby."

"Okay Dad?"

"I came to tell you that Rose, the lady that helped you that night, she died yesterday. She had cancer." My tears start to fall down my cheeks. "I understand Abby, I am so sorry. She helped you, she was a nice lady," Dad says. I am sobbing for her kids: a life gone. She was a beautiful person and I will never forget her. After that day, the feeling of depression started to get worse: my heart aches. School wasn't getting easier; the kids at school were bullies, thanks to Betty and Emily. They threw food at me and kicked my legs so I would stumble on my feet, or they'd call me names & making fun of my hair. Sometimes they even spit at me. I didn't want to go to school but this day was worse because watching Rick with them was the last straw. I couldn't take it anymore. Walking home I'm depressed and miserable. Going upstairs, running to the bathroom, opening the mirrored cabinet, I look for the bottle of aspirins. I grab a couple of them and put them under my pillow. I'm glad that the bottle is full. I had plans for them later. I don't want to be in this life. I'm done with feeling sad. I was so tired of feeling worthless. The feeling of not being wanted was gnawing at me. Megan always remarked we were lucky to not be in a foster home. Not getting hugged or loved is a huge factor in our lives. Washing the dishes, I watch Ma hugging Paul. She never hugs him; she must be in a good mood. Feeling a little jealous, I just keep washing dishes. Megan comes in. "What's up Abby?"

Rolling my eyes, I say, "Saw you kissing Josh's brother."

Her eyebrow lifts up in surprise. "Oh yeah?"

"Yes, sure did."

"So Abby, he's just a guy?"

"What's his name?" not that I cared much but still wanted to know.

"His name is Kyle Maxwell," she says. "He's so cute Abby. He has these beautiful huge green eyes. He's tall, my age, short jet black hair. He has dimples each side of his cheeks and he is also tan. He doesn't look like Josh, just his jet black hair."

"Boy you really in to him."

She rolled her eyes. "Well let's just say I like him. He goes to my school, we liked each other right away."

Waiting for Megan to fall asleep it felt like forever. "Good night Abby."

"Good night Megan."

My tears are slipping down my cheeks. As soon Megan is asleep I get the bottle of pills. I know Megan will be livid at me for doing this, but it's really for the best. I don't want to be here; my heart aches so much, I'm feeling depressed. Everyone at school hates me: all they do is make fun. Rick is no longer my best friend. All the nightmares from what Maria did never left me. Rose died; Ma never showed affection openly. And I missed Dad.

I'm better off gone. So I swallow one pill at a time until finally I take the last pill and I whisper looking in Megan's direction, "Love you Megan, and love you Dad and Ma and Pa, also Paul. God please forgive me." I close my eyes waiting for everything to disappear as I'm exhausted. My eyelids are getting heavy. A few hours later I'm feeling really sick. There are moans and groans as I am holding my stomach. Megan wakes up. "What's wrong Abby?" I don't speak, just moan. "What is it! Abby? Tell me what hurts!" Then she frowns. "What is this, an empty bottle of aspirins?" she stares at me. "Did you take all these pills Abby?" I just hold my stomach. "Why Abby? Why did you do it." She starts sobbing and runs and gets Ma.

Here I am in the hospital. They pump my stomach. I am feeling like shit! I just wanted to be left alone, I close my eyes. Someone is in the room asking me to wake up. I'm uncomfortable, tired and sick. I feel even more of a failure now that I wasn't able to die. I wasn't in the mood to answer these questions. Opening my eyes there's a lady sitting in a chair near the window. "Hi Abby are you feeling better?" Don't want to answer. "My name is Renee Wheeler. I'm a teen counselor, and I would like to ask you some questions, is that okay?" I still don't speak. "Why did you take all those pills Abby?" I'm biting my bottom lip playing with my fingers just watching them. "Abby could you answer me please!"

Tears started to fall down my face, I can't even stop them. "I DON'T KNOW ALRIGHT!"

Ma walks in my room. She looks at both of us, and tells Renee that there is nothing wrong with me.

"Mrs. Pena, you are wrong, sure there is. She tried to take her life; attempting suicide means something is wrong. She's depressed, she needs help and counseling." Ma tells her to leave and Renee puckered her brow. With a frown she says to Ma, "You are making a big mistake Mrs. Pena," and she leaves.

Laying on my bed at home, my hands on my forehead with my eyes closed, Megan walks in. "Abby! I know you're awake. Why, Abby? Why did you take those pills?"

God, I really wanted to roll my eyes. "Could you just leave me alone Megan? Don't want to talk about it okay? So please leave me alone."

She holds my hand, her eyes filled with tears. "Tell me what's wrong?" She stares at me like I'm going to tell her, but I just stayed silent. Ma comes in my room a few hours later and tells me, "Don't ever do that again, do you understand me?" Staring at me for a minute, she yells, "Answer me Abby!"

I just say, "Okay!" And she walks out of the room. Paul is next. "Not you too. Leave me alone!"

"Listen AB, don't scare us like that again! Life is boring if you're not in it."

"Yeah right." My tears start to fall. "God Abby, stop crying: you will be okay. You know that right?" Paul's eyes are watery and that makes my heart ache. He never sheds tears. "I know you are in pain Abby, because I'm feeling the same way." I had truly forgotten how alike I and Paul were. He gives me a soft hug and kiss. "Okay baby girl, you will see."

Ma let me stay home for three days from school and I was grateful. My hair was starting to look a little better, and I'm feeling somewhat better; at least my stomach is not that sore anymore. I walk into class trying to block the kids out of my mind. Hearing a smirk, I know who it's from: Betty Cox. I wished she stopped bullying me at least for one damn day! I notice Josh watching me and as I turn, I see Rick also staring at me. Boy! This is going to be a long day.

It's lunch time and I walk down the hall to go outside, I'm not even hungry. Feeling empty and lost in my thoughts, Josh comes and walks beside me. "Hi Abby." Of course, my face is getting red.

"Hi Josh, want to play four squares?"

"Not really."

"Okay, you know that your sister is seeing my brother?"

"Yeah!" Knowing you, you don't seem happy about it."

"That's on her to figure out if he makes her happy, not my business." Things at school got a little better. Josh and I were starting to hang out at school and at the park. Rick always stared at us. Boy, missing him was truthfully an understatement, but we no longer talk to each other. So Josh became my friend. He wasn't like Rick. As a matter of fact, he was totally different. Josh was fun in his own way. He told me his family was almost perfect and I was happy for him. His life was better than mine and Rick's. Ma and Megan and the whole family never talk about me taking those pills; they were happy to pretend, it never happened. I know Uncle Mario was very disappointed in me. He always said, "That's an easy way out, that's not God's will." I always respected Uncle Mario so I told him that I will never ever do it again. Ma and Pa went to some family gathering so as soon as they were gone, I went to the park. I liked being there by myself. I sat next to a big oak tree. The breeze on my face felt so good. I smile when I heard a familiar voice call my name. "Abby! Can I talk to you?"

I knew that voice anywhere. "No! Rick, not friends anymore."

"Just talk to me Abby."

"No go talk to Betty and leave me the hell alone."

"What happened to you Abby? You sure like to hang around with Josh."

"Boy! You have a nerve telling me who to be friends with."

"Come on Abby. No! Stop bugging me already." I was the one that got up and walked away from him this time.

Chapter 10

Time flies and three years had passed by. "Happy birthday Abby!" Megan exclaimed excitedly holding a cake that she made to mark the occasion. It was a vanilla box cake with white frosting topped with a few cherries. Paul was amused because it was smashed on one side. Well at least it was a white cake, my favorite. Megan looked at me with a smile dancing on her lips and said, "Abby, how does it feel to be thirteen?"

Rolling my eyes had become a hallmark as Paul would say. I smirked and replied, "How did you feel about me growing up Megan?"

"Come on, Abby stop being a stick in the mud."

Paul said eager to get a piece of the cake. "Blow the damn candles already, we never celebrate our birthday so what! Just blow the damn candles alright, did you make a wish?"

God he really is getting on my nerves. "Yes, I did now stop bugging me." Paul just snorts a laugh; we all started to giggle. I blow the candles out and cut a piece to give Paul and Megan. We dig into the cake with our spoons like we've never seen a cake before…

Paul spits the cake all over the place. "This cake is horrible."

Megan offended by the remark says, "You should have baked it yourself Master chef Paul." It did taste kind of funny but I would never say that to Megan.

Being in the seventh grade now, the school was far. I and Josh walked together to school and back; our friendship had grown by leaps and bounds. But he never kissed me like Rick did. He was a nice guy. We had outgrown the age of 'puppy love'.

I see Rick sometimes at school. He watches me like a hawk. I ignore him because despite all the time that has passed, he still acts hurt. I don't act hurt anymore because of his hanging out with Betty & Emily; I'm past that and don't hold onto what's gone. Rick has become an attractive young man and he could easily be every girl's dream guy, but as long as he's with Betty and Emily, he's going to be a puppy in their hands, playing into their whims. Good luck with that!

It's Monday morning and I'm getting ready for school. I am going to wear my short dark blue skirt with a fitted ivory white blouse that Ma made me. My hair is now at shoulder length with natural curls. It looks a lot better than it did three years ago. I put on lip gloss just to avoid getting chapped lips—most girls enjoy getting dressed with makeup: blush, lipstick, mascara. But I prefer looking like myself, natural. Megan also preferred it that way but she's become so pretty, she always was.

Megan and Paul are now in senior year; while Megan has grown more responsible, beautiful and wise with age, Paul seems to have gotten into more trouble than he used to before. The last three years, Paul has been in trouble. Ma caught him with drugs, and he is not doing so well in school. Hanging with the wrong crowd isn't helping him one bit. Megan still sees Kyle, Joshes older brother. They're always kissing and holding hands like two peas in a pod. I guess you could say that's her boyfriend. They have been together for three years. I even saw Paul with a few girls—well, more than a few. They' love to be all over him—my theory is girls like bad boys.

I walk down the hill and see Josh waiting for me in the distance. I'm glad for his company and friendship. We talk about everything under the sun on our way to school. I've worn a pair of short heels to complement my skirt and blouse. My shoes have a small heel from my six-grade graduation. Glad they still fit. The shoes were the only thing I liked. The blue dress Ma bought me was dreadful.

I get closer to where Josh gives me a huge grin and I smile back and then he says, "God Abby you look so pretty, not that tomboy anymore." He says with a chuckle. We both laugh and I slap his arm and tell him to be good. He gets my hand and we walk to school. It's half an hour walk. Josh walks in front of me. And then turns to walk facing me. He stares deeply into my hazel eyes and I can see that he's nervous and wants to say something. "What's up with you Josh?" I'm asking because he's acting funny now. "Well Abby, I wanted to ask you if you wanted to go to the school dance."

I stop walking raise my eyebrows. "You're asking me to go to the dance with you?"

"Don't be surprised Abby. We have been friends for three years, you know."

"I don't think Ma will let me go!"

"Well you will never know if you won't ask." We keep on walking. "Just think about it Abby."

"Okay," I nodded.

Josh went to class, giving me a lovely smile while I go to my locker to get a few books for the first class. I hear a familiar smirk. Knowing who it is, not turning around, Betty says, "Your hair is longer but you are still ugly."

I turn around slowly. "What do you care how I look? You must be really jealous."

Betty swallows on her salvia, almost chokes on it, and says, "You wish. Look at me and then look at yourself."

I can't help but roll my eyes. I admit Betty is pretty; she's the envy of many girls in school. With a bit of makeup, she's become a head turner in school and boys are putty in her hands. But I've seen and experienced her ugliness in person and the unkind things she says to people, just for the fun of it. That to me isn't pretty.

I tell her to move out of my way, hoping that Betty doesn't start pushing my button. I'm not the same girl anymore who can be pushed and bullied around. There was a time when I was like that, but if someone does that now, I'm more likely to twist their arms into submission and have a sharp response back than go away quietly. So for her sakes, it's better she leaves me alone. I'm not the same girl anymore. Betty always wanted Rick next to her and she has that now. And I couldn't care less who Rick was with. That's a done deal, so what was her problem now? I decided it wasn't worth my time or energy to invest in what Betty wanted or didn't want. What do I care?! I finish class without too many distractions and head out for lunch. I catch up with Josh who's waiting for me to join him.

I have money now to buy my own lunch because I babysit and wash cars in my spare time for pocket money. So, sitting next to Josh we start to eat. "Abby, how are your classes so far?"

"It's alright, how about yours?"

"Okay I guess."

We both have PE next. I really hate it because Betty and Emily have it at the same time. We are running track today in teams so I have to finish lunch early. I hurry up and finish my sandwiches & drink and say bye to Josh. He gives me a crooked grin. "Good luck with the mean girls." I roll my eyes in return. I get ready for it; red shorts, white blouse, white socks and white tennis shoes. I put up my hair in a tight top ponytail so that it stops falling over my forehead, which is so annoying!

I'm ready to run. I love softball, basketball and running. Competing with Betty and company really adds to the fun of it. I could see Josh is grinning from ear to ear, giving me a look over from head to toe. As I was turning around, I see Rick watching me too.

Even though I don't talk to him now and we're in different friend circles, he makes me nervous when he looks at me like that. Not sure, what's on his mind. Betty isn't afraid to cheat anywhere, whether that's in sports or in exams or with boys. She's addicted to winning by hook or crook and doesn't care much for fairness. That's where I begin to piss her off because I like winning too, but I like playing fair. We get ready for the race and position ourselves at the start line: we both bend over, hands on the ground, left leg back, steady and so ready to go. Betty is gawking up at me. I return her scowl with a wide grin, knowing that it'll piss her off even further. I don't let her nastiness distract me from the race on hand. And the whistle blows! And we're off! Betty is trying very hard.

And we're off! I take off looking straight ahead to the finish line. I start running in a moderate pace and then speed up towards the end. Betty on the other hand runs very hard right from the start and gets tired mid-way so that when she's near the end, she slows down, unable to run any faster.

It was close and I could hear Josh yelling, "You can do it Abby!" I'm motivated from all the attention now, running faster, keeping up with the pace I'd planned just like I said. Betty slows down. I run past her and I win! I could hear Josh, "Alright Abby!" Abby, Abby, he starts chanting as if I just ran the Olympic marathon. I was blushing red looking at his reaction. I'm standing there, catching my breath when Betty comes at me with full force, pushing hard in my chest. I remember the time Maria did that, I fell helplessly onto the floor, unable to defend myself because I was so little. Not anymore. I shove Betty back with an equally forceful punch in her stomach and she slops to the ground. Betty glares at me and calls me a bitch. I watch Betty and give it to her back, word for word, "You're the bitch ugly Betty." Everyone from class noticed the ongoing exchange and reported it to the Dean. We were separated before it could become a full-blown scuffle and taken to the Dean's office.

Now we are at the Dean's office waiting for our punishment. Betty is still gawking at me, I just ignore her.

Mr. Evans opens the door tells me to walk in his office and have a seat. Mr. Evans is a short, lean and bald man in his early fifties. His blue eyes are framed with a pair of black rimmed reading glasses, a contrast to his fair skin. "So Abby, what happened?" he asks peering through his glasses.

"Well, Betty is a sore loser, I won on the track race and she got upset. She pushed me hard on the chest so I pushed her back."

Mr. Evans sits back on his chair, puts his fingers together. "You know Abby, you have good grades. I wouldn't want you to mess that up."

"Well, she really started it."

"Don't let it happen again." I just nodded out of respect for him. "The next time this happens Abby I am going to call your parents."

Now I really wanted to roll my eyes. What parents?

Josh is waiting for me. "So, what happened? Are you alright Abby? You didn't get in trouble, did you?"

"No, he gave me a warning." So we walk to the next class.

I'm walking upstairs changing my clothes when Megan rushes through the door almost hitting my face. "Abby! I heard he asked you to the school dance??!"

"Who asked me?" I have a smirk on my face.

"Don't act dumb with me Abby! He told Kyle that he wanted to ask you."

"Yeah, Josh asked me."

"Well, are you going?"

"You know that Ma won't let me go Megan."

"Maybe if you say you're going with girlfriends."

"I don't have any friends, remember?"

"Well, Ma doesn't have to know that." Megan said with a sly smile.

I don't have a dress or any money to buy one of those fancy things girls wear for such dances. Megan reads my thoughts and says, "I'll fix you up Abby." I welcomed her enthusiasm though I don't entirely trust her with the job at hand.

That night Uncle Mario came to bring sweet bread for Ma, so I took advantage of the pleasant atmosphere at home to tell Ma about the dance. Of course, as predicted, Ma said no so I played it off, telling her with a frown, "Ma all my friends are going, please!" If she only knew! I didn't have any friends. Uncle Mario smiles at me. God, he could see through my game. Mario tells Ma it's okay to let her go and so Ma agrees!!! I can't believe it! She never gives in that easy and I'm just grateful to Uncle Mario for buttering her up to get a YES! Thanking them and giving both a peck each, I run up the stairs to tell Megan. I'm so excited!

It's the night of the dance. Uncle Mario is will be dropping me off at school, that was the only way Ma would let me go. With all the things that had happened in the past, I could understand Ma being protective of both me and Megan. We were young ladies in the making, and it didn't hurt if Ma was careful about where she was letting us go and with whom. Josh and I had agreed that he'll wait for me at the entrance of the school. I can't contain my excitement for the dance and neither can Megan, who's right now helping me, get ready for it. She's curled my hair and is lightly dusting my face with blush. She puts makeup on me with a light hand, just like I prefer it. It has a very classic silhouette and makes me look elegant and classy, just two things a lady should always be. I wear sheer pantyhose before I slip into my shoes which match my dress. Megan picked it out when we went shopping with Ma. Megan puts her final touches on my makeup by putting pink lip gloss for a more natural look. "Okay Abby, you should see yourself in the mirror now!" I smile at my reflection in the mirror, pleased with the way my makeup complemented my hair and dress.

Seeing myself I remarked, "Wow! Megan, Yeah! You clean me up pretty good."

We both giggle, "Josh is not going to recognize you."

"He's just a friend, Megan."

"Don't you realize, Abby, that Josh has a crush on you?"

"He always treated me like a friend though and that's what he is."

"Well you look amazing Abby!"

"Thanks Megan."

Uncle Mario gives a nod of approval when he sees me in my dress and then proceeds to caution me about certain rules I should be mindful of when it comes to boys. Things my dad should have told us but never did. So I listen to him intently on our way to the school dance, grateful that I and Megan have someone like him around to guide us.

He looks up at me. "Be careful Abby and you look beautiful. When the dance finishes, I'll pick you up in front of the school."

"Okay Uncle Mario." I smile and hug him.

Walking to the steps, I see Josh is already waiting for me at the top of the stairs. I'm amazed by how polished he looks today. He was good-looking but today he's just looking his best! He's wearing a brown pull-over V-neck sweater. I could see his white t-shirt underneath brown slacks. His jet-black hair was combed back with gel. I think he's cropped his hair for the dance. I could see his gray bluish eyes shine with his light skin. The guy stands out already; I see other girls eyeing him like he's the best candy. I step up to give him a big hug.

He stares at me. "Abby you look so beautiful. I mean, you are beautiful." Now I'm blushing a shade of beet red. I bite my bottom lip as he squeezes my hand and walk to the gym room.

There's an assortment of party lights in the form of big stars covered in sparkly glitter and colorful balloons. There are tables lined with plastic bowls, cups and glasses and chairs which are tied around with big bows. The atmosphere inside the gym room was crackling with excitement. I'm captivated by how beautiful everything looks when my eyes stumble upon Betty Cox. She's worn a little black dress with high heels, her blonde hair flattened straight to frame her pretty face. She has a ton of make up on though and looks harsh under the glaring lights of the dance floor. Not my favorite look on her.

Rick is her partner, looking dapper as ever. He's wearing a white dressy shirt and has paired it with black slacks and matching shoes. They looked rather nice together. Rick looks at me intently when Betty notices it. She drags him across the dance floor to dance because she cannot stand him looking at anyone, and definitely not me.

Seeing that, Josh asks me to dance. Of course, I say yes. The whole point of dressing up and getting here was to be with Josh. I enjoyed my time with him, he was a decent boy. Though I was unaware of him having a crush on me and brushed it off lightly in the beginning, I think I'm hopeful though cautious. I don't trust people. It was a fast song; this was my first dance, so everything was new. I was really having fun with Josh. He was actually different tonight; he seemed a lot more free and sweeter than he usually is. We went to get some punch after our first round of dancing. We were drinking punch and giggled over the jokes he made. Josh stayed by my side for quite some time and we just relished each other's company. We didn't even realize how many glasses we drank because we were so lost in our conversation.

Josh's best friend came. His name was Brett Fox and his girlfriend was Brandy Torres. They looked good together. Brett was tall and lean, with blue eyes and tan skin. He had light brown hair with a loose curl. He dressed the same as Josh only his clothes were blue. Brandy was a brown eyed, red haired beauty who was voluptuous and pretty in every way. She already had huge breasts. She'd worn a short navy-blue pleated skirt with a powder blue sweater that suited her tanned complexion beautifully. We all were talking together when I felt someone watching me. I tilt my head to the side and see Rick was watching me intently, like he always did. I've never managed to figure out what he wanted or what he got out of eyeing me like this when he was putty in the hands of Betty. I looked away, puzzled and eager to avoid him. Josh notices my change in posture and asks me to dance again. This time, it was a slow song; Josh holds my waist and I can feel the strength in his arms. He stares into my eyes as I put my arms around his shoulders and neck. I loved the way Josh made me feel, he was like a warm blanket on a cold winter's night. I could feel the warmth of Josh's cheeks next to mine and knew he'd kiss me. I had butterflies in my stomach and I felt Josh lean in to kiss me. I closed my eyes, surrendering to the sweetness of his kiss when both of us were pushed to the floor. We fell hand in hand.

Chapter 11

I should've have known that things in my life could never go smoothly. Even the simplest things could become complicated. It was Rick who pushed me and Josh on the dance floor; his anger and jealousy had gotten the better of him but it's Josh and me who took the fall. Rick punched Josh and obviously, Josh wouldn't turn his back when he's challenged like this. He's furious and punches Rick, not once but twice.

Rick yelled at Josh "Don't ever touch Abby. She's mine you hear me?"

Josh laughs at first and then he smirks. "She's not yours idiot. Remember! Your girl is Betty Cox you jerk!" They kept beating each other. Brandy comes and helps me. Finally, one of the teachers breaks them apart and escorts them outside. They are talking to them after they finish. Josh comes for me and we start to walk when Rick grabs my arm so harshly and rushes me down the stairs. At the bottom, Rick pushes me against the wall. He holds my face gently with his hands and kisses me with all he has to offer. I pull away, repulsed at his sudden passion. Where was all this when I really needed a friend, where was he when Betty and others in class were tearing me apart like I was nothing. Did he feel something tonight when I was with someone else, which he hadn't felt in the last three years?

I was furious, "What are you doing Rick?" I was angry and there were tears sliding down my cheeks, ruining the little make up I had on. "God! What do you want Rick?"

"I'm sorry Abby." With his thumb he wipes my tears away. "I don't want to hurt you. I've missed you Abby. I've been missing you so much that my heart hurts so badly." I'm not amused with this latest display of affection that was absent in the presence of Betty Cox.

He goes for another kiss when Josh comes down the stairs with full force. He yells at him, "You don't learn. You listen punk!"

And he punches Rick in his face so violently he falls to the ground. His lip is bleeding.

"Why don't you do you a favor dude and leave Abby alone?"

Rick stares at Josh. Rick wipes his mouth with his palm and says, "Let her decide who she wants!"

"You treated her like dirt, like a piece of shit! Punk! And now you want her to choose, are you crazy? Come on Abby, let's wait for your uncle in front of the school."

I take Josh's hand and walk away from Rick. I don't look back. "Sorry Abby that this night didn't work out the way we wanted it to."

"Not your fault Josh."

"I really like you Abby! Ever since picking up your pencil."

Josh stares into my eyes. I could see his lips part to kiss me, something he was stopped from doing earlier, thanks to Rick. I let him and close my eyes to savor the moment. He is kissing me so sweetly, slowly and with so much tenderness, that I'm melting in his arms. He breaks away from kissing me momentarily and holds my face with both his hands. "Be my girl Abby?" he says with pleading eyes and all I could do was to nod coyly like an idiot. We seal this with another long kiss and end the night on a memorable note.

Waking up in the morning, Megan was on top of my bed bouncing up and down. "So how was it Abby?"

Rolling my eyes at her, I ask, "Don't you ever stop?"

"Come on Abby, tell me: did you have fun?"

"Yeah, I had fun!"

"So what happened? Did he kiss you?"

"OMG! Megan you are too much." Of course, I grin from ear to ear recollecting Josh and my kiss. I start to tell Megan what happened, how Josh and Rick started fighting and how they both kissed me. Megan had the nerve to ask who kissed better and who did I like the best. Well, I didn't tell her who kissed the best—I don't want to kiss and tell. I was very confused about them, thinking about what happened last night about the kiss with Josh. I was thinking more about Josh, did I really like Josh–like more than friends? And what about Rick? He was sorry and he missed me so much but he's also hurt me just as much. What am I going to do? Well, I don't have time to put things in perspective about that, just yet! Because I have to clean the house like we do every Saturday or every day for that matter. Uncle Mario is telling Ma that he's planning to get married. I didn't even know that he had a girlfriend or was engaged. He really looked happy telling Ma that he wanted me and Megan in the wedding. We say ok. He gives us a huge smile and a bear hug. Maybe Dad will come because the last three years he only came a few times when he and Maria were fighting. He would get drunk until he fell asleep. I never saw Maria ever again, thank God!

Walking down the hill, I see Josh was waiting for me. When I see him, I feel weak in my knees and my stomach feels funny. He looks so cute, why am I feeling this? I'm so confused. "So Abby are you going to be my girl or what?" What else could I say: he's so cute, and I'm blushing and shyly say yes? He gives me a gentle kiss. We hold hands and we walk to school. We talk about our classes. He's holding my hand so tight; my stomach is feeling like a garden of butterflies are fluttering. Then he lifts the palm of my hand to his mouth. Rick used to do that. Why am I even thinking of him? Because, that was such a sweet gesture. Now Josh is doing it. We get to school and I go to get my books from my locker, when Rick gets really close. "Abby I'm sorry about Friday."

"Just stay away Rick, it's best for everyone."

"No, it's not Abby!"

"Why?"

"Won't you listen, because I don't want to fight with you anymore Rick."

"Abby just listen."

"Okay well I'm listening."

"I really miss you Abby."

"Same story Rick." God he's making me roll my eyes.

"I am so sorry Abby, I want to be friends again."

We just stare at each other. "Rick, Josh is my boyfriend now."

"No Abby he's not."

"Yes, he is!"

Rick slams on the locker with his fist so intensely I almost jump!

"Abby I don't want Josh next to you, damn it!"

"Of course you don't, you're with Betty and you are telling me what to do and who to see. Does that make any sense to you?"

"I've never been with Betty!"

"Are you for real? I don't care what you do Rick but you have to stop harassing me, got it!

Or do I have to spell it out for you? Josh has been my friend since coming back, really when I truly needed a friend. You were so furious for something I had no control of. What did you do to me? You got back at me in the meanest way and that made me lose my best friend and you with those mean girls, they bullied me and threw food at me, made fun of me. So I really couldn't care less if you're Betty's boyfriend or not."

"Abby I'm not with her."

"Are we doing this same story again, Rick, because I'm going to be late for class."

"Please! Abby let's be friends and I promise not to hurt you."

"Sorry Rick it's too late for that! You already did."

And with that I turn and walk away once again. Meeting Josh at lunch we share our food. He holds my hand and we kiss. Josh walks me to my classes. He truly is a nice boyfriend. He's sweet in every way. We walk home from school. We're at the bottom of the hill. He turns me around and holds my waist. He looks straight into my eyes first and then he kisses my forehead then my cheek then he leans in to kiss me. We kiss, his fingers caressing my cheek. "See you tomorrow Abby." Smiling at him, he knows we can't walk together up the hill because Ma is waiting for me, and we don't want to rock that boat.

We are getting fitted for our dresses for my Uncle Mario's wedding. Today, we are going to find out what kind of dresses and what color we'd be wearing. Uncle Mario and his girlfriend are taking us to the boutique. Uncle Mario introduced us. "Megan and Abby, this is Anna Sosa."

She is a sight for sore eyes. Almond skinned with light brown eyes, short black hair and full lips. We smile at her and give her a big hug. So, we find out that the dresses are going to be ankle length, in soft pink satin with a silver sash. Uncle Mario tells me that my partner is going to be Anna's brother. I'm not very excited about that idea as I wanted Josh and Megan wanted Kyle. We agreed reluctantly knowing that this was Uncle Mario's wedding, not ours…! So Anna has four brothers and they are all going to be in the wedding. Uncle Mario turns to me and says, "One of her brothers is two years older than you, so he's fifteen."

"So what's his name?"

"Martin Sosa."

"Ok!" I nodded. I really don't care, and Megan's partner, her brother is three years older than Megan, his name is Steve Sosa. Megan just rolls her eyes. She tells me, "If we're lucky, they will be cute, because can you imagine if they are ugly the whole day would be wasted, and the pictures!" I just shake my head in disbelief, I can't believe she just said that. Oh well, just have to wait and see. Uncle Mario said on Friday we will meet them. They are hosting a big family dinner.

The week went fast. It's Friday. Anna's family is on one side of the restaurant and our entire family are is on the other side. Ma pushes me and Megan to the table; it was so embarrassing. Megan looks around and turns to me. "God they are so cute. We are so in trouble. Don't stare Abby! They are staring at us."

"Then how do you want me to see?"

"Take it from me, they're so cute."

"Why do you care Megan? You have Kyle, remember, your boyfriend."

"Abby you are a stick in the mud. We both have boyfriends."

"Yeah! We do." Giving a chuckle

Uncle Mario nudges me and Megan to get up so he can introduce our partners to us. Megan was right, we were in trouble because these two brothers were more cuteness than we could handle!

Uncle Mario says, "This is Abby Pena and this is Martin Sosa." He gives me a hand shake with the most beautiful smile I ever seen. He has light skin, brown eyes, light long brown hair; he's sporting one of those 'I just woke up from bed' kinda of looks. He was tall and masculine. He wore a blue shirt, with the sleeves rolled up and some black trousers. I look over to see Megan already talking with Steve. He is tall and lean, with light skin, brown eyes, and dark brown hair, very nice, he wears it short and pulled back. He's a looker. Boy, she didn't waste any time and of course Martin is just smiling at me. Oh God why does this have to happen to me?

My face is reddening up. Glancing at Martin, who looks a lot older than fifteen, he says, "So Abby, what grade are you in?"

I shyly say, "Seventh grade."

He frowns. "You are young."

Now I'm rolling my eyes. "Well so are you. You are only two years older."

"Has anyone told you that it's rude to roll your eyes like that?"

If he only knew Ma hits me all the time for that. "Are you going to be annoyed with me all night?" Martin is smiling again–not again that beautiful smile; now I'm really blushing, and I am turning so he won't notice. Martin says, "Could I have your phone number?"

"Ma doesn't let me use the phone"

"Do you have a boyfriend?"

"Yes, his name is Josh. Do you have a girlfriend?"

"No."

So we sit to have dinner, then we meet Anna's other two brothers. They are much older, in their early twenties. We all say our goodbyes after dinner. Megan seems elated. "So Abby did you like him?"

"He's okay I guess, he is just a partner for the wedding Megan, that's all,"

"Well I like Steve, he is nice, smart and cute."

"And what about Kyle? You know, your boyfriend."

"Stop Abby! You're always spoiling my fun." Then she winks at me. "We are young Abby, we should have friends you know." Since when does she feel this way? Then we all go home and all Megan talks about is Steve Sosa all the way home.

Chapter 12

It's Saturday, day of the wedding has arrived. It's fairly sunny today for a November morning. I and Megan are getting dressed in our room. Since I have to be dressed in a similar way as bridesmaids, we've decided to put our hair in a high bun. Our dresses are pink with silver sashes so we pick out similar jewelry in silver that also goes well with our pale, cool toned skin. A light but decent amount of makeup, a little mascara, a brushing of eye shadow, a dusty pink lipstick touched off with a bit of gloss, and who could forget a deep brown-pink blush? When we finish with our makeup and dressing, Megan and I look at ourselves in the mirror to inspect our final look. We both are pleased with what we see. Megan has always been the prettier one among the two of us, and she looks exquisite today, the pink really suits her and brings out the color of her skin. She looks at me and remarks, "Well Abby, you look real pretty today."

I say, "Thanks. We do clean up well," I said with a smile and then Megan gives me her famous wink. Putting on our silver shoes that we'll in all likelihood never use again, we're ready to go downstairs to join Ma, Pa and Paul. We had spent the whole night making pink flowers out of tissue to be used as decorations for the car and even our bouquets. It turned out well. When we got down to the living room, Ma had already hurried off to the church. We decide to go together then. I step outside and see Josh. I'm delighted to see him and show off my hairstyle and pink dress. Josh wasn't very happy about the wedding because of Martin. He runs to our fence as soon as he sees me. He stares at me for a minute and gives me a smile. "You look so beautiful Abby." Josh gets the palm of my hand and I feel his mouth leaving sweet kisses. "Have fun okay?" I nod my head like a moron.

Megan yells, "Come on Abby, let's go okay!"

"Stop yelling!" I glance back at Josh as he watches me walk to the car–Megan promptly pulls me in the car so that we can reach church on time. We finally get there in 10 minutes flat. Uncle Mario looks handsome and happy. He's dressed in a black suit with pink carnations pinned to his left pocket. He's beaming with joy and both Megan & me agree that he really deserves it. He's been the sweetest to us and is Ma's favorite as well. I notice that all the guys are wearing black suits. They all look so handsome, every single one of them. We are all going to walk hand in hand with our partners in the entrance procession. The flower girls go first, then the bridesmaids with their partners. Martin takes hold of my hand and whispers in my ear, "You are the most beautiful girl here."

"I bet you tell that line to all the girls." I say with a sheepish smile.

"No, just the pretty ones like you." He says with a wink.

I feel my cheeks getting flushed and remark coyly, "You don't look too bad yourself," He reciprocates that with his beautiful smile. Martin is quite a charmer and I know for sure that girls would be all over him if they had a chance. I get weak knees when I see him smile like that, not that I don't get weak knees when I see Josh. But really, I don't know how I'm going to survive the day if he keeps smiling like that all the time. Everyone is at the church. All are families except Dad and Paul. Uncle Mario wanted them to be part of the wedding as much as anyone else. Paul had refused the invitation and said no; he's never home and keeps hanging out with the wrong sort of people. He's become such trouble. Dad's drinking didn't help. He's drinking more now than ever before. While we wait for Anna, I glanced at Martin. He is very handsome with his hair combed back, his full lips and brown eyes that are twinkling with delight. The music for the ceremony begins and wakens me from my thoughts about Paul and Dad. The music for the bride's entrance has begun and I see Anna walking down the aisle. She looks amazing in her wedding dress. So beautiful: it's a princess line dress in a deep, vintage ivory with silver sequins embroidered all over. She's worn a bridal tiara studded with rhinestones and crystals which sparkle under the light. Her veil flows a foot behind her wedding dress. Her wedding bouquet is a mixture of white and pink carnations with silver ribbons and bows. It's perfect! I could see Uncle Mario beaming with pride and joy seeing beautiful Anna walk towards him. Seeing Uncle Mario and Anna's love, I secretly wished that for myself. I'm sure every unmarried, grown up girl would've teared up with joy at the sight of this lovely couple. When the ceremony ends, everyone goes and takes pictures and we all leave to the hall they rented for the wedding party. It was decorated with pretty pink flowers, silver accents and ivory-white curtains. Silver glitter covered candles were part of the centerpieces on each table. It was so beautiful. Martin holds my hand and we walk to our table. Megan and Steve are already sitting there talking and laughing. She's really having fun with him. Martin holds the chair out for me, like a thorough gentleman and I respond with a courteous nod, saying, "Thank you."

Martin gives me that mega-watt smile again. "You are so welcome Abby."

God, does he have to smile like that every time! Is it just me or does weddings bring out more emotions than usual?! The lovey-doveyness of it all is rubbing off on me. Steve brings a cup from under the table and gives it to Megan, and I ask her, "Are you drinking?"

"Don't start Abby! Just one cup. Do you want one?"

I stare at her in disbelief "Are you crazy?".

"No, I'm not!"

I feel Martin's hand over my hand and I glance up to see what he thinks he is doing! He gives that mega smile then asks me to dance in a bid to diffuse the tension between Megan and me. How could I say no to that smile? I just nod and he leads me to the dance floor. We dance for two-three songs and head to our table when I see Dad stumble onto our table in drunken stupor. He calls out my name so loudly, "Abby!" he says in a high pitched voice. Oh! God! I'm mortified. Martin lets go of my hand and I don't blame him. My face is red with embarrassment, but no, he's my Dad. Ma was also slightly drunk so she couldn't fully comprehend the drama that was now unfolding before our eyes. I doubt she'd allow Dad to walk in at a wedding like this. And if this wasn't enough, Paul walks in like the cherry on the icing of the cake to bring this party down. He looked more than just drunk. He had a girl with him, and she was holding his waist, in a vain attempt to keep him standing upright. Paul was dressed in a white button shirt and black slacks. The girl was dark haired and looked messy, she'd worn a very short dress, her lady parts were barely covered; I haven't seen her before and presume that she's one of the many girls Paul hangs out with. The high heels she'd worn made her balancing act difficult because she kept stumbling just as badly as Paul. What a couple! My eyes scan in despair for Megan to keep this drama from getting worse, in the hope that Paul and Dad wouldn't make a spectacle of themselves. And more than anything else, this will hurt Uncle Mario so much, because this is his day! I can't see Megan; I search for her in the immediate vicinity. Where did she go? She's never around when these things happen. Uncle

Mario got some of Anna's older brothers to take Dad and Ma home. Paul was another story. He sat at our table so drunk kissing his date all over her face. That girl looked like she was the one doing drugs, not Paul.

Martin was still beside me. He knew I was uncomfortable. "Come with me Abby, let's get some air." We go outside and I'm grateful for the temporary respite it provides from seeing Paul in the state he's in. It's cold and the evening breeze was making my body shiver.

"You're cold." Martin says as he slips on his black suit coat around my shoulders. It smelled of him: musk and soap. I'm not nervous with Martin like I was with Rick and sometimes with Josh, and that takes me by surprise. "Abby was that your Dad?"

"Yeah! That's my Dad alright." I was staring at the ground, lost in deep thought. I wondered why Dad bothered coming, he seemed reluctant enough when Uncle Mario invited him initially. Martin had one hand on my cheek and the other lifts my chin. He stares into my eyes then he asks me, "I'd like to kiss you Abby," and there it is, his beautiful smile again.

"Why, me?" I ask, lightly protesting his request.

I said yes before he could even answer, but he was twirling my hair that was lying loosely around my face. He says, "You're so pretty."

I smile shyly at him and then he slowly but deeply, kisses me. It was passionate and he didn't want to stop; neither did I. That's when it hit me. I'm kissing Martin but my boyfriend is Josh. This is wrong but I barely have the courage to pluck myself away from Martin right now because, in this moment, right here it feels beautiful. When we stop, he could see that I'm blushing. "You're so innocent Abby. I really like you but you're so young."

"Martin you do know I've had a boyfriend for a while?"

"Then why did you kiss me Abby? Don't know? Silly girl." And he lifts my chin and starts kissing me again and again. Martin is shamelessly charming and seductive, a very dangerous combination for a guy. I simply didn't want to stop him from kissing me, his kisses were wonderful, his touch was gentle but his mouth full of passion. He was a great kisser. When we say our goodbyes, he gives me his phone number. "Call me whenever you want Abby!" Martin is smoothing my loose strands of hair with his finger. "I hope to see you soon." He says with a wink.

"Yes, soon." What else could I possibly say? My mind wandered with thoughts of Martin till I thought about having to take Dad home; he was drunk out of his senses and singing some song I couldn't make out.

Megan gets in the car just as we're about to leave. Her hair is down; some of her makeup is smeared. Who knew what she was up to? I didn't even want to know. Megan speaks. "So Dad came to the wedding after all?"

"Yeah! He did, it was so embarrassing."

"I'm mighty glad I wasn't there." Megan had the nerve to smirk and wink at a time like this. I just gave her my now famous eye roll.

It's Sunday morning and we wake up to a cloudless blue sky. It didn't get chilly until evening this time of the year. By the time we'd got in bed last night, it had gotten pretty cold. We cozied up in bed with two layers of blankets and slept off. I look out the window and then walk to the mirror and take a look at myself. I thought of the time with Martin, Anna and Uncle Mario, and then Dad & Paul. I'm exhausted merely thinking about it all. The planning and decorating related to the wedding took its toll on us as much as the event itself. Physically, I could be in bed for another whole day and wouldn't complain but Megan and I had a whole lot of cleaning up to do today. We didn't go to church either; Ma woke up late. Paul didn't even come home. I thought about last night, about kissing Martin. I felt a pinch of guilt for doing that. "How could I have done that? How will I feel about Josh now? And what will happen if he came to know? My mind starts to panic and I try to pacify myself with common sense. I'm not going to tell him because, well… I'll hurt him. Don't want to do anything to hurt him, this is not me. And this isn't right."

I finish cleaning up when I see Ma & Pa leave together to go visiting some family friends. This was my chance to go to the park and breathe in some fresh air. I welcomed that thought and got ready to go walking slowly, lost in thought when I heard someone say, "Hi! Abby!"

I didn't have to know whose voice that was. I turn around and see Rick. I purse my lips together because I don't want to fight with him again. "Hi!" I manage to say back, coolly. Rick stares at me with a heavy heart, it makes me ache for him but I'm determined to not get sympathetic towards him.

"Where are you going?"

"You know where, I'm going to the park." I say in a matter-of-fact kinda voice.

"Come on then, I'll walk with you Abby." So we walk. We sit on the bench. No one is at the park yet! So we're alone when I turn to face Rick. He has a fading black eye.

"What happened to your eye?"

"Had a fight with my brother." I just nodded: what could I say? We were not friends anymore, so being nosey is was out of the question. There's a minute of silence between, then he turns to me and says, "Abby, I really want us to be friends again!"

Staring up from my thick black lashes I look back at Rick trying to gauge him. I felt for him at times but then I recollect the times he had a chance to be there and didn't. Did he deserve another chance at friendship, maybe? I keep looking at him and reconsider. Rick's eyes are so glossy like if he wanted to suppurate.

"Okay Rick, we could be friends."

"Really!" he quips with delight.

I smile at him. "Yes really."

Rick lifts me up from the bench and gives me a tight bear hug. Turning me around and around, I can see he's positively excited about us becoming friends again and his enthusiasm is making me giggle. "You're hugging me too tight." I say to curb his high spirits.

"God I've missed you so much."

"We are just friends Rick, and what about Betty, she's not going to like you being my friend."

"Abby, I don't care what she thinks. She doesn't choose my friends okay."

"Don't want drama from her, Rick. I have enough to deal with her on my own."

"She won't bother you Abby, I won't let her. And what about Josh?"

"What about him?"

"Abby, he hates me, and you know it!"

"Don't worry about him." But in my mind, I was wondering how Josh would take this piece of news.

Telling Josh about Rick being my friend was a huge mistake. He was yelling at me, "You're not going to be his friend Abby! Don't forget the way he treated you for God sakes!"

"Don't be telling me what to do Josh! Got to go! Going to be late for class."

"Wait Abby! I'm going to walk you."

"Don't Josh! Just leave me alone for a while."

Josh rolled his eyes. "So it begins right Abby! Yeah go, don't want you to be late for your class." He leaves me in the middle of the hall. I walk slowly to the locker, wondering what just happened. He's so angry, and I'm just as furious too. I had lunch alone that day. I even walked home by myself without Rick or Josh.

I'm cleaning the large restroom at home when I hear someone making weird sounds in the toilet. I slide the door quietly, careful to not intrude. I rush when I see it's Megan; she's bent over and is vomiting. I'm worried, and I ask, "Are you okay Megan?" She starts sobbing, wrapping her arms around me. "What's wrong?" I ask again in a soft voice because I didn't want to alarm anyone. Not yet. She just nods her head back and forth, and then she vomits again. When she finishes, I help her to our bedroom and sit down beside her. At this point, though I'm unsure, I'm pretty darn worried seeing her sick like this, "What's wrong Megan?" Still crying she tells me that she's pregnant. I gasp, "Oh my God." I'm in shock and can't believe what she's saying. Still trying to process what she's said, I blurt out the obvious question, "Who's the father?"

Then Megan gets angry. "Who do you think? Abby, do you think I'm sleeping with every guy? It's Kyle's. I'm scared Abby. What if he doesn't want the baby?"

"Goodness gracious, Megan! You shouldn't be worried about whether Kyle accepts your baby right now; you should be more worried about Ma. She's going to be furious as hell! You need to tell Kyle, immediately."

"I'm scared Abby." I could see the fear in her eyes and we weren't quite sure how Ma's going to react to this. Megan called Kyle to meet her at the front of the house. He comes promptly and I watch her go to meet him from the bedroom window, praying that things don't take a turn for the worse. He always looks at her with a megawatt smile. I believe they truly loved each other and wanted the best for both of them. I could only hope that everything worked out the way we imagine it to. I continue to keep myself busy with the chores, thinking about how the conversation between Megan and Kyle goes. When Megan comes into the room, she seems at peace. She looked ecstatic–and I only assume he was as delighted about the news Megan gave him as I and Megan were. I was so happy for her, that's one prayer answered. Megan grinned ear to ear saying, "He's happy Abby!"

"I'm really glad, Megan but Ma won't be."

"I don't care, she's always angry anyways." I was worried about Megan but she's so in love and I love to see her happy and hearing her singing was always such a treat. Megan sang only when she was really happy and that happens quite rarely. Today was one of those days. My mind wanders to thoughts about Josh. He's Kyle's brother and technically would be an Uncle to Megan and Kyle's child; that makes me an Aunt! I was feeling so positive about all this but I'm assuming Josh is–probably still angry with me about establishing a friendship with Rick again. Oh! Well he's going to have to accept it. The next day, I walk to the park to see a softball game.

It's kind of windy and the breeze feels so good; this is heaven for me. I can feel goose bumps pop all over my skin, I love inhaling in the sweet fragrance of autumn. I close my eyes taking in the fresh air when I hear Josh say, "Hi Abby." Opening my eyes, I see him smiling as sweetly as only he can. Taking hold of my hand, he says, "I've missed you Abby."

"Well maybe you shouldn't get angry so much."

He holds my shoulder and turns me to face him. "You are too stubborn for your own britches Abby."

Stubborn or not, Josh still wanted to be my boyfriend. He made sure I knew that. We were at the park the whole day and everything was starting to come together again. But in at the back of my mind, I was waiting for the shoe to drop—you know, the storm that threatens to wash out every beautiful thought you've ever had.

It's December, and the first rumblings of the storm I fear, is here. It is the day, Megan and

Kyle are going to tell Ma she's pregnant. It's one of the days when the skies mirror the emotions running through our minds: dull, dark and grey. Like something sinister was in the air. It was that same feeling that I had leading up to that dreadful Christmas morning when all hell broke loose. My gut was sending out the same signal, something was going to happen. I help Megan clean up and push out all negative scenarios out of my head. Ma was making us an amazing Mexican dinner from scratch: rice, beans, some chili, and tacos, and her best red salsa–it's really great, and happens to be one of my favorite comfort foods. Home cooking over restaurant food anytime! Megan was nervous, she was nauseas and sick. I was eager to taste Ma's food as I was hungry. But seeing Megan's unease, it just didn't feel right to indulge. I was looking out our bedroom window when I see a lot of guests at Josh's place. "He didn't tell me family were coming to his house." Megan was still waiting, anxiously for Kyle. We all walked to the table to have dinner.

"It was getting cold," Ma says, "Let's eat."

Megan didn't want to eat now. She's worried so I try to console her. "It's okay, he's just a little late."

"God Abby! What if he's changed his mind?"

"He loves you Megan and you know it! They have lots of guests visiting today."

"What you mean? He didn't tell me anybody was visiting."

"Well maybe they didn't know either. Stop worrying."

"Okay let's go eat dinner."

We are eating dinner when we hear a knock at the door. I sensed something oddly wrong about that knock. My stomach is in knots but I go to open the door. I'm surprised to see Brett. His blue eyes look gloomy. "Hi Brett, what are you doing here?"

"We need to talk Abby."

"Is there something wrong?"

He knit his brow and frowns at me. Ma yelled from the dining room, "Who is it Abby?"

"Got to go Brett. Ma won't let me talk. Give me thirty minutes, and then meet me in the back yard."

He nodded. Walking back, I knew something dreadful was to come. I felt more and more at unease and suddenly the food in front of me lost its hold on me. I lose my appetite and my mind is churning, wondering what could be the matter. Ma asks, noticing that I haven't eaten a spoon of food that's on my plate, "Well who was it?"

I just say it was someone who was asking for a person that didn't live here. Megan was just staring at me, blank. She lifts her eyebrow and looks at me with questioning eyes. She knew better that it was best not to say anything when Ma was around. We started to clean up after dinner which I managed to finish rather reluctantly. I could see Megan's face grim with worry because Kyle didn't turn up.

Chapter 13

I go to the backyard with my heart pounding out of my chest; even though I wasn't sure of why Brett came to meet me at such an odd time, I knew something was up. It's raining outside; what started out as a light drizzle was now turning into a full blown thunderstorm. I finally see Brett waiting for me in the backyard, taking cover from the rain under a tin roofed shed. I brace myself for whatever it is that Brett was going to say because right up to this moment, my instincts have gone into an overdrive saying something is terribly wrong. Brett takes a deep breath, and then speaks with a heavy voice. "Kyle died today Abby."

"What!" I almost fell backward in shock. I couldn't believe what I heard. No, it can't be. Megan's waiting for him back home. No, no no…this can't be true. I can't breathe, I catch hold of Brett's collar and shake him. "Tell me, this isn't the truth." I plead, with tears pooling out. He didn't say anything but his silence spoke more than any words could. He holds me up, to keep me from collapsing down. I'm feeling weak and the blood has drained from my body. What happened to Kyle? How did this happen? I wanted to know everything, but I still couldn't believe this was happening! And the big question of how to tell this news to Megan?! My head was spinning with worry and sadness. How is Meg going to take this? My heart screamed 'No' having our happiness defeated by the hands of fate, yet again.

Megan will be devastated, and what about Josh? "Where is Josh, Brett?"

"He's distraught Abby!" Oh My! God! I cannot take this, two of my favorite people in the world are going to be broken by this. I finally muster the courage to ask Brett how he died. A drunk driver ran over him. He was walking home alone. They said he was coming from the store. They found him clutching a baby toy in his hand. This can't be happening. Tears were coming down my face and I'm unable to accept this bitter reality. Saying I'm in a state of shock would be an understatement. How would Megan overcome this? Brett says he has to get going.

Delivering the news to me was hard for him as it was for me to hear it. Kyle and Brett have known each other for years. We both cry, knowing that nothing could console us right now. We hug each other and he leaves me, standing in the rain, pondering over the sorrow and bitterness of what lay ahead for Megan, Josh, me and an unborn child that is breathing in Megan's womb. Megan and I had known the pain of having our mother die early; we grew up without her maternal love. Would this child's fate be the same? There were a thousand questions running through my mind, but most of all, I couldn't escape the pain of this moment. I didn't want to be the one to break the news to Megan. She was so blissfully happy in the days leading up to today and she's still hoping that Kyle will walk in that door anytime now and deliver the news of their baby together, to Ma. Why do things have to be this way my God, why? It was so unfair! What about my sweet Josh? How did he cope with this? I wanted to see him. My heart ached for my sister and him. I'm pacing back and forth while the rain poured relentlessly. I was crying, heartbroken and feeling hopeless all the same time. I wasn't sure how to tell all this to Megan. I wanted to be there for Josh but I wanted to be here for Megan too. There was no decent way of doing this, I feel torn and unable to decide. Megan finds me all wet and pacing frantically. She's both concerned and anxious about why Brett had come.

"What's the matter Abby?" she asks holding my hand. She warms it up, then looks at me "You are all wet. Let's go home before you catch a fever." I silently follow her lead back to the house. Megan hands me a towel to dry my hair and face. I nudge her to go upstairs and told her I'll come up soon. My heart was weighed down and I knew Megan was going to be shattered when she hears what I say. I walk up the stairs to the bedroom, quietly, knowing that the next few minutes will change my sister's life forever. How I wanted to see her happy, how I rejoiced in her song.

I push open the bedroom door to step inside and see Megan sitting up on the bed, her head slightly resting on a pillow she's plopped up for support. I shut the door behind me, my face distraught with the task at hand.

I look straight in Megan's face and she knows something happened. "Tell me Abby? Just tell me?"

I go and sit beside her, unable to contain my tears. She holds me tightly and asks again "Abby, what's the matter? You know you can tell me anything, I'm here for you."

"Megan, Kyle died today." I blurt out, tears flowing down my cheeks.

"Stop being a liar Abby! Just stop!"

"I'm not a liar Megan! I wouldn't do that."

Megan fell on her knees on the wooden floor. and I wrap my arms around her. "What Happened Abby? Tell me please! Answer me! Where is he? Tell me!" Megan was sobbing, her eyes pleaded with me for answers but she was crumbling. I held her tight; I prayed she'd have the strength to live through this.

"That's why he didn't come to dinner. He met with an accident when he was walking back home from a store. They found his body by the roadside clutching a baby toy in his hand."

"Oh my God Abby! Nooo, noo......Kyle..."

Megan moaned in sorrow. She knew Kyle had received the news of her pregnancy with great joy. She dreamed of a future with him and their child. Everything was shattered in a single moment. It was too much to bear.

"I loved him Abby. I loved him! What am I going to do without him?" she said sobbing inconsolably.

"I don't know Megan." I said, trying to comfort her.

"He was happy Abby when I told him, and our baby is never going to get to see his Dad." I just hold her tight knowing that nothing I did right now would comfort her. It was difficult for all of us to believe he was gone. And I still hadn't reached out to Josh; I don't know how I'm going to do that. This was one of the most difficult, sorrowful nights of my life. I never felt so helpless. This was the storm my gut instincts were hinting at. Even with a prior feeling of dread leading up to today's dinner, nothing could have prepared me, Megan or Josh's family for something like this. My thoughts were with Josh and his family, the sadness and grief they'd be feeling at this time is unimaginable. Kyle was such a promising young man with a bright future ahead of him. I thought he was perfect for Megan and would've made for a wonderful father. Seeing so many dreams and so many people's hopes & expectations of him be wiped away in such a manner was a poignant reminder of the unpredictability of life.

Megan wept till her eyes were bloodshot and painful. Her head ached, her body was weak and at that moment, she wasn't sure if she could even stay alive. Kyle's death had left a void in her heart, and it may take years, even decades to heal. Exhausted and unable to cry anymore, she fell asleep. I stayed by her side, caressing her beautiful face. Words wouldn't help in a time like this. I looked out the window, feeling the autumn wind go its way. The sky was dark but the rain finally stopped. I turned to look at Megan. She was sleeping and while she looked at ease now, I knew her spirit was crushed. She wasn't prepared for the way her life was going to turn around. Tomorrow morning, her new reality will set in. We hadn't yet broken the news of her baby to Ma, and Kyle's death has also not been shared with anyone. Only I and Megan knew. Knowing what lay ahead of us, I couldn't sleep all night. I tossed and turned wondering how Josh, Megan and Josh's family would cope. I whispered a silent prayer holding of them in my heart, pleading with God to show mercy.

The next day, Megan stays back at home, her health deteriorating overnight. She looks strained and sorrow is etched all over her face. I go to school because that's the best way I can reach Josh or Brett. I find Brett waiting for me near the hallway of my class. He gives me details of the funeral and walks me to class. I ask Brett how Josh is holding up and meet with an expected response.

"He's not okay Abby. He won't talk to anyone. What about your sister? She's hanging in there?"

"Megan isn't doing so well either."

"Hope she feels better. Abby, I'll see you on Thursday night."

"Sure, I'll be there."

I spent the rest of the day at school in a daze, not paying attention to anything or anyone. I walk as if I'm walking through a nightmare when I bump into someone's chest. I say sorry only to find it's Rick.

"Hi Abby!" He smiles at her.

"Hi! Rick, didn't mean to bump in to you."

"It's okay Abby. We both are not paying attention. Heard about Josh's brother—sorry! Knowing he was with your sister. So how are they?"

"Well really don't know how Josh is doing, haven't seen him. Megan is not doing so well."

Rick puckered his brow. "And how are you Abby?"

"I'm doing fine." I didn't know what else to say. He was being thoughtful and I appreciated his asking me how I was. But deep inside, I wasn't fine and neither was I going to be. Thinking about Josh and Megan, I don't think I could ever be fine. We are silent for a minute. He holds my hand. "Come on Abby, I'm going to walk you home,"

It is Thursday evening, the second week of December. We are getting ready for the funeral. I'm keeping a watch over Megan because ever since the news of Kyle's death, she's been depressed and sometimes so lost in thought, that I'd have to pinch her to draw her attention back. She still hasn't told Ma about the pregnancy and that Kyle was the father of her child; it didn't seem like the right timing but nothing worse could happen than what has already happened. My heart ached for her. I had to call Uncle Mario so that he could take me and Megan to the funeral because Ma won't let us go alone. Uncle Mario is waiting in his car. He came alone. I don't know where Paul is. We haven't seen him in days so that can't be good. "Come on Megan, let's go!"

Megan holds my hand then squeezes it so tightly, it starts to hurt. I tell her nothing because I know the anguish coursing through her veins right now.

"I can't do this Abby, I don't want to go."

"Are you sure? Because you should be there!"

"Not anymore Abby!"

"Don't then." She sobs again. "It's okay Megan, don't come with me." I understand how she felt but I tell her about Josh and his family. About the loss they're feeling too, just like her. When she hears that, she reluctantly walks to the car and gets in.

We reach the church and walk inside. The church pews are lined with white flowers. You could feel the sadness in the still air. Megan tightens her hold around my hand and continues walking, trembling slightly. Uncle Mario holds my hand tightly and I'm clutching Meg's hand tightly. We sit right beside Brett and Brandy. We are all wearing black clothing. There were so many people. I can't see Josh from where I was seated. I see Rick a couple of rows ahead with his brothers. Kyle's father takes to the stand and talks about him with affection, about his childhood, his dreams and how often they had remarked that they were lucky to have a son like him. The people gathered there knew he was saying the truth because everyone was so fond of him. He was amazing with Megan. I really had to speak to Josh. A few more people talk and then the priest concluded with a short sermon on death, its inevitability and how every moment was precious. He speaks highly of Kyle and reaffirms the many good things other people said about him. Everyone walks to the coffin to say their final goodbyes to Kyle. Kyle's family, his cousins, Aunts and Uncles and many others present there were inconsolable. They mourned his loss quietly. I finally see Josh, has his hands covering his face, weeping for his brother. My heart breaks for him. I wanted to hold Josh and comfort him. When I manage to get close to him, I wrap my arms around him then whisper in his ear, "I'm so sorry about Kyle."

He's nodding his head and whispers back in my ear, "Get away from me! There's not a damn thing you could do or say to bring him back Abby." Josh pushes me backwards which takes me by surprise. Rick was standing behind me and catches me from losing my balance. Josh was angry, hurt, distraught and so sad. I was at a loss for words. I couldn't see this, I run out of the church, crying while Rick watched on helplessly. Outside, I cry out, unable to contain my sorrow. I didn't expect such a reaction from Josh but I knew what he was going through and what Megan was going through, would change them forever. Rick finds me outside and puts his arm around me to comfort me. I take comfort in his warmth and his silence. He was being the friend I needed him to be.

The next day, it was hard to just wake up. I had cried most of the previous day and night, Megan even more so. We went to bed, exhausted and heartbroken. I open my eyes, events of the previous day going through my head. Josh's reaction, the funeral, Rick…it felt surreal. I hear Paul's voice coming from below, much to my surprise because he doesn't turn up home too often these days. I hadn't really seen him after his disastrous entrance at Uncle Mario's wedding. I turned my thoughts to Josh again. He's heartbroken and grieving, how else should he be behaving? I wanted to comfort him and console him, but it wasn't going to be of any use right now. I pray that time heals us all because it's a wound that's cut all of us deeply. As these thoughts are running in my head and I look at the ceiling above us, I sense Megan wake up. She looks distraught and tired. I was beginning to worry about her baby. She hasn't eaten much in the last few days and if Ma begins noticing, we'll have to let the cat out of the bag.

"Well Megan it was dreadful, really horrible."

Megan, asks me, pained and concerned "Abby do you think Kyle told anyone about the baby?"

"I don't think so, no one even talked about it or assumed anything. Megan you need to tell Ma about this today! It can't go on like this"

"Abby NO!"

"Why! You have to tell her."

"Give me a few days."

"Okay then."

It's Friday. I walk to school slowly, my heart heavy with all the things that have happened in the last few weeks. I cry often when I feel overwhelmed, it's the only way to release the sadness I felt. I knew Megan felt similarly and she had a bigger headache to worry about, breaking the news to Ma. I wipe my tears and continue to walk, fraught with worry about what more is to come.

I feel someone's palm slip into my hand when I turn sideways to see Rick. I give him a faint smile. "Hi" I say.

"Let me walk you to school Abby." We don't say anything as we walk in silence.

Here I'm in class and the teacher is saying who knows what. "Abby did you hear me?"

Staring at him, I say, "I'm sorry, I didn't hear."

"Okay Abby! I really don't like repeating myself."

"Sorry sir," I say in a faint voice.

You have been picked for the pageant, and if you win queen, you will go to the dance with the winning king."

I roll my eyes and wonder whether he's even being real because it felt like an inappropriate joke, if it was one. Apparently, he wasn't kidding. He was serious. I walk to my locker with so many things going through my mind.

I see Josh as I get close to my locker area, he's looking at me but I'm unable to make out if he's still angry and hurt or he wants to talk to me. I was surprised seeing him in school so soon. I wanted to talk to him, hold him and console him. His reaction at the funeral left me a bit reluctant to approach him. He looked terrible, like he hasn't slept in days. No one could blame him. Kyle's loss has devastated him and Megan so much; it's taking a toll on both of them.

"Hi Abby," he said, in a muffled voice. It caught me off guard but I nodded in return. What could we tell each other? I waited to see if he wanted to say something more. and I just nodded. I have a bad feeling about this but I take a deep breath and inch closer to him, to hear him more clearly.

"Sorry Abby, about the way I treated you at the funeral."

My mind heaves a sigh of relief and I respond warmly. "It's okay Josh, you lost your brother. You are hurting right now."

"Yeah, but it doesn't give me the right to hurt you. That being said, I can't be with you anymore, now or ever."

I'm thrown back by this new development. He's saying he's sorry and then he breaks up with me?

I'm looking at him in disbelief.

"So you don't want to be my boyfriend?"

"No!" he said. I just nodded silently. He lifts my chin with his fingers gently. "I'm sorry Abby." I see tears welling up in his eyes.

He put his arms around me and whispers in my ear, "I don't want to hurt you Abby, but a piece of me is gone with Kyle. I'll never be the same." He holds me so tight, that I could barely breathe.

I love him so much and I whisper in his ear, "I don't want you to let me go Josh."

He gives me a kiss on my forehead and then softly kisses my lips. He looks into my eyes and says he'll miss me. I could feel not one, but two hearts breaking at that moment. He loved me and felt like he could not be the boyfriend I'd hoped he'd be because he was now a changed guy. Kyle's death has changed all of us one or another, but not more drastically than Josh and Megan. I understood that and knew his decision was a difficult one. I open my locker as Josh walks away from me. I weep helplessly, unable to stop these tears. I turn around sensing someone was standing behind me. It was Rick holding his arms wide open. I hug him and he urges me to go.

"Come on Abby, let's just go!"

"Where?" I ask.

"Anywhere but here," he says.

"You want to leave school."

"Yes! Abby let's go." So we turn to the exit from the school.

Then we hear a voice. "You whore, you will regret this," I've heard that voice a million times before. It is Betty Cox yelling from who knows where. Rick holds my hand tightly, looks into my eyes and gives me a smile. He completely ignores Betty. The scene looks almost comical and as we leave, she shouts even more loudly all the expletives she knows in her vocabulary. But it doesn't stop Rick from taking me farther. I didn't fear Betty like I used to when I was young, but I knew she could make things miserable for me at school. I had too many things to worry about as is, she was the last thing on my mind. This is my first time missing school but it hurts too much to stay. We walk to the park. We sit under the oak tree, my favorite place to be. That's where Rick and I used to spend time as friends. There were many memories we had of this place. We shared our first kiss here. So much has happened since then and now I found myself crying for Josh. Rick was trying to be a good friend despite all that we've been through. We sit under the oak tree till I'm crying no longer. Rick walks me halfway home and I'm grateful for his company and friendship. Ma is waiting for me at the door, and I am saying to myself "Now what?" She stops me at the door. The way she's staring at me it feels like I've committed a huge crime. Grabbing my arm she tells me to clean the restrooms and the kitchen because Megan wasn't feeling too well. My heart was pounding; I was scared for her and the baby. She's got to tell Ma about the baby. The more she delays telling Ma, the more terrible the outcome would be. I started cleaning as soon as I get home so as to not anger Ma anymore. I change into my old clothes and finish cleaning up before I go upstairs to check on Megan. She's fast asleep. What could I possibly do for her but be there for her like the way she was for me when we were kids? She was my Mom, my friend and my sister. Megan has lost weight and there's only a little bump in the place of her stomach now. And it's growing bigger with each passing week. She could hide it for a few days, but not forever.

"Are you awake?"

Megan sits up and says, "I'm ok Abby."

"Just brought you some food." She frowns at the plate I'm holding in my hand. "You got to eat Megan." I say forcing the plate in her hands.

Tears start falling slowly down her beautiful cheeks. "I miss him Abby!"

"I know you do, so do I." I smile, trying to hide my sorrow.

"It's okay to remember him but you have a baby to take care of too."

I'm walking to school thinking how terribly things have fallen apart in all our lives. Josh and I broke up, Megan and Josh lost Kyle, Rick no longer was with Betty and I... I was just feeling lost. It was difficult. People always leave me, and my life sucks. Just got to be stronger and perhaps hope that happy days will come again. I was losing interest at school and my grades began to drop. I felt hopeless and I didn't learn anything. I'm just about to walk back home when I see Rick running towards me. I smile at him, oddly pleased by his company.

"Abby, I wanted to walk you home."

"You don't have to!"

"God Abby, I want to."

He holds my hand and I let him. We talk and laugh like old times. He makes me forget everything, he makes me happy at least for a while.

When I get home, Megan is on her knees crying and holding her stomach. I run to her. "What's wrong?"

"Don't know Abby? I'm having lots of pain." She grabs my arm tight. "I can't lose this baby!"

"Is anyone home?"

"No one."

I am going to call Uncle Mario. Getting the phone as fast as I can, I had to tell Uncle Mario the truth that Megan is pregnant. He couldn't believe it. "It's true, but just hurry! She's in a lot of pain."

I hang up, running back to Megan. Uncle Mario came bursting through the door, got on his knees to help her. He lifts her up gently and takes her to the hospital. I wanted to go but I had to wait for Ma. A few hours passed and there was no word about Megan. I'm walking back and forth like I usually do when I'm nervous. I was going mad with worry about Megan. And now Uncle Mario knew the truth as well.

I get down to clean up the house as it takes my mind off Megan. The wait was getting longer and more frustrating. My heart was telling me that something terrible is going to happen. I get on my knees and pray for Megan. I'm alone or so I thought when I feel a pair of strong hands hold my shoulder and lift me up. It's Paul.

"What's wrong? Abby, who hurt you?" My eyelids are heavy from crying and I tried to explain the whole story. Paul holds me so tightly reassuring me that Megan would be alright.

Chapter 14

The day Megan had gone with Uncle Mario to the hospital, she had lost the baby. Two precious lives were snuffed out two weeks apart; with Kyle and the baby now gone, Megan seemed like the walking dead, a ghost of her former self. Her mourning & grief had etched itself permanently on her once beautiful & radiant face. She'd lay motionless for hours on her bed with her eyes open, looking into the distance. It was a heartbreaking sight to see my sister numbed by so much pain that silence was all that accompanied her existence. She grew more and more distant; any attempts to talk to her proved futile. I even coaxed her to get back to school, hoping a change of environment would help nurse her back to some semblance of normalcy. I find her on her bed, looking out the window. I hold her hand and whisper to her, "You have school still you know?"

She ignores me and pretends like I don't exist. It was her way of telling me to leave her alone. Ma discovered about Megan's pregnancy when Uncle Mario had called her from the hospital, when things had gotten serious. She was furious at Megan but also concerned about her. She let out her anger on me by confronting me with the news; she slapped me hard for keeping such an important thing hidden from her. While she was still screaming and hitting me, there was another call from Uncle Mario that the baby had died. This news saddened both Ma and me; the anger had temporarily subsided and was replaced with grief and pain. Ma blamed me for the baby's death, reasoning that if I had told her sooner, Ma could have given her the proper care and ensured she'd be in good health to get through this pregnancy. I cried for days, wondering if Ma's reasoning had any truth to it. Megan was so nervous to tell Ma because she had anticipated the reaction to be unwelcome. And though Ma would've furiously reacted to the news & blamed Megan for her irresponsible behavior, she would've finally warmed up to the idea of welcoming a baby into the house. I remember when Ma welcomed me after I came home from Maria's abusive physical attempt to kill me. She had enveloped me with such love, something I had never witnessed before. Now in hindsight, it felt like perhaps Megan or I should've let Ma know instead of waiting for things to have gotten this bad and unbearable. The storm that was churning for a few weeks had now gone, having done the damage it had intended to cause. Life would never be the same. But the show must go on.

I get to school with a heavy heart, going over what could be different if I or Megan had made those difficult choices earlier. I replay the consequences to see if things would've indeed been different. I go to my locker and fetch my books when my eyes go wide; I'm seeing Josh making out with Emily at the bottom of the staircase. I stare in disbelief before I look away and walk as fast as I can to class. It felt like a knife had stabbed me through my chest, talk about a punch in the gut but nothing had prepared me for this. I was fuming throughout school hours. Here I was thinking that Josh broke up with me because he felt he couldn't be the boyfriend he wanted to be to me because Kyle's death had changed him in a way that he couldn't undo. Those were his words. What was I supposed to assume now that he's got half his tongue in Emily's mouth?! If there was any sympathy for his reasons to break up with me, it had gone out the window. It's lunch time and I didn't bother eating, though I had enough lunch money stashed in my skirt pocket to down four sandwiches and maybe even a dessert. I thought Josh was going through a really rough time after Kyle's death and for whatever reasons, he chose not to be with me. I thought he needed this time to recover; this was his period to mourn and make peace with a deep loss not going after some new chick you never even fancied in the first place. Josh disliked Betty & Emily as much as I did and to see him warm up to her in the way I did, it was unbelievable.

I finish classes for the day and head for the school exit when I hear a familiar voice calling out my name. I turn around to see Josh. My face is red with anger that he even has the audacity to bother with me after what I witnessed today. I give him a stern look & stare at him as if I was going to strangle him. I didn't ask him for an explanation and didn't want one. So what he says to me next, did not amuse me one bit. "Abby, just wanted to say sorry about Emmy."

He's grown thin and there are dark circles under his eyes, a sign of long sleepless nights he's had no doubt. That's when the word 'Emmy' struck my mind.

"Josh you already have a pet name for her? Guess that didn't take too long now, did it?" Only someone tone deaf could miss my sarcasm. Taking a deep breath, I respond as objectively as I can. "You don't have to say anything to me Josh. You let me go remember?"

"Just let me say it Abby: I'm so sorry about everything."

"Okay, you're sorry. Josh, we don't need to talk ever again. You made it crystal clear that you don't want anything to do with me." I step backward to turn around and make my way towards the exit when I feel his hand catch my wrist.

"I will always care for you Abby!"

"Yeah, why don't you keep telling yourself that and day dream about it?" I say as I wriggle away from his hold. I quicken my pace to a half run, wanting to get out of there. I walked back home alone, relieved to be just be by myself. I see Ma standing at the door waiting for me. I knew I was late by a few minutes and could anticipate a slap from Ma to be the cherry on the icing of what has been a rather forgettable, painful and disappointing day.

"Well, you know what happens when you are late," Ma says as I walk inside without looking up at her. "You know the rules Abby." And with that she plants her palm on my face in a hard slap. What else is new?

I get upstairs, numb to the stinging pain on my face. I look into the mirror to see four fingers clearly make its mark on my right cheek in a bright shade of red. I roll my eyes at the predictability of it. I hear Megan sobbing in the bathroom and knock at the door, hoping to offer her some solace. She shoos me away saying "Leave me alone Abby." I was getting used to it. I knew Megan will take time to recover from this period of her life, perhaps a few months or a few years. Time will tell. But I'm going to be here for her, no matter what. I try to forget the day's happenings and go about cleaning the house mindlessly. Cleaning has become my way of escape.

I eat dinner alone and go to sleep, too exhausted to stay up and think about anything though I didn't look forward to going to school the next day. It was a chilly morning; I dressed in all blue attire for school. It consisted of a navy-blue sweater, a grey blue blouse underneath and a striped navy-blue skirt; it mimicked my state of mind: I was feeling the blues. As I walk to school, I see

Rick suddenly catch up, "Hey Abby!" I give him a best reluctant smile in response, events of yesterday still fresh in my mind. I venture to tell Rick about Josh & Emily; to my surprise, he already knew and apparently, I was the last one to know. I was bitter at Josh and all the love I had for him seemed like it was another lifetime. Rick tells me to stay away from Josh, because he's come to know that Josh has been doing drugs these days to cope with Kyle's loss. That explained his change in behavior and 360-degree turn. He was no longer the Josh I had known. I felt so sad and helpless. I'd seen Paul go that route and unable to help him in any way and now Josh too. I had no idea if Emily could be the light and love he needed to get through this dark phase but I'd hoped she'd rise to the occasion and shed her bitchy, inconsiderate and shallow self aside for once. She was known to be a player in school and she had no business playing with the feelings of someone who's going through such an emotionally difficult time. This bit of news has made me sober and the rest of the walk to school is engulfed in pensive silence. Rick didn't say much because he knew I was processing all this in my own way.

The first two classes at school go without major hassle though I'm hardly paying any attention to what's been taught. I've been so distracted by everything that studies have taken a backseat. The atmosphere at home doesn't make it any easier. I try to catch up on reading a few subjects either in the library or the lunch area. I enjoy reading my history book when Rick settles into a seat in front of me with two servings of lunch. I look up to him, appreciative of this gesture. He was looking out for me and being the good friend, he had promised he'd try to be. I put my book aside to savor the warm lunch with him. We eat together and talk; he makes me laugh. I could sense the old camaraderie return. Suddenly, there's an angry female voice that thunders down our quiet time. It's Betty. "Rick, what are you doing with this pathetic whore?" I stare at her, pursing my lips together, trying to exercise some form of restraint but with the way Betty is provoking me, I don't think I could hold myself together any longer. She launches into an expletive ridden tirade calling me some choice words like 'bitch'. I get up, anger coursing through my veins. I've been through hell and back in the last few weeks and the last thing I needed is this insensitive, arrogant and pretentious girl talking down to me whatever she felt like. "I'm tired of this, and of you Betty!" I'm going to kick her ass like right now when Rick gets in front of me to prevent a scuffle because things could have gotten really ugly. She threatens me in her trademark snooty way and yells, "Watch your flat ass Abby."

She wishes my ass was flat; it's firm as a racehorse. And I could kick really well, may be at some point I'd have the privilege of letting her know of my lower body strength! She's one jealous nut. After lunch break and all the adrenaline rush of an almost fight with Betty, I get ready for PE, changing into a white tee shirt and red shorts. I love the challenge of a good race and I knew Betty would try her best to get back at me on the race track. I see Emily chewing gum when I get to the track and Betty is making her way behind me. There are five girls ahead of me in position on the track. They look at me as their arch rival number one. If they even try to physically hurt me, they're going to get it back in full measure. Paul taught me some cool moves to defend myself after the Mexicano tried to get at me years ago. But now it wasn't a male, it was an all-female troupe of sour bunch of losers. I get ready on the track and glance sideways at Betty. I'm pretty miffed at her antics during lunch time earlier. It was good that Rick stood between us as a wall but there's no Rick on the racetrack so I knew things could still get ugly here. I hear myself speak to Betty in no uncertain terms "What do you want Betty, too cowardly to fight your own battles?"

The rest of the girls, including Emily, express amusement. They won't be laughing for long. Betty takes a step forward, chewing her huge gum, her hand on her hip, warming up. She looks funny when she jumps up and down because every part of her body is bouncing, it's quite a sight. I redirect my gaze to the track ahead. I've had enough of these girls and my palms roll up in tight fist thinking about Betty & Emily. I position myself and double down with one leg forward, hands down in the start position when I'm pushed to the ground sideways. It's Betty and this time when I snap, it felt like a dragon had been unleashed. All the four girls come down on me and I go down on Betty. Three of the girls pull at my hair and while it hurts, I was only tightening my hands on Betty's collar. I'm atop her and punch her face with full force. She was a pain in the ass for so many years; she really had this coming for her for a long time. Emily tries to hit me when I kick her with my leg and I keep punching Betty till I'm satisfied. We're separated from our fighting fest by our PE teacher and a few other students. The guys in the stands had a real good time watching this unfold. We're lined up in the Dean's office but it's just Betty, Emily & me. I look at Betty and almost let out a laugh. Her hair looks like a tangled bird's nest; her eyes look black and blue, a swollen lip and scratches around her rosy cheeks. Emily doesn't look that bad but she's bruised in enough places for people to know she was in a fight. Because there wasn't a mirror around, I could only imagine what I'd look like.

Emily looks at me and says with a wicked smile "Look at you: so ugly, you are so delusional if you think they would really stay with you." I just ignore them and couldn't care less what they thought. Our parents & in my case, guardian were called. Betty & Emily portrayed themselves as my victims when the reality was that she started the fight. I knew they'd believe her and I didn't have anything to say in defense. I shut my mouth because my mind was on what Ma was going to do when I got home. A few more knocks and I'd be out. Ma's deathly silence on the way back home even after I attempted an explanation to paint a more realistic version of what happened, didn't comfort me much. I get home and run upstairs to take a shower. I look at myself in the mirror and see that I'm bruised all over my body with a particularly ugly one near my eye. Ma was getting ready downstairs to welcome me with a belt. She was literally whipping me left, right and center. My whole body was aching and red. At the end of it, I look like a boxer who had lost the match. It doesn't look that bad, considering five girls beat me up. It could've been worse. I wake up the next morning, wincing in pain and unable to even walk to the bathroom. I was sore and achy. I almost want to go back to bed when I think of Ma; she'd not have me taking off from school for what was in her head, well deserved punishment. I get ready for school reluctantly. I was slow to get to my first class and had forgotten to go to the locker to take my books. So I head towards my locker when I see Rick. He holds me by the shoulder and asks, "Are you okay?" I roll my eyes at his pretentious concern, like he didn't know a damn thing about what transpired yesterday.

"What do you want Rick?" I say nonchalantly.

"What Happened Abby?"

"Well let's see: your girlfriend and her bunch of mean girls want to ensure that I stay away from you and you stay away from me. So point taken—stay away from me Rick. I'm done with this drama. I have enough drama in my life without these girls."

"Don't push me away Abby!"

"Go tell that to Betty Cox and Emmy or Emily whatever she calls herself. Just leave me alone please!" I leave him standing alone and don't turn back.

It's Saturday morning which means no school. I was glad for the off day after the week's share of drama. But we had to go to Uncle Mario's house for a party he's having. I didn't think Megan would have wanted to go, given how depressed she's been feeling. I couldn't blame her; the poor thing's been through much. But I decide to ask her if she wanted to come with us. Her face brightened up a bit, thankful to have a chance to go out of the house. She always felt safe around Uncle Mario, he was beside her when she lost the baby and made the whole experience a little less dreadful & painful. He'd stood by her and managed the situation with Ma so as to minimize damage. She was incredibly grateful for the kindness he had shown and the prospect of visiting him had cheered her up in a way I hadn't seen her be, in weeks. I was grateful to Uncle Mario as well, if he wasn't there to help us at that time, I don't know how things would've turned out. It could've been much worse without him. I'm glad for this trip to Uncle's house because both I and Megan seemed to be in dire need of a change of scenery. So we decide to get dressed for the party. Megan is wearing a pretty blue skirt with a white sweater. I finish up my hair with a pony tail and a white hair band. With a bit of luck, the entertainment will be worth playing dress up. We looked forward to see Uncle Mario no doubt, but were even more eager to see Anna. It had been a long time and she was as kind & affectionate towards us as Uncle Mario was. I and Megan walk in to the party and see almost all the guests either dancing or drinking. Everyone seems to be in high spirits. The party décor is impeccable. Tables were lined with expensive cutlery, centerpieces of flowers and candles; it looked rather classy. Uncle Mario & Anna greet us with a warm hug and help us to our seats. Our food arrives soon after even though we aren't that hungry or eager to eat. I was still sore from yesterday's fist fight with the girls. I scan my eyes through the room when my eyes recognize a familiar pair of men: Steve and his brother Martin. I suddenly perk up in my seat and make eyes at Megan, pointing her to their direction. Megan's face lights up seeing Steve and she gives a smile, suddenly remembering the time she had spent with him at Uncle Mario's wedding. He was attractive and a total eye candy. And at this point, a much-needed distraction for Megan. God knows she could've done with a bit of love and laughter. Megan gives me a sideways glance and winks at me as if she followed my mental cue. She stands up as Steve makes his way through the crowd recognizing her. I see her leap into his arms eagerly as he takes her to dance. I watch them in delight, hoping this would turn out well when I see Martin grin at me with mischief written all over his face. He was seated across my table and makes his way to me.

"Do you want to dance Abby?"

"No thank you."

"Why not?"

"Do I have to have a reason?"

"Umm no. Not really! So, what happened to your face?"

I take a deep breath. "Let's just say some girls don't like me."

He nods his head. "Okay, don't tell me then." Smiling at me again, he says, "I like you Abby."

"Well, you're the only one."

Martin laughs out loud and makes me laugh too. "Do you still have a boyfriend?"

"No Martin I don't!"

He gives me a huge smile that makes my stomach flutter and makes my heart beat faster. Martin takes my hand and pulls me to the dance floor. It's a slow song and he gently puts his hands around my waist. I put my arms on his shoulder, leaning my head on his chest. It felt so good because no one ever hugs me. I hadn't felt like this in a long time and I didn't want him to let go. I had missed

Josh but I knew he was more broken than me. Martin lifts my chin, breaking my thoughts away from Josh. I look into his eyes.

"A penny for your thoughts Abby?"

"I just need air."

He takes a hold of my hand and we go outside. We start talking and he proves to be a charmer. We see Steve and Megan kissing; I'm relieved to see her not deny Steve's advances but I wanted her to be careful too. The night was nice but all good things must come to an end. Martin leaves me with kisses and asks for my number; this I promptly give it, delighted at the prospect of hearing from him. Megan seemed like life was returning to her, she was flushed pink from the time she spent with Steve. They did look good together and I thought he was a gentleman, much like Kyle. Megan and I agree that the brothers proved to be delightful company and that we could do with some normal interaction whether or not our flings would turn into something serious. I knew Megan was trying to forget about everything in the past but hanging out with every guy that would catch her fancy wasn't the solution. She had to tread carefully so as to not repeat things from the past. With all the things that had happened, both of us had veered off from any expectations of permanence in our lives; it's been a pattern. Everything was temporary so all we could do was to make the best of what we had. If it was meant to stay, it will. If it didn't, we wouldn't hold but readily let go. That's been our greatest lesson in life. The harder we've tried to hold on to people, the more we were forced to let go. We simply couldn't plan for the future. We just had to focus on taking it one day at a time.

Time passed and my friendship with Martin had grown. We used to meet up with Uncle Mario's help because Ma wouldn't allow it on her watch. But after a few weeks, she found out and put an end to it. I had to break up with Martin through a letter I managed to send through Uncle Mario. Who breaks up with a letter?! Me! I was depressed about the way things had ended with him but from there on, I'd decided that I don't want to deal with boys for a while. I've just about had enough. The distractions at school had reduced and I was able to focus again on getting my grades up. I never got to be queen because it was honestly the last thing on my mind, but Rick became King. When I found out who won queen I just wanted to gag! It was Betty Cox. They will have a dance for the king and queen soon but I won't be there.

Once in a while, I would see Josh. He was no longer with Emily or Emmy, whatever he called her. He found out about what Betty & Emily did to me on the racetrack. He promptly left her, having some sense return to him. He didn't waste much time moving on to the next girl though. Emily seemed to have changed after her relationship with Josh ended; she kept mostly to herself and had lost a bit of her nasty edge. As for Rick, he gave me my space I was grateful for it because being drama-free was number one priority. I was more at peace this way. I didn't see much of Paul though he was happy in a relationship with a pretty girl. I'm in school, walking for my first class. I hear the girls' gossip about some new guy that they thought was cute. I see Rick and Josh are sitting in two corners of the classroom; I spend most of my time in class reading books. I remember both the boys fondly but it was in the past and some things are never meant to be. I've outgrown them and I hope they're happy with where they are. I hardly had any friends in class now but it was better to be alone than have fake friends for company. I see the classroom door open and all the girls are looking to see whether it's their fancy new boy who's going to walk in. Sure enough, a cocky looking, young guy walks in with an air about him. I roll my eyes. Our teacher introduces him to the class as Cory Hendrix and I couldn't care less. Ignoring all the drama surrounding our newest entrant, I carry on with writing notes and thinking what else could be added. I sense someone's eyes on me when I glance up to see Cory grinning at me.

"Hi doll!" he says, beginning to introduce him. I hold my hands up in front of him.

"I don't want to know your name and please, leave me alone."

"Don't flatter yourself doll, there's plenty to go around."

He's cocky and conceited. Whatever! The bad boys were never my type. All the kids are laughing. I'm looking down at my notes with strands of my hair covering my eyes.

"Hey doll, don't cover those beautiful eyes." He grabs my strand of my hair and moves it at the back of my ear. I'm caught off guard by his audacity, we just met! I roll my eyes and I can see him getting nervous. I pay him no attention and in my head, I'm wishing the class was over already.

I see Rick come at me with an odd question. "Are you coming for the dance Abby?"

"NO! Rick I'm not going, why? Are you kidding me! Take Betty, after all, isn't she queen?"

I'm sufficiently pleased with my answer because I see his hopeful eyes sadden.

I take a quick look up. The new guy is just staring at me. Seems like I've caught his fancy but he hasn't caught mine. I intend to keep things that way. The bell rings, and the class is over. I'm literally running after class when I bump into Josh. He's become so thin but his grey blue eyes are still pretty as ever.

"Sorry Abby…"

"It's okay!" I say, managing a smile.

"How are you Abby?"

"Good." It had become so awkward to talk to him.

"I've got to go Josh. Nice seeing you."

It's my last class. I walk to my locker to put my books away when the new guy quips in to say, "Hi doll."

The mere fact that he called me 'Doll' and not my name had annoyed me.

"What do you want?"

"Abby I'm the new guy on the block. I really would like to take you to the dance."

"Why? Because I chose you okay. Will you go?"

"Sure why not."

"That's my girl."

"I'm not your girl."

Cory smirks. "You'll be my girl at the dance." He walks away, cocky as hell! I have no idea why I said yes. Was it because I wanted to see Rick see me with someone else? It all seemed so pointless and did I get that petty about things? I didn't have the time to ruminate on these because I already said 'yes'.

I get ready to go to the school dance. Megan helps me slip into a black dress. She's curled my hair and pinned it in place with a sparkly hair pin. My makeup is fairly subtle. I put on my stockings. Megan seems pleased with how I look. "You so pretty Abby," I delight in her compliment.

"Megan you're corny." I say.

Uncle Mario takes me to school; that's the only way Ma lets me go. Cory was waiting for me. WOW! Did he dress up good. He looked dapper in a black suit and his hair slicked back with gel. He smiles as I walk up to him. "Hi doll, you look lovely." He holds out his hand to take me to the dance.

I looked at him and said, "You look really good today"

"I knew you'd like me." he said with a chuckle and we both laughed out loud.

"Don't flatter yourself," I say as I walk with him to the dance room. If only things could be this good every day. Once we were in the hall, we went to take our seat. Everything is beautiful: flowers on the tables, all colors there, little butterflies lights throughout the room on the wall, a huge poster with glitter that says congratulations to king and queen. Cory smiles at me and asks, "Would you like something to drink?"

"Sure."

"Be right back okay."

I start to stare around, seeing Josh yet with another girl. He's kissing her. I turn away. It's a sight I'm jaded with. I feel someone's hand touch my back, I turn around to see Rick. "You came Abby."

I'm really trying not to be rude, "Yes, I'm here."

"So you came with the new guy?"

"Yes I did, so go away."

Cory came with two drinks in his hand and passed my glass to me. He looked up to "Are you bothering my date?"

Rick snickers and walks away. Cory asks, "Are you okay?"

"Yes, long story," and I blush again.

The music starts. Betty looks lovely. She's wearing a long pink princess dress. Her hair is up in a bun. She really does look like a princess. If only her heart matched the beauty on her face. She's holding Rick's hand and leading him to the dance floor. I could tell Rick didn't want to be there because he's busy looking at me, which visibly annoys Betty. He is gorgeous his light brown hair combed back. Cory is observing my reaction to Rick and Betty when he leans into my ears and whispers, "Would you like to dance or you still want to be gawking over your ex?"

"Sorry yes, let's dance."

We're dancing. Betty is looking so attentively at me. What else is new? Then we watch them get their crown. They take lots of pictures and Betty tries to flash her fakest smile ever. I get away from the crowd. Cory proved to be good company thus far and even though he seemed like the quintessential bad boy, he probably wasn't all that bad. However, he's never going to get rid of that cockiness. Josh comes to our table rather unexpectedly. He's looking at me intently and touches my hair. He says, "You're beautiful Abby, just wanted to tell you that!" I get up and hug him. He put his arms around my waist and he puts his face in my hair. For a moment, it felt just like the old days.

Cory visibly disturbed by this sudden display of affection from both Josh and me exclaims in anger, "I'm out of here. God Abby, all that surrounds you are your ex's and drama," and with that he leaves me standing alone to face the music. He had a point. Before Cory, all I was trying to do was damage control and keep the drama at bay. My whole life was a futile exercise in keeping people at arm's length. Josh, seeing what a mess he made by his affectionate display is feeling guilty. "Sorry Abby" he says with a puppy face.

"Just, don't say anything." I respond looking in the way of Cory, who's left the party. Josh leaves, sensing my being upset. At this point, everyone was staring at me like I'm an alien in the wrong planet. I have to wait until Uncle Mario comes for me. I sit down ignoring the hushed remarks and blank stares to finish my punch. Rick makes his way amidst all this and takes a seat next to me.

"I want to dance with you Abby."

"No Rick, go with Betty."

Rick yells at me as if to conclude this otherwise forgettable evening on a pathetic note. "I don't want to dance with Betty, do you understand? I want you Abby. It's always been you Abby!"

I can't believe this is happening. I snap! "Please! Rick, I'm sick and tired of all this drama."

I don't see it coming. Betty had somehow come from the side when Rick was talking to me and right now, it's too late; I feel her fist punch into my right eye. I grab hold of her hair in defense to keep her from striking again. I look straight into her eyes. "Make it the last time you hit me or touch me because you'll regret it!" And I smack her face and let go of her hair. I turn to leave when Rick comes running after me, again! "Wait!" he calls out.

I'm flustered, exhausted and out of my wits end at this point. "What do you want from me? This is the drama I was trying to avoid. Can't you see?!"

"Sorry Abby, I just want to be friends." He lifts up my chin and gives me a kiss. He then puts my face on his chest. "You are my girl Abby. Can't you see that!" Tears fall slowly down my cheeks. He kisses me. This time I open up my lips to him. He's holding me tight, real tight. He wipes my tears away and I hold him with all my might. We stay like that for a while away from prying eyes; I've been in the arms of three boys, all of who I adore but right now, this felt right and I didn't want to fight the feeling. But I knew reality would soon serve a wakeup call.

Chapter 15

I woke up with a black eye and my head was dizzy with a headache. Am I in a dream or was this real. I was feeling too dazed. I vaguely remember the events of the previous evening. And strangely, I remember Dad being around when I came home after the party. I hear his voice echo downstairs and I'm sure I'm no longer dreaming. The last thing I remember before I fell asleep is Megan asking and barraging me with questions about how things went. I was too tired and drained to answer. I walk past the mirror without seeing how gross my face looked; I turn on the shower in the bathroom, allowing the warm water to awaken me to my senses. I began recollecting everything more clearly and the reason as to why Dad was here. He's getting divorced from Maria is what I remember gauging from his conversation to Ma and he'd be staying with us here. I love my Dad but at this point in time, he's nothing more than a man in drunken stupor like 24/7. He sings mindlessly all the time. It's Saturday, so it's off to the races for Dad, Ma & Pa. I shower and dress, eager to get out for some fresh air. In between all this, I remembered kissing Rick and the lovely black eye Betty has given me as a parting gift. My mind shifts to Megan, she seems happy to be with Steve, she's handling herself well and is slowly returning to things she used to get excited about. She doesn't talk about Kyle much now because she doesn't want to linger on her past. Paul seems to be doing alright as well. In hindsight, I believe Megan, Paul, Dad and I are all damaged one way or another. It's our reality. I look at myself in the mirror before I walk out the door, touching my right eye and seeing how badly I've been hit. The makeup I've used to hide it isn't going to hold up too well. I snort, seeing how comical last evening had been; it didn't seem so amusing yesterday when it was all coming down. I'm able to laugh at it and that's a good thing, humor makes living a lot more tolerable. It's sunny outside, and I am happy to see the clear skies.

Megan comes behind me. "Where are you going Abby?"

"To the park."

"You better be back early, Steve told me Martin was hurt with that letter you sent."

"What do you want me to do? Ma told me not to see Martin so I won't." Now I'm just angry—more like furious. She doesn't get it! Ma will beat me if she found out I was going to see Martin again when she's prohibited me from doing so. She never knew about Rick and Josh or Cory. Well, I'm going to the park now. I roll my eyes at Megan to avoid her prying questions and tumble out the door.

I sit at a bench under the tree, grateful for the shade. It's a beautiful, windy day and the grass has been freshly mowed. I can see people having fun, kids playing on swings and slides. It was the perfect day. I looked up at the sky and inhale the fresh air. It feels wonderful being out here. My mind wanders to Rick; I'm confused about him and the kiss we shared. Is it so easy for him and me to keep going from one guy or girl to another? It may seem harmless at times but I could no longer differentiate what was really right. I was always basing my decisions on what I felt at the moment. I close my eyes hoping to hear my conscience and open them slowly. My eyes widen as I see Rick looking down at me with a grin. I get up, we embrace each other. This felt warm, nice, like a beautiful summer day. We were best friends, knew each other, it feels familiar. Always together since we were six. Rick touches my black eye. "You still look lovely even with a black eye."

All I could say is, "You think?"

"Come here Abby." We cuddle again and share a lot of kisses. We walk together, go up and down the hill at the park, like old times. It felt happy for once. He walks me home. "You're my girl Abby, you will always be my girl." He watches me walk away.

I return home with a day well spent at the park; Megan notices my flushed cheeks and leaves me in peace, without asking anything. I change and get into work clothes to help her clean up before Dad, Ma & Pa come home from the races. They return but Dad isn't with them, he told Ma he'd come later. It's evening and Dad finally makes a drunken entrance, singing again. Ma wasn't too pleased. What's a girl got to do to get some sleep around here? Megan was fast asleep by the time I got into bed. I can't bear his tuneless singing, he sounds like a lunatic. I use a pillow to cover my face and try to yell in frustration. Finally, Dad goes to sleep. Sunday morning, we're up before Ma is tempted to kick open the door to wake us up. I barely managed a few hours of sleep and looked as groggy as a frog at 3 am. We had to go to church so Megan and I get ready reluctantly. The new routine with Dad at home falls into a predictable drunken routine.

The seasons changed, what comes around goes around; before we knew it, two years had passed.

The past two years were so tough for Megan: the loss of Kyle and the baby. She started to go with so many guys. I was so worried about her, then she met Miles Wright. They met at the market reaching for a rocky road chocolate candy. They're the same age. He was handsome in a rugged kinda way. He made her laugh and she fell for him hard. Their relationship reminded me of the love stories we read in novels, the once-in-a-lifetime kinda romance. Paul got married last year. Their love is complicated and predictably so, ridden with problems. Then there's Dad, still the same, only now he's single & is drinking his life away. Ma didn't let me out of her sight. I felt like a prisoner in my own house. No boyfriends, thumbs down for any possibilities for friends. Rick got tired of waiting. Who could blame him? It was school, straight home, and house-work. Ma beat me here and there but that was nothing new. I was depressed when I thought about my life; there was nothing to look forward to. But I'd not miss my sister's wedding for anything in the world. She was a bright spot in an otherwise dull routine. She was getting married and was pregnant with a baby. Her happiness was in striking contrast to my sadness, but I was ecstatic about all the happiness she's going to have. God knows she's been through hell. Megan would be leaving to live with Miles in another apartment, they'd move on Saturday. The mere thought of it made me cry. She's been my best friend, mother, sister, partner in crime, everything; we both were with each other through thick and thin and I couldn't imagine this house without her. I was going to miss her. Truth be told, I felt miserable. With Megan gone, Paul already married and Dad in a permanent state of drunkenness, I was hanging on to life by a thread.

Saturday came and Megan's all ready and packed with her luggage to go. Megan holds me with both arms. We start to bawl like babies and then hug each other real tight. "I love you Abby, do what Ma says so she won't hit you. You better stop being the stubborn lass you've always been!" she chides. I squeeze her and sob. In my head, I'm almost pleading 'Don't leave me please! I need you' but all I say in words is "You take care Megan, I know you're going to be happy," Megan smirks.

"Look at us weeping like babies. Everything will be okay Abby."

"Yeah whatever." I say, pulling her to the side to hug her one last time. I shed bittersweet tears over her departure, and raise my hand to wave her goodbye. Now, there was no Megan or Paul, just Ma, Pa & Dad. None of them shower me with hugs or affection. And neither did anyone understand me. To say I felt lonely would be an understatement. I'm determined to leave this house at some point when I have my chance. I know it's a long journey and it'd be baby steps but I have to, else I'll go crazy. Uncle Mario has kids now and visits us only once or twice a year. His visit always comforted me as I share a close connection with him. I always looked forward to going to his & Anna's house when I got the chance and when Ma allowed it. Uncle Mario had some parties I went to occasionally. Martin didn't ever speak to me again and who could blame him for that, I'm the one to blame. I didn't talk to no one anymore; I kept to myself. I did what was asked of me. All I could think about was when I'd be able to run away. I started hanging around the wrong people at school and no longer cared what happened but stayed vigilant enough to stay away from drugs and drinks. I always felt I needed to be more in control of myself and my body. I had dreams to meet the love of my life and give him the gift of my virginity. I told my closest two friends at school about my thoughts on leaving home. They encouraged me to do it and even offered to put me up in their homes if needed. I felt this might work. I made up my mind to leave in two months or so. I didn't really have much to pack and carry as luggage other than the emotional baggage I was holding onto from so many years. I was nervous about Ma's reaction the most and that it could easily end any dreams of leaving home. I became more conscientious at home in a bid to please Ma. I did my cleaning, went to school, kept to myself and started planning my escape. A month passed and I was beginning to get excited about the prospect of leaving this place. I could almost taste the freedom and everything would seem bearable.

At school, my friends invited me to a ditching party during school hours. Something I haven't done before. Not wanting to disappoint them, I decide to yes.

We leave with one of my friends, whose brother is driving the car. "Okay get out, we're here." I realize he's really rude but handsome in a very masculine way. He had brown eyes and tanned skin, short and well built; he was at least a couple of years older and it showed through his countenance. I open my side of the door. He grabs my arm. "Hey, what's your name?"

"Leave her alone, his sister rolls her eyes."

"Shut up! Terry, I'm talking to your friend."

I look up at him. "My name is Abby." I respond with a straight face.

"Okay Abby, don't let the guys in there get next to you." I just knit my eyebrow. "And by the way my name is Angel, since you didn't ask."

"Stop Angel! Leave her alone."

"Going to the store to buy beer. Be back."

He winks at me and it takes me by surprise. I blush as Terry notices it and grabs me, remarking, "Look at that blushing cheek Abby, you look like a flower that just blossomed" she said giggling. I smile shyly and walk with her to the front porch. I've never been here before and I see Terry knock on the door. Some guy tells us that the party is in the basement and shows us the way in. We walk down the stairs. Everyone is drunk or dancing. Terry hands me a white cup. I told her I don't want to drink. "Come on Abby! Just one, loosen up okay!"

I take a sip. Whoever lived in this house fixed the basement and had some color lights. The place was cleaned and there were posters of girls. I take another sip of my beer then hear his voice. "What are you doing here Abby?"

To my surprise, I see Rick! "I could ask you the same thing! Don't be funny Abby, you don't belong here." He remarks chiding me.

"Oh! But you do, right? Leave me the hell alone okay."

"These guys just want one thing from girls, come on I'll take you home."

"Nope!" I need another beer I say protesting his attempt to take me out of the basement. He really is pissing me off. What does he think telling me what to do? I'll do what I want, thank you. Rick looks at me with worry etched over his face.

Rick knew all too well that these parties are to get girls in bed. He was one of those guys, but he cared about me and didn't want me to be taken advantage of. I was feeling the effects of the beer and was doing a few dance moves with Terry. I was really having fun when Rick comes close to me; it was a slow song and he twirls my hand and holds me real close. I stare at him, unsure of what's happening and then he kisses my cheeks, inhaling the perfume of my hair. He whispers in my ears, "I miss you so much Abby." I smile because the truth is that I missed him more than I could tell in words. I was in a very lonely place in life. Rick held me close to his chest and I could smell his cologne and feel the softness of his black sweater "Come on Abby let's go!"

I nod in agreement. I'm so ready to go. I think it's the beers I've drunk down. He takes hold of my hand. Going up the stairs, I see Angel coming to stop us. "Where are you going pretty girl?"

Rick puts his hand around me. "She's with me."

Angel smirks. "Really? Since I'm the one that brought her dude."

"Just move out of our way." Rick says.

"Are you sure Abby you want to leave with him?"

I was feeling light headed. "Yes, I'm leaving with him."

"Too bad baby, you could have had some fun with a real man." He gives us a grin and then moves aside. Rick and I go to the park. We started to kiss, like really kiss: his soft lips all over mine. We kissed before but this was way different. We keep kissing. Rick starts to touch my hair softly. He caresses me, kissing my neck. I feel butterflies in my stomach. It's starting to feel good. His hand goes to my breast. He pulls one out. He kisses one then I moan. It feels really good; he's so gentle. Then, suddenly sensing how this was going to end, I snap out my romantic reverie and I hear myself say, "I can't do this Rick."

"Why Abby? I loved you ever since you were six."

"Sorry, I just can't," and with that I leave, running home. That was the first time I let anyone touch me. That won't happen again: it's not wise to drink alcohol. I should've known better. I have a plan to leave and that's all I'm going to focus on. Knowing Rick was disappointed, I felt badly for leaving him. But he did exactly what he was trying to protect me from; from being taken advantage of. I wanted my body to be a sacred gift for whoever marries me and I know the man who marries me will respect me for it. I wanted that kinda love. My mind wanders back to the plan for leaving home. It's still a month away. To tell you the truth, I was anxious and a little nervous. Being a young lady never had its perks. The world out there was a nasty one and I was fairly naïve even though I've seen the worst in people.

There's just two weeks left for my escape plan. I saw Rick at school and avoided him like a plague even though he always tried to speak to me. I was embarrassed about the whole episode and I'd pretend he was invisible. I knew that'd hurt him and may keep him from getting close to me. I hadn't told him that I was planning to leave.

Though Dad was living with us at home, he was mostly outside, drunk in bars and would come home late. I can't recollect when was the last time we sat together and had dinner where he was present and not drunk. The times when he wasn't drunk, he'd show me fatherly affection and I cherished that. I felt like he was a good man but alcohol was a sickness that's hard to get rid of; this is the way he chose to spend his life and there was nothing I could do to stop it.

I knew I'd miss everyone when I leave from here. I was suffocating living here and had to go. I'd be leaving a piece of my heart behind with them. I had come to love Ma, Pa and Dad but without Megan and Paul around, things had gotten unbearably difficult. Ma always saw me as a liability so I doubt she'd complain or miss me when I left. We have just one life to live. My journey has been far from satisfactory; I've survived one nightmare after another in search for freedom which I only experienced at the park. I longed to break free from the shackles of this house, its loneliness and lifeless existence.

The day I'd been waiting for, finally arrived. Deep down I'm terrified but on the outside, I'm trying to stay as calm and normal as I can possibly be. I dress for school in blue Levi jeans, a white tank top, an off-white sweater and some tennis shoes. It's chilly outside and feels like a storm could be on the way. Dark clouds were rolling in the distance and the cold winds whipped my face. I walk to school excitedly. I'll be meeting Terry and from there, hopefully everything goes according to plan. I only take a small backpack with me that held my favorite clothes—two pairs of jeans, four blouses, two bras, five panties, and three pairs of socks. I pack in a few items Megan and I've used over the years like a handheld mirror, an old picture of Mom framed in a locket, a sweater that Ma had knitted for me. I wanted to pack light on purpose. I was nervous as I began walking towards my destination. I looked back at the house I called home and paused briefly. My stomach was doing a double as I remembered the first time I came here with Megan. The horrors we endured, all the memories. A tear rolled down. I knew I wasn't going to miss the drinking, Ma's belt or beating, the smoke and beer Dad had filled the house with…I wouldn't miss any of that. I turn around and start walking hurriedly. I see Terry waiting for me in front of the school, she smiles at me. "Ready?"

"I guess."

"Abby my brother has come with me. He's waiting in the car."

"Angel is here?"

"Yep he wanted to come. Think he likes you Abby?"

I roll my eyes "Well lead the way."

His car is across the street. He's standing next to his Nova. It's dark blue. He smiles at me. I frown. He smirks at me and we're on our way to their house. Their house has three bedrooms. No one is home. Their Mom is working. Their Dad passed away so it's just them three. "Come Abby let's go to my room." Terry says excitedly.

Following Terry to her room, Angel stops me. "So Abby, I'm going to like you staying here."

Sneering at him, "In your dreams."

He grins. "Believe me, I dream Abby!" Then he starts to laugh. I run to Terry's room to escape this awkward encounter, this was going to be tough.

When her Mom comes home she's not happy about me staying the night. I didn't think I'd be harming anyone if I stayed so I couldn't comprehend Terry's Mom's disapproval of the idea. I want to make a graceful exit but I ask for time. Terry asks her Mom and she reluctantly agrees to let me stay for two days. I didn't have to see much of Angel around for those two days as he hung out a lot. I picked a time when he was out to leave. I tell Terry and her Mom thank you and say goodbye. Terry promised to stay in touch. As I walk out of Terry's house, my mind is in survival mode. I have no place to stay and I don't know who to ask. I didn't want to be trouble. There was no way I was going to return home but I hadn't a clue where I should turn or go to for shelter. The first night was awful. I slept right next to a dumpster. It was dirty, stinking and more uncomfortable than I could put in words. I could hide myself easily because my frame was petite. At five foot one and weighing just a hundred and ten pounds, fitting into narrow spaces was like second skin. I have very little money from my savings. The next morning, I skip breakfast, preferring to save whatever little I have and keep walking till I see a gas station. I use the washroom to clean myself up; at this point, I smell like the dumpster only sweatier. I try to untangle my hair and get it into a decent ponytail. I buy myself some mini doughnuts which are easy to carry and will fill me just enough. I walk and take occasional breaks to drink water and clean up. If I get too hungry, I munch on one of the doughnuts and then resume my walking. It's evening of the third day since I left home. I reach a spot where I see there's some kinda party going on. There's a live band. I decide to halt since it'd be night soon. I'm also hungry and the only way to find some food is to blend in at this party and pretend like I'm supposed to be here. I get my act on, saying hello to complete strangers as I make my way for the buffet. I get myself a plate of warm food and savor its aroma. My backpack is secure between my feet and I watch the band belt out one song after the other. The singer is a cute blonde guy. He suddenly looks my way and gives me a broad smile. After he finishes the song, he announces a break. Some record is put on and the party continues. The singer guy sits right next to me. I'm gazing at my food, not wanting to look up. "Hi there!" he said. I pretend like I didn't hear him and he says it again. "Hello there!" I glance at his face. He's older to me, has a medium built, brown eyed and in his late twenties. "Would you like to dance?"

I smile. "Don't you want to know my name?"

He grins. "Yes!"

"It's Abby, what's yours?"

"Julian." He holds out his hand for to me take. My cheeks are blushing, knowing because they're warm. We dance a few songs. He tells me to watch him sing. He sings really well. Some guys ask me to dance. I just say no, eating some cake. The party goes on for some more time and then it wraps up. Julian comes toward me. "I'll take you home."

Frowning, I say, "No! That's okay!"

I don't want to tell him that I don't have a home and don't want anyone's pity; that's for sure.

He watches me intently. "You're a runaway, aren't you?"

I snicker. "You don't know nothing about me."

"Listen sweetie come home with me."

"I don't know you."

"I won't touch you okay? It's dangerous for you to be alone in a strange place like this. Come on now!"

I go with him against my lady senses. I know I have to be careful but something about him seemed like I could trust him. There was kindness in his eyes and it put me at ease. I could be wrong but I'm hoping he proves me right. We drive to his house. His house is old, white, a one story edifice with a red porch, huge windows and beautiful flowers growing out in the front. All I could think of is taking a shower. It's been a long time since I've had a warm shower or bath. He opens the door for me and we walk inside. It's pretty nice. He has a brown couch, a wooden table with a vintage lamp and a ivory-cream rug. That's it for that room. The kitchen is small with an all-white stove, a fridge and a few plates. He tells me there are two restrooms. Showing me the room, I'm staying in he says, "It's my daughter's room when she visits." Again, he assures me that I'm safe and he won't harm me. Julian lets me shower and I scrub myself until I'm red. I wash my clothes and feel relieved that I had a chance to refresh myself. I step out feeling clean and grateful. I know that he will want something from me eventually because though he was kind and hospitable, he was still a man. I stay with him for three days before he asks for sex. I knew it had to happen and so his request didn't take me by surprise. But I refused. He didn't know I was a virgin so I told him. He looked at me with a certain amount of respect and didn't push me for anything. But he did tell me to leave, handed me a few dollars and told me to stay safe. He said keeping me there at this house would be a risky proposition given that I was still a minor. He didn't want any trouble. I understood and thanked him for his kindness. I left relieved that things didn't go south with him and for once, my instincts proved right. I'm glad I took a chance on him. But I'm also glad that nothing terrible happened. Not every man was going to be like Julian. I understood being free came with a price; as I kept walking in an unknown direction, I knew I had to muster up the courage to confront everything I'll face. I had to make sure I was safe throughout this journey until I reached a place I could call home and start my life over.

Chapter 16

It's been a month since I ran away from home. Nothing had been like what I expected this to be. I was no longer scared though and I was sure I could defend myself. I went days without food or water and could only wash myself in dirty gas station restrooms. Someone tried to rape me on two separate occasions. Talk about 'survival of the fittest'. I had fought back both times and though I was badly bruised on account of this, I was glad for all the training Paul had given me in my younger years. He had taught me moves to defend my small frame; that's how I learned to deal with Betty & Emily through the bullying years of school. However, these men were nothing like Betty or Emily. They were fully grown men, much stronger than me. The first time the guy forced himself on me; I tore at his hair and punched him in the chest when he tried to unbutton my clothes. When he finally pulled himself away from me, I knocked him in the eye and ran. The second time it happened at a gas station rest room.

The guy was in his twenties and seemed to be drunk or on drugs. Guys who were on a high are always easier to hit since they're always off-balance. A couple of knocks and he went down like a pack of cards. I didn't know if I could be more careful if I tried but I had toughened up. My clothes were dirty, my muscles ached with pain from days of walking and my skin was tanned under the sun. If I missed someone, it was Megan. If only I could see her right now. I'm unable to walk any further when I collapse from weakness in front of a burger stand. I was hungry as I inhaled the aroma of fried chicken cutlets and warm burger buns & cheese. But I was too tired and without a cent & I'd faint hallucinating about a burger. I close my eyes, feeling dizzy headed and being blinded by the scorching afternoon sun. I feel a gentle hand touch my arm. I try to open my eyes and the sunlight made it difficult for me to see. I blink three times to see the figure in front of me. It's a lady and she's smiling down at me. "Hi! My name is Kate Bell, what's yours?"

"Abby Pena."

"That's a nice name. Going to have lunch, would you like to join me?"

I'm surprised by the kindness of a complete stranger. I motion to my empty hands to indicate that I have no money. "Come on. I'm buying, don't want to eat alone. Come on!"

Kate didn't care that I was dirty. Her pretty brown hair shone in the noon time sun caressing her shoulders. Blue eyed, olive skinned and petite, she was just over 3 inches taller than me. She looked like she was in her early thirties. To me, she almost appeared angelic; I was bone tired and almost about to faint when she found me like a guardian angel. I walk awkwardly behind her as she leads me to a quiet corner at the joint. We both order a cheeseburger, fries and a shake. She watches me eat. I was practically stuffing my face and that wasn't a very good idea: my stomach was hurting with the sudden intake of food, but didn't care. I can't recollect the last time I ate such a sumptuous meal since leaving home.

"Abby would you like to go home with me?"

"You don't even know me?"

Kate smiles knowingly "Look Abby you need help! I don't know why you're alone or someone that you're running away from for some reason, I'm just scared something may happen to you. Please come to my house. You could clean up, you could help me take care of my kids, clean house. So come with me?"

I thought it was heaven sent. A place to stay, I could clean up well, cook decent; I nod yes, it was better than living out here on the streets with zero safety. You don't come across people like Kate every day. I'd be a fool to say no. I clutch my small backpack and huddle into her car. She reminded me a lot of Rose; she had turned up out of nowhere to help me when Maria was beating me black and blue. She seemed nice enough. It's times like these that I feel that God is watching over me and making sure I was safe. We've reached Kate's house. Her house looks like a quaint little modern cottage that had big yellow windows, a white picket fence, and daises growing all over the front yard. We walk inside and find the house kept neat and tidy. The living room was spacious and had two couches, a center table, a large television, along with pictures of her family hung on the walls of the hallway. She has two children, a boy and a girl aged five and seven. Her husband is handsome. Kate tells me to go upstairs to shower. I'm taking in this new house and cannot believe my luck. I wanted to be part of a normal, functional family and seems like this would be a nice place to experience that. Had Kate not found me today, I'd be pining after a futile dream. I felt hopeful. I'm woken up from my thoughts by someone yelling downstairs. I pay attention and realize its Kate and her husband.

"Jake her name is Abby."

"I don't care Kate, she's a runway. She won't stay in this house."

"Please! She needs our help Jake, she's going to help with the kids and clean the house. The truth is I need her okay?"

"Kate if something happens this will be on you! She's a stranger."

"Thank You Jake!" He hugs his wife. I wanted to be the last thing or person to be an actual point of argument in their otherwise picture perfect life. Hearing Kate speak up for me has warmed my heart; it's not very often that I get that.

I hear her call me, "Abby could you come downstairs we are going to have dinner."

I'm nervous thinking about how everyone's going to react to me. I seat myself at the table and all eyes are on me. Jake is staring at me with curious eyes, gauging whatever he can from my countenance. "Abby, we have rules in this house." He says. Here we go with the rules yet again. "Kate wants you to stay." My head is down staring at my fingers.

"Abby! Look at me when I'm speaking to you!" This is the first time I see him eye to eye. He has short dark black hair, brown eyes. He's clean cut, thin pale lips, tall and thin. His son looks a lot like him. Jake is wearing dressing clothes. "So Abby the rules…." His eyebrow lifts up. "You have duties to do: take care of the kids when you are asked. In return you have your own room. Keep it clean all the time. You are welcome to eat anytime. Help Kate when she asks you to. Any questions?"

"No sir." I reply with a straight face.

"Don't call me that! Jake will be just fine, you already know I don't want you here; Kate likes you so I trust you will respect our home, yes? Please finish your dinner." He says motioning to my plate.

Without a word further, I eat all my food and clean up the kitchen. I take the kids out to play. Kate's daughter Cathy is just five years old: she's adorable. Brown eyed with fair skin and red lips, she's a beauty already. Jackson her son is seven, he's like his dad, dark haired and pale lips. The kids didn't seem to have a problem getting along, I was happy for their innocent laughter and curiosity. We had a great time playing. They both had very different personalities and I looked forward to knowing more about them.

A week's gone by. So far so good, everyone's getting along well. I think Kate's family is as sweet as her. And she was more than generous. She bought me new clothes and underclothes. She'd give me hugs to express her appreciation at a work done well and the kids have learned to be affectionate, just like their mother. I'd play with the kids and they'd always shower me with hugs and kisses. I felt like I was in heaven. Kate tried her best to make me feel part of the family and leaved no stone unturned. My initial reservations about Jake had disappeared like the morning dew. Though he didn't want me here he never treated me badly: he wouldn't talk to me for long but he'd make sure he'd say "Hi", ask me how the day went or say "Goodnight". I knew and felt the love in this family. This wasn't just a house, it was a home. They were heaven sent. They even took me places: to the movies and the beach. Things I'd never experienced when I stayed with Ma. Of course, I always helped with the kids, and that was fine with me. I quite loved my time with them and often remembered Megan and the niece/nephew I've not yet seen.

Two whole months passed and it's been going great. I always did what was required of me.

Kate and the kids went with her in-laws. I cleaned up the whole house. I'd sing and dance whenever I was by myself; I'd never been so much at peace and it showed. It's only when I'm in bed that I start thinking about and missing Megan, and Dad. Someday perhaps, I'd go home to see them but for now this is my world. This is the family I always dreamed about. Though I couldn't be here forever, I knew I'd cherish every single moment spent here. They felt like family even though we weren't related in any way. I dream about having a family like this someday of my own. I'll wait patiently till that dream comes true. I snap out of my day dreaming when I hear someone knock at the door. When I open it, there's a glorious guy grinning. "Is Kate here?"

"No, she's not"

"And who are you pretty girl?"

My cheeks are so flushed by the sudden remark! "I'm Abby."

"Could I come in Abby?"

"Who are you? Don't think Kate will like that…"

He doesn't let me finish. "Sorry my name is Andy. I'm her brother."

"Oh! I didn't know she had a brother."

"Well here I am in the flesh." Then he winks! Megan used to do that all the time. He really looks like a movie star: tall, well-built, green eyed, light brown hair, so clean cut, tanned skin, wearing a suit. In my head, I was like Wow! But dare I show that on my face. "So Abby, hope we could be friends. If Kate let you in her house she must like you a lot." I felt shy with this complete stranger who's now talking about being friends.

"Okay pretty girl you're going out with me on Saturday."

My cheeks flush. "I am?"

"Yes, you are, you could trust me pretty girl, so be ready by seven." He was a sight for sore eyes and it was hard for me to look away.

"See you then babe." With a low voice I say "Okay" again, rolling my eyes at myself.

When Kate came home she was always so happy. Telling her that her brother visited she smiled at me. "So, what did you think about my brother?"

Telling her the truth. "He's very cute."

"Well don't start to like him Abby. He could be a good friend."

I frowned, "What do you mean?"

Kate put her hands on both of my shoulders. "He's gay Abby."

"Okay, he's a happy person."

She shakes her head back and forth. "Abby you don't know what gay means? You are so naive and innocent." I was totally confused. Kate grins. "He likes men Abby!"

"Oh! Okay, I never knew men could go with men. And who am I to judge anyone?" I stare at her eyes, slightly shaken by this sudden revelation. He seems very nice though. She gives me a huge hug sensing my disappointment.

It's Saturday night and Kate is helping me get ready. She's already bought me a nice dress. She fixes my hair and puts on some makeup. "WOW! Abby you look so pretty. Go look in the mirror." She says excitedly.

So I do. I really felt pretty. "Thank You."

Kate says to Jake, "See how pretty Abby's face is?"

"Yes! Abby you look pretty." Jake says, nodding his head in agreement with Kate.

Shyly I smile saying "thanks". I knew he didn't like me as much but he was decent. As long as he didn't make any trouble for me, I was cool. Andy came fifteen minutes early. I had found he's older to me by a few years. He looked dashing in a black suit. Even though he was 'gay', I just couldn't stop looking at him. He was so charming. When he saw me he said, "WOW! Pretty girl you look older, and that's good."

He squeezed my hand. He bought the car around and drove to the night club. The music was pounding. He bought me a drink.

What I didn't know is that it was a gay club. Andy and I danced and since it was a gay club, I didn't fear for my safety. There was a huge bar at one side of the club and people were lined across stools, talking and laughing. Andy handed me another mixed drink. I was underage so I wanted to be careful. I remembered the episode with Rick when I was drunk and allowed him to get to second base. I didn't want a repeat of that under any circumstances. I wanted to save myself for marriage and a love that was pure and would stand the test of time. I was frowning and lost in thought, when Andy interrupted "Are you having fun Abby?"

I'm flushed and shy by his question, all I was able to say is, "Yes thank you for bringing me here."

"Listen pretty girl, do you feel like talking?"

"No."

"Okay, then let's keep dancing." Giving him a huge smile, he's pleased "That's my girl."

It's a slow dance. He knows how to dance. "Babe would you like to go shopping tomorrow with me?"

"Sure."

He grins and holds me tight. After that night, we became such good friends. He bought me nice clothes, took me to the park, dinner sometimes, and even to the movies. He was so sweet. Too bad he was gay: he was perfect. When we talk, it felt nice. I could share everything with him and he understood. He shared his struggles too and I understood how much he needed a friend when he was being isolated sometimes on account of his orientation. Both of us were broken in a way and that's why we understood each other so well.

I told him I missed my family at times. I shared my dreams of having a family like Kate's when I'm old enough. He listened quietly and assured me that I'd have my chance.

Kate's whole family is going to long beach. I've never been there. They called it the pike.

They have rides and games. They made me part of their family and I went everywhere they went I always went. Andy was also coming with us so I knew we'd have an amazing time together. That night, I lay down thinking how lucky I was to have Kate find me that day, how blessed I was to be part of a family as loving as this one. I hadn't felt so much peace anywhere else. Everyone cared about each other; there was no selfishness, petty dramas or beating. I haven't seen Kate beat her kids even once, she disciplined them with sternness and lots of love. It's when I saw Kate in her maternal avatar that I begin missing Megan. The last I saw her was when she left with Miles to the new apartment. I hadn't told her anything about my wanting to leave home because I knew she'd do everything to stop me from leaving. But I missed her terribly wondering how the baby was, whether I was an Aunt to a niece or a nephew. I don't think she'd be too pleased about me leaving; she'd be worried about me. If there was any way of letting her know, I would. I could call her but I was scared of her reaction. What am I going to do? What can I do? Maybe they don't care about me or are happy that I'm gone. I suddenly feel miserable and sob into my pillow. The next day was kind of tough. I wake up with swollen eyes. I go about my routine like everything is normal. Kate's family has been amazing to me and I've enjoyed every bit of my stay here.

Chapter 17

It's been six months since I ran away from home. Life in the Kate household has been memorable and fairly peaceful. I've learned so much and more than anything else, I've realized what it feels like to be part of a normal loving family. I'd been pondering about giving Megan a call and letting her know that I was here. I've missed her so much and I've had to muster the courage to even make a phone call to her because I was so nervous. I hadn't told Kate about Megan or about my plan to call her. I wanted to see her so badly. I wait patiently for Kate and Jake to leave the house for shopping. Andy was playing with the kids so I was finally free to make the phone call. It was going to be difficult and I have no idea what am I going to hear at the other end of the line. Will Megan scream at me in anger or be relieved to know that I'm alive and well? I didn't have much time to think about consequences. I pick up the phone and dial Megan's number, anxious and wrecked. The phone rings. After the fourth time, I hear Megan's voice "

"Hello! Hello! Is anyone there?"

My throat was dry. I force myself to speak. "It's me Megan."

"Abby! Is that really you? My God Abby! Tell me where you're at, are you alright?"

Hearing her speak, I just start crying out of happiness and relief. "Yes I'm okay." I mumble.

"Tell me where you're at. I'll pick you up!"

I told her I was at Echo Park. I gave her the address. "I'll be there soon."

Knowing Megan, she wouldn't waste a minute.

I pack quietly but I knew it was even more difficult to tell Kate, Jack and Andy about this decision. They have not seen this coming. They have been so kind to me, I hope they are not angry at my sudden departure. I wait to tell Kate, unsure of her reaction but hoped it'd go smoothly. I was going to miss them and the kids but I longed to be with my own family too. I see Kate and Jake take the bag from their car. "Abby will you help us please!" As soon as she sees my face she frowns. "Abby what's wrong?" I see Jake roll his eyes because I know he won't miss me one bit. She puts down the bags and holds my shoulders. I start to shed tears. She hugs me. "What's matter sweetheart? You're not feeling well?"

"I'm leaving Kate."

"What?"

"My sister is coming for me."

"Why Abby? Aren't you happy here? They don't want you so why are you going to punish yourself? Why? Abby don't go honey."

I cry, feeling guilty and grateful at the same time. "Sorry Kate I'm so thankful for your help." I whisper.

Kate lifts my chin.

"I did more than help you Abby. I saved you out there in the streets alone. You were broken Abby! We loved you Abby! We don't want you to leave."

We both started weeping then we hear a loud honk! We both wipe our eyes with the palm of our hands. I knew the honk was from Megan's car

Kate whispers in my ear, "Good luck Abby honey, we love you. You are always welcome back here." I whimper and manage a feeble, "I'll miss you so."

At that precise moment, I feel a twinge of regret and guilt. I don't have the strength to say goodbye to the kids. I say, "Give the kids a bear hug for me. Tell Andy goodbye for me." I give Kate a forced smile, unable to bear the pain of parting with this beautiful family. I clutch my backpack, now filled with things Kate has given along with the many memories I've had of her and their love. I run across the street and see Megan wave out, standing next to an orange Nova. Looks like a new car and she looks much better than I remember seeing her. We fall into a long embrace. I cried so much because I missed her. I held on for the longest time. She helps me into the car and stayed quiet for some time. I know Megan will barrage me with questions when we get home. "Okay Abby why?" she suddenly muttered, checking into the rearview mirror and then looking sideways at me. "Why did you run away? Why?"

We haven't reached home yet and she's already started. I roll my eyes and keep looking straight and answer, "Why don't you take a guess Meg?"

"Come on Abby you could have been raped or killed or something."

Turning towards her I say, "Don't make me regret calling you Megan."

"What is that supposed to mean?"

"It means I don't want to talk about it!"

"Why were you living with those people Abby?"

Man, she's not going to let this go so I tell her what happened from the beginning to the end. For a brief moment, she was so deathly silent that I had to touch her just to see if she was actually here. I see tears run down her cheeks as she continues to drive.

"I'm sorry Abby! I miss you so much! Ma didn't even look for you." Megan frowned. "I was so angry Abby, nobody cared that you were gone. No police report, nothing."

Well that didn't surprise me.

"Megan, I don't want to live with Ma. I'm going to tell her that we both can't live together under the same roof, anywhere but not with her." Megan nods in agreement but looks concerned. Well can't promise that: Ma will say what she wants, you can come and live with me."

Megan hugs me. "Love you girl, never do that again okay?"

All I could say is okay. We're halfway through the drive home and I'm exhausted. My head is aching and long to just nap for a bit. Megan and I decide to go first to Ma's home to avoid complicating things. We reach home and I step out the car to see the house looking pretty much the same. Did I expect anything to change, no, but did it bother me that nothing changed? Yes. When I walk in, Megan squeezes my hand. "It's okay Abby you will be alright." I nod not knowing what lay ahead. A feeling of dread was coming upon me and I was beginning to regret having come here. It felt like a good idea then but standing inside the house, seeing Ma, it doesn't feel like such a good idea at all. Megan tried to tell Ma that I would live with her; Ma was angry hearing that and said no! She said she was going to make me work for my room and board if I wanted to live in her house and food too. Just being fifteen years old I didn't really care anymore. Someone told Ma that I was sleeping around, that I was basically a whore, and that she was disappointed with me. She would never trust me again. Megan tried telling her it wasn't true but she just wouldn't hear about it. Ma says that I'm going to start work on Monday.

"No more school just work you hear me Abby?"

"Yeah! I hear you."

"And half your check will go to me and no more boys for you."

I wanted to laugh. If she only knew that I was still a virgin. It saddened me that no one believed me; so what else was new? I was pretty sure now that I should not have come back. I'm already missing Kate and the kids. I feel so torn and I feel sad thinking about not saying bye properly to Andy and the kids. I'm…Yeah, my life sucks. It breaks my heart that I won't never see them again.

Megan surprises me with a big hug. "So happy you're home and safe Abby. Love you girl and you're an aunt now!"

"I'm sorry Megan, what? Did you have a boy?"

"Yes Abby, his name is Kyle."

"You named him Kyle?"

"Yes, Abby I did."

"Are you happy?"

"Yes Abby." She said with a happy smile.

"Well that's what counts in the end right?" She nods. We both smile. At least someone is happy. I wanted to see my nephew but that would have to wait. Megan takes me to my room and sets my backpack down. Nothing's changed; it looks like a museum preservation of a bedroom. It looks exactly like the day I had left it. My thoughts go back: at Kate's house my room was beautiful. The walls were a cream color it had pictures of flowers, even the comforter had a floral pattern and smelled fragrant of fresh soap. I felt free there in every sense of the word. Those six months felt like a dream, a beautiful dream.

It's Monday morning. I wake up at 6 am and get ready to work at Ma's friend's company. Ma lets me know that they're happy to let me work there. I roll my eyes. There is a honk outside! Ma yells, "Do good Abby, work hard!" Is she for real! Dear God I'm never going to hear the end of it. I see a woman waiting for me in the car. She's Ma's friend Maggie. I get in the car and wish her good morning.

She greets me with a smile and says 'Hi'. She'll be picking me up for work every day from here. How Ma managed that is beyond me. Maggie is an older woman. She's been Ma's friend for so long. Ma worked at Maggie's company for way too long. Ma retired now I guess so I'm the lucky one to carry the family baton. I can't help but roll my eyes hoping that Maggie doesn't notice. Maggie is quick to show me what to do; it's a shoe factory. "So Abby, this will be piece work: the more you do the more money you make. You'll be doing a variety of things. Mind your business so no one will mess with you. Count the shoes, put them in boxes, doing different things." I thought time will go quickly if I keep myself busy with work here but it seemed quite the opposite. A majority of those working here were older with only a handful of girls my age. Work went slowly as a result. Most of them seemed curious about their new work mate, I for my part kept to myself. I get by the first day at work, bored and tired. I'm grateful for Maggie's lift back home.

Maggie drops me off after work. "See you tomorrow Abby! You did very well today."

"Thanks." If I didn't know better she was surprised that I could work. She doesn't know how hard we worked at home with Ma.

Waking up the next morning was easy. Maggie picked me up at the usual time. I did what was expected of me and tried to do my best. Ma made lunch for me so I didn't go hungry like I did at school. That must be because half the check was Ma's.

Weeks passed by like a breeze. Though I settled into my routine fairly quickly, I was beginning to feel depression and gloom come over me. I felt alone and misunderstood. I had dreams but I also didn't have much choice. I saw Dad three days after I got home. He looked much worse than he was before. He had kicked off his drinking habit and stayed sober for a while before he started again. He quit his job and now drinks full time. I wished he was able to sustain himself without the drinking; he would be so much better and productive if he did. It was painful to watch him waste his life like this. But he was still my Dad and I still loved him, all the same. I was surprised by the new Dad I was seeing. I love him and he was sure glad to see me.

Chapter 18

It's a dull, grey and cloudy Saturday morning. I feel oddly different today. Most days I wake up feeling like a wreck, tired of this insipid existence. Then there are days when I knot up like someone just kicked me in the stomach. It's an ominous sign that a disaster lay ahead of me or my loved ones. Not today. I feel there's a sense of peace and calm. I look out the window and feel the cool breeze caress my face; it never ceases to amaze me how little things like this could bring me so much happiness. Life always hands out little pleasures to make up for the misery and mundane. I've got a lot to do, like clean up the house and tidy things around before chaos descends over the household; it's going to be the usual serving of drinking, card games and mindless bickering. I've never enjoyed these and keep to myself. I remember how different things were when I was living with Kate. They felt so much more like family even though they weren't related to me by blood. I feel my heart ache as I think about how often I got to laugh my heart out and play, how comforting it was to be with Kate & Andy. And the kids, they were a special joy. I missed them and perhaps with time, the pain of being away from them would diminish. It's evening and as expected, most of the family is here for their night of 'fun'. I just roll my eyes. I don't find their idea of 'fun' amusing in the least bit. I see Dad walk in with a smile.

"Hi! Abby want to give your Daddy a hug for good luck?"

He knows how I hate their game of cards and drinking bouts. They make the house look and smell like a bar! It annoys me to no end but since I have no say in it, I leave it. I reciprocate Dad's request with a small peck on his cheek and give him a hug.

"Love you Abby."

"Me too Dad"

I run upstairs to Ma's room before the living room turns into a loud, smoky night bar. I enjoy reading a book at times like this to keep myself distracted and educated. The sound coming from below isn't blocked out despite closing the bedroom door and is now giving me a headache. That's when I hear the phone ring.

I pick up and hear an unfamiliar voice.

"Hello! Is Cindy there?"

It's a guy's voice.

"Cindy is that you?"

"I really think you have the wrong number Mr., I'm sure that no one with that name lives here." I roll my eyes, what a lame guy!

"Wait! Don't hang up!" he said.

At this point my head is throbbing with pain and I don't have the patience to talk to a total stranger.

"What do you want?"

I ask, my voice sounding visibly annoyed. Why would this guy not want me to hang up?

"What's your name baby?"

Is he for real?

"I'm not your baby."

"Just don't hang up!"

"What the hell!"

"Tyler Miller, so what's yours?"

"I am not going to tell you my name, I don't even know you."

"Come on, you have an amazing voice. I'll just keep calling you so tell me your name please!"

"You're very persistent and obviously very annoying." He gives a deep hearty laugh.

"I have things to do! And you are simply wasting my time."

"Baby just tell me your name, please?"

"It is Abby. There, satisfied?"

"Pretty name and a pretty voice, can't wait to meet you."

"That's not going to happen."

"Oh! Baby it will, believe it. I'll be calling you baby, and then we can go out on a date later baby."

He hangs up before I could protest any of the nonsense he just mumbled. Gawd, his nerve! I stare at the phone in disbelief over what just happened. That was a wrong number, does this kinda of thing happen for real? I shake my head and laugh it off as a silly prank of sorts. May be some guys get a kick out of it? I certainly don't.

One week passed. It's seven pm on a Friday night. I've just finished taking a shower and settle into bed to read a book. I'm just about to take the bed covers off when the phone rings. I pick up because Ma isn't home.

"Hello." I say softly.

I'm half expecting Mr.Wrong number at this point and as if on cue, I hear his voice on the other end of the line.

"Hi baby."

"What do you want?"

"That's not nice Abby baby..."

I smirk rolling my eyes.

"Did you miss me, baby?"

"Huh?! No! I don't even know you?"

"Come on baby, you're hurting my feelings here! Want to meet you Abby?"

He sounds serious. He had a voice to die for but that doesn't guarantee a heart of gold. I had seen so many boys with superficial good looks and zero heart, that I almost feel jaded. "My Ma won't let me."

"Let's write a letter with pictures attached to it. What do you say baby?"

Okay what else could I say; taking a chance is kind of difficult for me these days but my curiosity gets the better of me & I hope to God it doesn't get me killed, like it did the cat.

We exchange letters as suggested and I receive his letter with a picture after a week. I open excitedly because I wanted to see how he looks. Well it wasn't what I expected. This guy was skinny, messy haired, brown eyes, with huge mole on his cheek and thin lips. He was so not my type. I'll still be his friend I decided.

I unfolded the letter he sent me.

"Dear Abby baby, looking at your picture, words can't describe how beautiful you are. I want to meet you so badly; perhaps if you give me a chance, something could come from this. Every time I call you and hear that sweet voice of yours, it makes me want to go through that phone and touch you. There's something about you and I won't stop until, well ... getting to know you will be my mission in life. Okay baby talk to you later. Abby I'm serious; I want to meet you soon Tyler."

This was more like a note than a letter and there was nothing I could glean about him from just the note. I still didn't know him any better or about his likes or dislikes, nothing. And the main part, I am not interested. That ends all potential for anything other than a platonic friendship which I doubt he's interested in. He kept calling for two weeks after the letter arrived; Ma picked up and hanged up every single time and not being to talk to him proved to be a blessing in disguise. I wasn't good at saying 'No' and this was easier. I did feel bad but perhaps this was the best way forward, why promise him something that I can't do.

I had a horrid day at work today. One of the girls at the factory got into an unnecessary scuffle with me in the restroom. I didn't understand a word of Spanish she was mouthing out at me. I didn't talk much with the other girls who came to work there. We both ended in Maggie's office and as in all situations, I took the blame even though I didn't start it. I protested halfheartedly knowing that she wouldn't believe me.

"Didn't do anything wrong. She pushed me first," I said motioning towards this girl who played the victim card all too well.

Maggie sent me home early. Since Maggie was the one who usually dropped me off home and she wasn't going to do that half way through work, I had to walk back. I hoped Ma wouldn't be around when I got there else I'll be questioned and I'll have to tell her everything. Then she won't believe anything I've said because that's just the way it is when it came to me.

Thankfully when I get home, Dad and Ma have gone out shopping somewhere. So I change into clothes and get to my cleaning duties a little early. I was sulking throughout and all I wanted was to go and lay in bed. I finish up and take a nap as I intended to. It's just been twenty minutes since I was asleep when the phone rang.

I rub my eyes, still half asleep and super annoyed at the call. "HELLO!" I say in an irritated voice.

"Hi baby."

Oh no! It's him again.

"What do you want Tyler?"

"You really want to hurt my feelings Abby."

"I'm just busy right now!" I lie because I want to avoid this conversation like a plague.

"Told you baby that I wanted to meet you, so come to the corner."

"What! You're here?"

"Yes Abby! Came to visit you baby."

"Why are you here?"

"Abby just come out!"

"Okay just give me a minute!"

I was wearing a pair of blue jeans and a black blouse. I looked myself in the mirror and thought it didn't require me to change into something new. It's not like I want to impress him because I wasn't even interested in him. I run downstairs eager to get this impromptu meeting over with. I walk out the door onto the road, hoping to see him somewhere at the corner, like he said. I don't see him. I walk all the way further down the road near a store and I see a guy come out. I don't recognize him from the picture so it's probably not him. But he looks gorgeous, tall and chiseled with slanted green eyes. There's a mischievous grin playing on his lips and I see a pair of dimples pop out on each side. He's dressed in black shorts, a white tee and black sneakers. I see a few tattoos etched on his left arm. He's a total eye candy. I look at him with curious eyes and ask, "Are you Tyler?" I blush a beet red and hoped it wasn't so obvious.

"Yes baby that would be me." he quipped with a smile.

"You don't look like that picture you sent." I said eyeing from top to bottom.

He chuckles like I missed something.

"Abby you are beautiful just like your picture." I feel the blood in my body warm my cheeks. "Aren't you going to give me a kiss baby?"

"I just don't give kisses to strangers." He smirks at me again, what does he think? I'm lost in this visual feast of looking at him and blushing in all shades of red when I hear a voice of terror boom down my ears. It's Ma!

I turn my head and see Ma standing in the distance yelling out my name. "ABBY!"

I'm mortified; this is not going to go well. I look at Tyler and say "I've got to go, like now!" I say that and turn to run when I feel his arm grab hold of my waist and his other arm lifts my face. He gives me a long, deep kiss. If Ma weren't standing there watching me like a hawk, I'd be lost in the passion of this kiss.

I pull myself from him, overcome by his sudden display of passion.

"You taste like strawberries and are so sweet baby. I'll be calling you."

All I could mumble is "Sure." He laughs and turns away to go when I'm momentarily interrupted with Ma's fanatical scream. I had not a minute to waste and quickly run back; I hear the sound of a motorcycle whoosh by and I'm like, OMG, he has a motorcycle and he came on that to see me. I blush but right now my heart is pounding at the prospect of a confrontation with Ma. Ma is standing at the front door and as expected, she's furious as hell.

"What do you think Abby? Being on the corner like a whore. Only whores stand on the corner."

"But I'm not one okay. GAW! You think the worst of me Ma. Can't you just trust me?"

She just pushes me inside the house.

"No boys Abby, he looks old for you."

"He's not!"

"You will not see him again Abby!"

"Ma!? He is just a friend!!"

I run up the stairs, tears pooling my eyes. I'm frustrated with the amount of rules and limits she imposes when it came to me. I wish she trusted me more but all I could do is cry into my pillow. Then I think about Tyler, Ma was right about one thing, though cute, he did look older. It didn't matter to me much because there was something about him. He wasn't traditionally attractive and he could pass off as a bad boy, but then there was still something tender about him. Or was it just me?! I was just overwhelmed by the passion I felt in that one kiss, I could feel butterflies in my tummy. I tingled all over thinking about it and it's been a long time since I felt that way about a guy. And surprisingly, there was no big mole on his cheek.

I brush aside all thoughts of Tyler when I see Megan come home with little Kyle cradled in her arms. I rush in joy to hug them both and kiss my nephew's cheeks. He's so cute, I can hardly resist from taking him into my arms. I look at Megan, glowing from within. "Where is Miles?" I ask, still holding onto little Kyle.

"He had to go to work." She says with a frown.

"What! You don't want him to go to work?"

"Yes, I do, but just miss him so much! That's a good thing, right?"

"Megan you look so happy. I'm so glad for you." I say, relieved and thrilled for at the same time that she could have a life outside of this place.

"Let's talk about you Abby, Ma told me you were with a guy."

I glance at her, gob smacked. "Is that the reason you came, because Ma told you about Tyler?!"

"Well Abby, who is Tyler? Ma said he seemed older."

"So what! I really don't care if he's older Megan, he's so cute!"

"How did you meet him Abby?"

"Wrong number," I say sheepishly.

"You gave a total stranger your address."

"Calm down, we wrote to each other first and exchanged our pictures."

"That's beside the point Abby; Tyler could be a murderer or rapist who likes young girls."

"He's not Megan, he likes me." I say confidently but underneath all my vote of confidence for Tyler, Megan's concern seemed genuine and had a point. After all, how long did I know Tyler? And honestly, I still don't know anything about him other than what he looks like and him being a good kisser.

"Sorry Abby we just care about you that's all."

I see her face, creased with a mix of worry and mother-like concern only an older sister could have.

"Be careful okay?" We hug each other.

A few days go by. The phone rings and I answer.

"Hello baby."

"Hi Tyler."

"Did you get in trouble?"

"Yeah I did."

"Sorry baby, that wasn't my intention. I want to see you again Abby."

"Tyler could I ask you a question?"

"What is it baby?"

"Who was Cindy? You know the girl you were calling when I answer."

"She is just a friend Abby baby. I want to see you again, there is something about you. You're so sweet and beautiful."

"Well you're not that bad yourself."

He laughs and the sound of him laughing makes me giddy. I'm pushing my naivety aside and falling for a fool's adventure. I tell Tyler to meet me at the movies the day Ma goes to the horse races, which is on Saturday. Tyler manages to call me almost every day. He's twenty-two, has a younger sister and lives alone in a two-bedroom apartment while his sister lives with her parents. They own a convenience store and he helps around with the work there most days. He dreams of opening a motorcycle shop. Since I've seen most of my childhood dreams collapse like sandcastles, I've lived one day at a time not thinking much about dreams. Besides, no one cares enough to ask if I even have any.

A month passes quickly. Tyler is my everyday distraction and consolation from the mundane existence in this house. We talk almost daily and haven't had any regret yet about meeting up this total stranger. He doesn't know I'm a virgin because I haven't told him. This guy is so different, maybe because he's older? I've never felt this way before and it feels amazing, or is this love? Tyler is going to pick me up from work today and I can't wait to see him. I hurry up with my work and finish as efficiently as I can. By now, my ears are accustomed to knowing the sound of Tyler's motorcycle so I don't lose much time making for the exit, knowing he'd be waiting for me. I see him; grinning ear to ear and those dimples make me weak in my knees every time. "Get on baby." He says extending his hand to give me a helmet I climb on to the back seat, slip on my helmet and hold fast to his waist. I feel his muscles tense up in response to my touch.

"Where are we going?" I ask, just happy to be with him.

"It's a surprise baby. First, let's get you something to eat, okay?"

That was thoughtful of him.

We are sitting at a Jack-In-Box fast food place. "Abby what would you like?" I stare at the menu because everything looks so yummy. I've never been here before so that makes me unsure of what to order.

"Abby!" He interrupts my thoughts.

"Anything will do."

He tells the girl, the order went something like: two jumbo jacks with cheese, some fries, two vanilla shakes and an apple turnover."

Wow, that sounded like an order for the crowd! My mouth salivates at the idea of gorging into all this. Our order arrives and I can't believe how great the food tastes. It's really good. "Yumm...." I exclaim with complete satisfaction of devouring the last bits from my plate. Tyler is smiling, happy that he brought me here. "Tyler, this is wonderful. Thank you for bringing me."

"Abby, you never been here before?"

"No. Ma doesn't let us go out to eat. She makes food fresh for us every day. She's a wonderful cook."

Tyler just stares at me with a frown. "Your Ma is pretty strict."

All I could say is, "Yes!"

His surprise was taking me to his apartment. We reach there in ten-fifteen minutes, being a short way from where we had stopped to eat. He helps me from the motorcycle and I take the helmet off and shake my head; I'm relieved to be breathing freely again, having the helmet on is kinda of funny. My hair tumbles down from being held up so long because of the helmet. I can feel Tyler watching me and my cheeks redden as he takes my hand, leading me to his apartment. It's a cozy little space with light blue walls, pictures of motorcycles, some old cars, a poster of a girl with a bikini at which I rolled my eyes. Tyler keeps looking at me to gauge my reaction at his place. I continue walking along, taking in his living space. The living area has a long, navy blue couch with two small side tables holding a lamp each and a television. The kitchen is quite small. It has an all-white decor: a white fridge, white stove and a small dark wooden square table is the only contrast to the white theme. Then we turn left to walk a short hallway to Tyler's bedroom: a full-sized bed is lined with a navy blue bedspread. There are nightstands on each side with blue & white lamp shades. The walls were a pale powder blue. He tells me that the other bedroom is empty and is hardly ever used. I stand in the bedroom, nervous and wondering what exactly I was doing there. He then proceeds to show me the restroom which is done up in a similar blue & white theme.

He holds my hand walking me to the couch. I breathe a sigh of relief in my head that we're no longer in the bedroom. He motions me to take a seat on the couch.

"So Abby like my pad?"

"It's really nice."

"Yeah it's nice not living with my parents."

Tyler moves closer to meand lifts my chin and looks into my eyes. I look back innocently and peer into his hazel green eyes. He's really handsome. I see his lips part as he tightens his grip around my waist and holds the back of my neck. I cannot resist touching him feeling the full intensity of his passionate kiss; my fingers start grazing down his neck and chest. He moans, delighted at the sensation and starts kissing my neck in response.

Then he lifts my blouse. I'm wearing a white cotton bra. Then he begins caressing my breasts; we can't keep our hands off each other.

Then Tyler says, "Want you so badly Abby."

He grabs my waist as if to make a point.

"I can't Tyler!" I say, resisting the idea of losing my virginity to him.

"What do you mean you can't?"

"I have to tell you something. I haven't! I mean I've never been with anyone before." My stomach is in knots. I'm so embarrassed, I feel like my cheeks are on fire. His eyes widen and he's looking at me in quiet contemplation like a monk. Unable to take his silence anymore, I say "Tyler say something?"

"What do you want me to say? You are young Abby, you're a virgin. I'm not happy about that fact!"

He walks to the fridge to get a beer & diffuse the rather awkward situation.

I feel hot tears flow down my cheeks.

"Well sorry, I'm not a slut. I was saving myself until I get married."

"Are you for real Abby?"

"Could you please take me home? Ma will be back soon?"

"Yeah! That's a better idea. Let's go Abby. I'm not good for you, but I want you so badly. There's something about you."

"Yeah I've heard that before." I say, disappointed and hurt that he wasn't respectful of my decision to save myself for that one special guy and marriage. Instead he mocked at me and asked me if I was for real. I wanted to be out of here.

Tyler takes me home promptly. My feelings are all over the place. I cry a couple of hours and wonder why things like this happen to me. Perhaps I should've listened to Ma & Megan, they were right. I was in a pity party half way through midnight. I woke up the next morning thinking maybe he'd call and things will be okay.

Two weeks passed; he didn't call me. I was heartbroken; disappointed yet again for letting myself fall for someone I barely knew when I should've known better. I loved him and hoped there'd be a future with him but he doesn't want a naïve, young girl as his partner. It broke me. The fool's adventure ended exactly like it would for a fool. Sadness had engulfed my heart and I had no one to blame but myself for this ordeal.

☐

Chapter 19

It's 1st of November, 1978. The sky is dark and cloudy, a gentle drizzle has already begun and storm clouds are gathering in the distance. I'm still partially in a pity party for myself ever since Tyler drifted away from me. I know I'm damaged but he didn't even give me a chance. I had work to do, so I get ready to go to the factory, pushing away all thoughts of Tyler and what was a short-lived romance.

I worked hard and that was my escape from my reality. I focused only on what was in the present and required my attention. The past was behind me, the future before me and nothing that I can change. I can only be mindful of making the right choices, something that I haven't been too good at.

I walk home after work because Maggie is sick and recuperating at home. It's just my luck that I have no lift to get me home on this stormy, dark evening. It's raining cats and dogs. I begin walking slowly, in a few steps,

I'm drenched wet. I trudge along a few more steps when I hear a voice calling my name.

"Abby, Abby."

I turn around and see a black mustang parked a little away from me. My eyes widen in surprise as I see Tyler get out the car and walk towards me. I can't believe my eyes and grin in delight, happy to see him. At that moment, all the heartache melted away. We're standing facing each other, staring into each other's eyes. It's like time stopped for a moment there.

I can feel butterflies in my tummy as he caresses my face in his arms. "You're mine Abby. Missing you so much was the hardest thing I ever felt." I can hardly believe that he said that. It felt like I was in some movie, it was surreal. He kisses me deeply and holds me so tight. He hugs me, then tucks my hair behind my ears gently and kisses me again. I felt like I was on cloud 9, I was so happy…! Is this what all those romance novels and movies are all about? I feel dizzy with love. This is the kind of love I had hoped to find;

the kind people would trade their lives for. I couldn't feel luckier! I was ecstatic and Tyler's face mirrored the joy I'd felt. We get into the car, overcome with emotion. My heart was bursting with love. He turns on the heater once we're inside. "We need to have a talk Abby; I'm taking you to my apartment."

"Can't stay too long Tyler, Ma won't be happy if I get home late."

"That's what we are going to talk about then."

He gives me a sly smile showing his dimples, holding my hand.

"Okay let's go for a while."

I'm really worried; he has no idea how much trouble I could get into if I turn up late. Ma's fury is legendary. He makes me some hot chocolate and for a moment, my mind is back to Tyler. I sip on the hot chocolate, relieved to have its warmth soothe my throat. "Thanks Tyler, it's so good." I say, continuing to savor the hot drink. "Glad you like it. Abby sit with me." So we are looking at each other for at least five minutes. "Abby would you like to move in with me?"

My eyes widen in excitement and surprise, this is proving to be a memorable evening for all the right reasons. In my head, I'm like YES! But I barely know him. We needed time, I needed time. When I try to articulate my thoughts, I end up choking on my hot chocolate and spill it on the floor. He's amused by my reaction and reaches out to offer me a kitchen towel. Cleaning up my mess, I say, "Tyler I can't live with you."

"Why not Abby? Why? I love you baby, don't you love me?"

"Yes, Tyler I love you so very much, but we really don't know each other."

"You are mine Abby and I want you with me. Come here baby." He cuddles me and softly kisses my lips.

"Think about it, okay baby? Just think about it, that's all I'm asking."

Tyler holds me for a while and I relish the feeling of being in his strong arms. Then he takes me back home. When Tyler brought me home, Ma wasn't standing at the front of the house and I was relieved. I hurry back into the house, my clothes still partially wet. All I could think about was Tyler's proposition about moving with him. I was quite taken aback by his request, saying it surprised me was an understatement. I was damaged and I had a history; would he be able to understand those things about me? Will this love sustain and stand the test of time? I and Megan had gone through much pain and struggle in our early years that we matured early. Though we preferred being naïve about the world, hoping and believing in the good of people, our experiences were bitter. Megan found the love of her life and things are looking up for her. Her husband turned out to be everything she had hoped he'd be. I can't compare Tyler to him but would he be able to be the man I need him to be? What if I ruined our relationship with unrealistic expectations or he leaves me when things get really tough? There are a lot of 'if's' & 'buts' to get through in this scenario, but my heart was happy beyond I could put in words. He wanted me. Abby

Marie Pena, the girl that no one wants, the one that was always being left alone is finally wanted by someone!

I had to tell Ma that Tyler is now my boyfriend and it was the hardest thing. But I had to tell her sooner than later, having well experienced the full fury of not having told her about Megan's pregnancy a long time ago. I didn't want to be more trouble. As expected she was furious when she heard. She was washing utensils and cracked a glass when I mentioned about Tyler. Predictably, she began saying the things I had come to expect from her. "He's too old for you, guys only want one thing and they'll leave you when it's over...Etc..." I sighed.

"Mark my words they are all the same, or get you pregnant. Is that what you want?"

I don't want her to see me roll my eyes at her comment so I look away.

"No Ma that's not what I want."

We finish the conversation on a sour note, she says I'll regret. I didn't want to fuel her anger more so I left.

The days that followed were much like a dream. I couldn't contain my happiness. Tyler had planned to take me to the movies. I'm so excited and nervous at the same time. I'm dressed in a pale blue knee length dress and have a light dusting of makeup, touched up with a little bit of lip gloss. I leave my hair open because Tyler always liked playing with my hair. He comes to pick me up at my house in his black mustang and even opens the door for me, like a thorough gentleman. I appreciate the chivalry. We're delighted to see each other. We get to the movie hall but barely see the movie!! He's got his hands all over me and I don't resist. We kiss each other and mess around like it's typical for our age. We laugh and cuddle, just happy to be in each other's company. After the movie, he takes me out to eat to the place we first went. By now, I had my own favorite dishes in the menu and we talked, ate happily and tipped the waitress. When we get in the car, I want to kiss him deeply as a way of saying 'thank you' for letting me have such a wonderful time. But instead, he's asking me in a serious voice "Abby I want you to move in with me."

"Are we going to do this now?" I say, rolling my eyes.

"Then when Abby, tell me when then?"

He's miffed at me so he drives home quietly. He doesn't say anything even after we reach my home. I try to say 'goodnight' but he just drove back. I was hurt by the way he reacted.

Weeks passed, still no call from Tyler. I could imagine how frustrated he may have felt about me not agreeing to move in. But it didn't feel right, so early in the relationship.

I take out my frustration and energy on the work I'm entrusted with. I feel lifeless and all the enthusiasm I had felt was being replaced with a sense of dread. Ma's warning was ringing in my ears when one day, the phone rings.

"HELLO!" I say, annoyed.

"Abby it's Tyler."

"Hi!" I say reluctantly, not knowing what else to say.

"I'm outside of your house, come out."

I put my fingers through my hair. I'm in a pair of denim shorts, an oversized sweatshirt and my hair tied up in a messy bun: my classic work style clothes when I'm working my ass off cleaning the house. I walk out the house, anxious and nervous. I see Tyler dressed in dark jeans, a white t-shirt. His hair is messed by the breeze and he doesn't care.

We stare at each other. "Come here baby." He says and then gives me a big tight hug.

"I love it when you wear shorts Abby."

Then he kisses me so gently.

"Miss you baby. Come on, let's go to my apartment."

I leave after telling Ma. She threatened me to not return home if I go with Tyler. Though unsure of what Tyler was thinking, I wanted to take the chance. I loved him and if he turned up again for me, surely, he must feel the same way. Tyler and I are sitting on the couch. For a while, I try gauging what's going on in his mind but I'm unable to read him. What he says next changes my life. "Abby, I don't want you to go back home. I want you to pack your belongings and be here with me. I'm going to take you to meet my parents." I feel the earth move below me, I'm dizzy with happiness.

I had lost my job because Ma & Maggie thought I was sleeping around with Tyler, which wasn't the case. I had no way of proving that our love was real and not some game. Tyler's decision to take me to meet his parents vindicated me in some way. He drove me home the next day to pick up my stuff. When I got there, I saw Ma and Dad in the living room. Tyler walked in behind me and motioned me to hurry up with the packing. I go to my closet and find nothing. There were no clothes, none of my underwear, none of the medals I won in school; I searched for the silver heart necklace Rick had gifted me, even that was gone. They gave all my stuff away without even asking me! I was livid but I had to swallow my anger at this moment. I hurried downstairs with an empty duffle bag. Tyler understood that there was nothing to pack when he saw tears pool in my eyes. He held my hand and began to lead me outside when Dad said,

"You better take care of my daughter. If I find out that you hurt her, you will answer to me."

I'm grateful for Dad looking out for me in that way. Ma, though furious, looks me from head to toe, taking in how much I've grown. She gives me a peck on each cheek. She didn't say anything. It broke my heart.

"Baby let's go, it seems like I'd have to buy you clothes." As we turn to leave, I suddenly hear Ma's voice, having resigned to my decision. "Tyler, do well by her." With that Ma left the room. Though I didn't expect even that much from Ma, when she did say what she did, I knew she cared and may be this was her way of showing sadness. Something I knew all too well. I walk out the house with an empty duffle bag, holding on to Tyler's hands with a sense of freedom.

The day of meeting Tyler's parents have arrived. I feel nervous and go over possible ways of introducing myself; I find myself tongue tied and confused. What do I say? I've never done this before. I make all sort of excuses to not go and protest "I can't go with you Ty, sorry."

"You'll be fine baby. You look gorgeous in this dress. I'm sure they'll be as smitten with you as I am. Believe me baby they're going to love you."

"Yeah sure, they will." I say, trying to calm my nerves down.

"We're here baby." He says as he pulls the car in the driveway. Tyler's parents' house is a simple white house with a white picket fence. There are rose bushes lining the fence and red roses are in full bloom as if to welcome us. The front porch is a brick red and we walk to the front door. I glance sideways at Tyler, smiling but nervous.

His Mom opens the door, smiling wide until she sees me. Tyler hugs his Mom and then he turns to me. "Mom, this is Abby. Abby, meet my mother Anna Miller." I extend my hand for a handshake and she reluctantly reciprocate the gesture. This is not starting out too well. She looks young for her age. Tyler looks nothing like her; she had dark brown hair cropped in a short bob and had golden brown eyes. She was short but not petite. "Tyler, why have you bought this girl home?" she asks in a rude voice and a gaze that looks at me with contempt. "That is enough Anna," a strong voice says from behind her. It's Tyler's Dad.

"Hi Dad."

"Hello son, who do we have here?"

"Dad, this is Abby."

"Abby this is Tyler Miller. Just like me, right son?" his father quips with a smile. They're boxing each other playfully.

"Well Tyler, you didn't tell me how pretty your girlfriend is." He takes my hand and says "Nice to meet you Abby."

"It's nice to meet you too," I say shyly. I could almost hear his Mom gnashing her teeth. I resist the urge to roll my eyes; it's almost predictable that she wouldn't like me. Tyler's Dad is a different story. His Dad was right; Tyler got his looks from him. They have almost the same face, dimples; dark hair pulled back, his green eyes, tall and broad, just older. His sister comes out. I heard quite a bit about her from Tyler and I looked forward to meeting her. She looks a lot like her Mom: brown eyes, dark long brown hair, she's short but petite. Tyler introduces her to me.

"Diane this is Abby."

"It's my pleasure to meet you Diane."

She smirks. Like mother, like daughter. They looked and behaved the same way. Tyler wasn't too bothered about who liked me and who didn't. His Dad is sweet, and smiles at me when they're not watching me. We all step in to the house. I like the simplicity of their décor: brown leather couches, a wooden table, a few paintings and a coffee table make up their living room. Their kitchen is big enough to accommodate a stove, a fridge, four stools and a mini-table. Anna walks into the kitchen and I follow behind her, hoping to be of some help. She's cooking and I can savor the aroma of the gravy cooking off merrily on the stovetop. It smells amazing.

"Hope you like roast Abby."

"Yes I do. I'm not very picky."

"Well good, then let's sit at the dining room table. Will you help me with these dishes" she says handing me a platter of freshly baked bread rolls and a bowl of potato salad.

Tyler sits next to me and gives me his beautiful smile. Though I feel better seated next to him, I feel a general sense of discomfort. I felt unwelcome and Anna didn't try to hide her displeasure at my being here. She was tight lipped. I wish I didn't come but I couldn't let Tyler know that, so I played along. We're eating dinner as quietly as possible and there's awkward silence in the air. Tyler's Dad asks me how I met Tyler to break the ice. When I tell him that I was a wrong number, his sister snorts.

"Were you calling Cindy again Tyler?"

Tyler and his Dad both frown at her.

"Anything wrong Diane?" his Dad asks in a stern voice.

"No Dad."

"Then stop being so rude." He says.

"Alright, not to be a party pooper, but Gosh Dad, Tyler is always bringing girls here!"

"Enough Diane!" he says loudly.

As soon as she says that, I begin to get up.

I try my best to not make a scene. "Thank you for dinner," I say politely and walk away.

"Wait Abby." I hear Tyler calling me as I continue to walk out of the house. "For what Tyler? What should I wait for? So I could be told how many girls you've brought home?"

"Come on baby, that's my past." He holds my hand tight. "I'm taking you to Jack-in-Box."

And he huddles me into the car. I'm visibly upset and angry at this point. We find ourselves a table in the corner and order my favorites, tacos and apple turnovers which are to die for here. The food manages to calm me down and ease me into a more relaxed mood. Tyler smiles at me playfully and asks "Hungry?" I blush red in embarrassment because I really am. We left dinner at Tyler's place midway rather abruptly and I couldn't have asked for a more comforting meal. The food arrives and it's everything that I hope it is: delicious and satisfying. It manages to calm me down and ease me into a more relaxed mood. "We have to talk Abby." I've been sensing it for a while now but I can see how moving in with Tyler has increased his desire to have sex with me. So what he says next doesn't surprise me.

"It's been two months Abby. I want you and love you baby. You do know that right?"

I stare into his green eyes, hoping that he wants to make love to me out of his sincere love for me and not out of some lustful desire. His mischievous smile always makes my heart flutter and it's been difficult to resist him, when you're living with him under the same roof.

I do love him, so what am I waiting for? Do I give in, do I not?

"Okay, Tyler James Miller, we have a date on Friday." I say, finally giving into him.

"Oh! Baby, can't wait," and with that we go home. We just cuddle together. I like to be with Tyler. He holds me tight when we sleep, almost like he thinks I won't be there in the morning.

Tyler goes to work. I clean up, and then take the bus to the library to take some culinary books that'd help me cook better. I wanted to cook something nice for our date on Friday so that it's special and memorable in every way. Friday will be the day when I lose my virginity to a man that I've loved and wanted in every way. It had to be special and I was ready to do whatever it took to prepare and make it beautiful for both of us. I pick up two culinary books and a romance novel, from one of my favorite authors. I hurry home and make myself a sandwich before I sit down to read. If Ma knew that I'm eating sandwiches, she'd be so mad. She always thought of sandwiches as unhealthy and as a result, she always encouraged Megan and me to prepare meals from fresh produce and ensured that the meal would be balanced, nutritious and delicious. I was always a fan of Ma's cooking and I knew I couldn't come close to her natural talent at serving up great dishes. I was determined to learn how to cook. I finish up my sandwich and sit down to read the first cookbook. I'm immediately put off by the long ingredient list to make a single dish! I get to the kitchen to try out my first recipe. It turns out to be a disaster. No one gets it right the first, but right now I was frustrated that I couldn't cook a decent meal, if not anything fancy. I wanted to cry. The big day is tomorrow and here I'm in a messed-up kitchen with the most unappetizing meal I can serve up. I try to stay calm and collected even though all I felt was like a bunch of nerves. And I was scared. I was saving myself for when I got married but Tyler said he won't get married any time soon. Tyler comes home happy, telling me he can't wait for tomorrow. "It's only one more day." I say with a smile.

"I know baby. You're mine and always will be Abby. You're my baby you know that right?"

I nod my head trying to hide my discomfort. Tyler has a wild side to him: a bad boy image that doesn't surface too often but kinda lurks beneath. That mixed up with my feeling of not being good enough is making me feel all sorts of weird.

☐

Chapter 20

Today is probably the biggest day of my life; it's the Friday that will change my life forever; the day I lose my virginity. I whisper a prayer to God, hoping I'm doing the right thing. I've always treasured it like a sacred gift and I wanted to preserve its sanctity just the way God ordained it. I knew most guys were all about just sex and I've ignored it for the longest time. All my friends had sex; they used to make fun of me for the way I saved myself. I shift my focus to making the tacos, they were supposedly the easiest recipe I could find from the cookbook and required a minimal amount of ingredients. I finish up, pleased with the results and head to the bedroom to get ready. Tyler will be home in a bit. I take a quick shower and put on some jeans, a black t-shirt and leave my hair open. I pinch my cheeks in the mirror to give it a naturally flushed pink look. I put a cherry pink lip gloss. I toss my hair back and let it flow in natural waves. So far so good but I'm feeling uneasy. I go back to the living room. I decide to read a novel, just to make things feel a little normal. I just sit down when I hear Tyler come in through the door excitedly. He greets me with a big grin and then plants a kiss on my cheek. "Sorry I'm late baby. Looks like you've managed to cook something delish because it smells great!

I give his hands a squeeze and smile. "Going to take a shower baby, then we could have dinner." He quips and gives me a wink.

Tyler comes out of the shower and puts on a dark blue t-shirt and some Levi's. His hair is wet and kind of messy. He's all smiles as he comes to the living room and takes his seat, waiting for dinner to be served. I hand him his plate filled with tacos made from scratch, beaming at my successful attempt. His green eyes light up like glistening emeralds; he devours his plate and wipes it clean. I couldn't be more pleased. I couldn't take my eyes off him throughout dinner.

"Wow! These tacos are good." He says licking his fingers clean.

"Glad you like them." I said.

"Abby thanks for making such a sumptuous dinner." I nod in acknowledgement, feeling nervous about what the night would be like ahead. I clean up in the kitchen after dinner and Tyler turns on the music, holding out his hands to me saying "Let's dance." He puts on a song by Frankie Val Lie 'Can't take my eyes off of you' He holds my waist. "Baby you're so tense, relax baby. I'm not going to hurt you. Trust me, you look beautiful."

Tyler started with small gentle kisses on my hair, my cheeks, and then he put his full lips on my mine then carries me into the bedroom in his arms.

He kisses me ever so tenderly. His large hands slide slowly to my arms, then my breasts and then it's all over my body. I was tingling in excitement and nervousness. I knew I'd love him and he's the love of my life.

This man could make me happy or break me in to pieces. "I want you Abby, I love you so much." Then he takes my gift. It hurts. After it's happened, I feel tears roll down my cheeks to the pillow I'm holding tight. It wasn't anything like I expected. Tyler holds me so tight, kissing my face with sweet kisses, swirling my hair with his fingers. "Don't cry Abby, did I hurt you?"

"No! Don't worry, Tyler I'm fine. I love you Tyler with all my heart."

I don't know why I felt like I lost a part of me tonight and yet my heart was blissfully happy and at peace. I didn't want to miss these precious moments with him. I gave him my all and he gave himself as fully as he could. I snuggle up to him forgetting the pain and sleeping like a baby. The next morning, Tyler is up before me and walks into the bedroom with a breakfast tray: some fruit, a kettle of tea, two cups, some toast and butter.

"Thank you, Tyler, this is sweet of you." I say with a chuckle, delighted by his gesture.

"It's nothing; I'll be coming home early today okay?"

With a smile on my face and a slice of toast in my mouth, I nodded in glee.

The last three months were heavenly. We made love three times a day, always kissing and holding hands, I've never been this happy ever. This feeling of happiness often scared me to death because of a repetitive pattern ingrained in the past. It always felt like there'd be a storm that'd take away everything I hold close and dear, I was scared to dream of happiness and its permanence. I cherished each moment with Tyler and the thought of him, made everything of the past vanish like dew.

Tyler's Mom invited us to a party. I was uneasy about it from the moment she invited us because it was quite obvious she didn't like me but I'm with Tyler now for a good 3 months. I was however feeling anxious about the whole thing. I tried to push it away from mind thinking it may just be a case of nerves because of the dinner episode. But then there was that nagging feeling; the same one I had the morning of Christmas when Maria beat me black and blue years ago, the same one I had when Kyle died…I can't ignore it as much as I try to. The day of the party arrives and my stomach is mirroring the knots in my mind. I'm a wreck. I know something will happen tonight. I just know it. Tyler parks the car in the drive-way to his Mom and Dad's house. The house has been decorated with sparkly white lights and there are red roses placed in beautiful vases everywhere. It looks quite romantic. The most uncomfortable part of this scene was the number of people who were present. There are so many people and I naturally tend to veer away from crowded places or parties.

Tyler's Dad welcomes us in.

"Hello Abby, you look beautiful"

"Thank you, sir." I say respectfully.

"No don't call me 'sir' Abby! It makes me feel old." He says with a smile on his face.

"Dad you are old." Tyler jibes in.

"Tyler, stop hurting your Dad's feelings." Anna says, stepping in to hug Tyler. "Okay Mom." He looks at Anna amused.

"Well Abby, you look pretty."

"Thanks Anna." She said it like they were pulling her teeth out. Anna takes Tyler by his arm. "Look who is here Tyler, it's Cindy Walters."

Tyler's face grows pale. I clearly remember her name because the wrong number call he had placed to my house was to talk to this girl named Cindy. Cindy stares at me from head to toe and smirks. I return the head-to-toe scan. Cindy is blonde haired, blue eyed and has painfully thin lips. She's worn too much make up and it makes me wince. She's dressed in a black sweater; a super short skirt and her most prominent feature were her large breasts. I would've said pretty but she's trying too hard to be. And that's a turn off. Of course, I'm saying all this because I'm a girl but for a guy, a girl like Cindy would be a dream come true. I wanted to pull Tyler aside and ask him if he was nuts to leave her and be with someone like me. But then, he chose me for a reason, right? However, looking at Cindy a couple of times guaranteed me one thing; the night ahead was going to be long and miserable. I try and mingle around with a few people but no one cares. Some even pretended that I don't exist. I guess this was to be expected when the host of the party was herself guilty of doing this. Anna could have introduced me to her friends, neighbors or Diane's friends, if she wanted to. She chose not to and there wasn't much I could do about it. I spent the evening in a corner, quietly waiting for Ty to join me, but he wasn't around. Anna continues to make me feel unwelcome and I regret having come here. I just never feel like I belong here. I seat myself beside a lounge chair in the corner to keep myself away from any curious, prying guests. Everyone is drinking; no one even asks me if I wanted a drink?! A tall handsome guy makes his way to where I sit and motions if he could take the seat next to me. I nod. He looks a lot like Tyler, his hair was dark and his green eyes were strikingly similar to Tyler. He had a dimple, though only on one cheek. The resemblance was uncanny. They were even similar in structure, broad and well built. He was dressed casually in black slacks, a blue sweater and black shoes. I won't be surprised if he said he was Tyler's cousin. "So beautiful, what's your name?" Glancing up at him, I say "Abby!"

"Abby, I'm Tom" I just nodded my head. "Aren't you too young for Tyler and where is he anyway?" I don't answer and suddenly notice that everyone in the room is staring at me and Tom. Some people's eyes are on the bathroom door. I start to get up to see what that was about when Tom grabs my hand gently to stop me from going. "Don't go to that bathroom Abby."

I yank my arm roughly from him and walk fast towards the bathroom. When I open the door, I can't believe what I see. Tyler is having sex with Cindy. He stares at me in shock. Cindy's smile is so big and wicked; all I wanted to do is throw up in disgust. He just sits there on the toilet seat. I feel tears roll down my cheeks. I felt like someone had punctured a thousand holes into my heart. I run out, my heart unable to believe what I just witnessed. I could hear people jeering at me, I'd become a complete spectacle all because Tyler turned out to be an insensitive jerk. He was nothing I thought he was, I fell for an act!

Oh the horror of it all! My heart is pounding and aching as I catch myself from falling down.

How could he have done this to me? I finally collapse on the ground beneath me on my knees, hands covering my face. I groan in pain and sorrow, utterly devastated. I feel a pair of arms around me trying to hold me. I hear Tom's voice.

"I'm sorry Abby, you shouldn't have been with him. He goes with a lot of girls Abby."

"Leave me alone! Please! Mind your business." I say trying to fight his imposing but kind countenance. I don't have the strength to protest so I weep, grateful that there was someone at that moment to console me. I don't know how much time passed like this but I suddenly hear Tyler's voice.

"Get your hands off my girl Thomas."

Tyler lifts Tom up and hits him in the jaw. They're both fighting and beating each other.

"STOP IT! You're an ass Tyler! Leaving her by herself so you could have sex with a slut!

You have a beautiful girl here. If you're going to treat her like that I'll take her." Tom says, fighting Ty.

"Shut the fuck up Thomas, and get out of here. Leave us alone."

Thomas held my hand. "Bye Abby, don't stay with this punk."

He even smiles at me. I don't answer; I'm just overwhelmed by everything that has happened. A complete stranger whom I met for the very first time just fought with a jerk I call my boyfriend, to defend me. I see him wipe his blood stained lips with his palm. I really felt awful for him. Tyler starts to tell me he's sorry.

I lift my hand in front of his face. "Save it! I don't want to hear what you got to say. I think I've seen enough."

He grabs my hand and I panic but decide to take it head on.

"Don't you dare touch me Tyler! You were having sex with her. Gosh, I can't even bring myself to say her name. You have lipstick all over your face." He wipes his mouth with his shirt.

"I'm so disgusted right now with myself, let's go home Abby." It's then it struck me. I had nowhere to go. I suddenly feel sick; I'm crying, my head's aching and do not have the nerve to go with this guy who just cheated on me so shamelessly. He made me believe that he loved me. Or was I too naïve like Ma had warned me?

"I'm so sorry Abby! I love you baby."

"Well it's tough for me to believe you Tyler. You just had sex with Cindy. How long have you been with her? She's more than a friend Tyler!"

"Don't worry about that bitch, you're the one baby. It won't happen again."

All I could do is roll my eyes and weep some more. When we get to the apartment I sleep on the couch. Nothing will ever be the same again. I wanted to run and be anywhere else but here.

Chapter 21

It's been a month since the nightmarish episode at Tyler's parents place. I felt like a complete fool and was the butt of all jokes, literally. Tyler's Mom, Anna seemed to have had the most fun seeing me broken in pieces. I didn't say anything then but, in my mind, I wondered if she'd react the same way if it was Diane, her daughter who was in my place with some guy who she found cheating on her in a party with his ex. I know the answer. She'd probably be blowing fire and hopping mad. It's always fun until it happens to someone in your own family. I wouldn't wish an experience like this even on my enemy. After all Anna wasn't some mean girl in high school like Betty or Emily, she was a mother of two; such bickering and nastiness was unbecoming of her status in life. I tried to put the past behind me. Tyler for his part, tried to make up for his mistake, not one that I could easily forget. I'm naïve, always choosing to believe in the best of people. I thought I wasn't like the other girls and hoped that Ty would see that special quality. But I was so wrong, I was just like any other girl for him and that broke my heart more than anything else.

Every time he leaves for work, I think he will cheat on me with someone, how was I to trust him ever again? Trust is so hard to build and once broken, it's almost impossible to repair. Things are very different between Ty and me now. I spend my time alone and depressed. I torture myself imagining Ty cheating on me with someone else. I hadn't shared the experience of this with anyone else, not even Megan. I knew she'd be worried sick and tell me to go back to Ma. I wanted to leave as much having lost my self-respect and dignity, but my heart wouldn't let me go. Tyler was the love of my life and I could barely see things unravel in the way it did. I thought we'd be like two peas in the pod, like chocolate and strawberries. Little did I know that, love would be like a bottle of bitter poison; after all, this wasn't the first time I was heartbroken. Ty and I no longer fit together; suddenly we seemed as different as chalk & cheese. All the love I had felt in those three months before this party had all gone out the window. It was hard to resurrect something that was dead unless a miracle happens. Given the life I lived, miracles were hard to come by. But I had hoped things would get better eventually. I held on.

One day, Ty came home exasperated. He grabbed me with both arms so tight that I wince in pain.

"Tyler you are hurting me!"

"Abby you haven't even talked to me or made love to me, so I'm taking what's mine."

"Don't touch me Tyler!"

He's so angry; he picks me up and throws me on the bed. He kisses me roughly, devoid of any tenderness and affection that was between us before.

"Oh yeah Abby, you're going to give me what I want."

"No! I'm not!"

He grabs my face and slaps me violently having fully surrendered to the lust that had now consumed him. He doesn't show any sign of stopping or slowing down when he sees tears rolling down my cheeks. It's almost as if he got pleasure from seeing me hurt. I tried hard to free myself from his hold but he proved too strong for me. I could smell his breath and it reeked of alcohol. He tore my clothes off violently like an animal.

The next few minutes passed by like a nightmare. I was forced down and he took what he wanted from me with no consideration of what I felt. When it's over, I feel like I'd been raped, he made love to me, no, he had sex with me against my will.

Tyler sleeps off turned with his back facing me, like nothing happened; I felt like I'd become an object or worse, a slave whose sole purpose was to please him. I couldn't believe this was the love of my life that did this to me. How can someone you love so much, also be the reason for all the pain one feels? He could make me or break me at will. I felt like a helpless puppet. I'm still in tears unable to close my eyes. I've curled up on my side, sore and pained by the emotional and physical assault of it.

There was no way to justify what he did even if I tried to be understanding. It was unacceptable and brutal. I continue to sob into my pillow when I feel his hand slide from behind around my waist. He inches closer to me and whispers in my ear, "Sorry I was rough baby; it's just that you get me so furious." I can sense the frustration in his voice but I'm not softened by his explanation. It only made it all the more painful because now I felt like I was merely someone to let out his frustrations on.

"You're mine Abby, and don't you dare forget it." He says and rolls back to sleep.

I wake up the next morning and take a look at myself in the mirror. My hair is a tangled mess, my eyes are puffy from crying and I have a bad headache; my swollen lips have bite marks on it, scars of a painfully rough night. When did love become abuse? How did I get here?

I take a shower, blacking out everything that had happened the previous night. I didn't want to remember any part of it and wanted to run outside, to feel the breeze; it was my escape from the darkness that was beginning to consume my existence. I dress in a pair of Levi's, a black tank top and leave my hair open. After making myself presentable enough and hiding the scars with a bit of makeup, I leave for a nearby park. I take in the warm breeze and feel the humid air. It's a clear sunny day. I walk to a bench in the park and see a flock of starlings take flight; it's a beautiful sight. My heart wishes to fly free like them yet all I felt was that I was trapped in a nightmare, bound by invisible chords. I look around the park and see people going about their daily lives. Some folks are taking their morning run, I see an old couple walking hand in hand together, there are kids enjoying the slides and some others still waiting to get their hands-on popsicles. A perfect summer day, a striking contrast to the mindset I was in. I'm awakened from my day time reverie with a voice that causes me to jump. It's Cindy at her sleazy best. I roll my eyes; I wasn't expecting to see her of all the places, in a park.

"What do you want Cindy?"

She flashes me her trademark smirk. "You know what I want bitch! Want you to leave Tyler! He's mine bitch."

I look at her closely now that she has my full attention. She's worn a pair of tight jeans that makes me wonder how she's able to even move in them; this is paired with an equally tight blouse to enhance the silhouette of her large breasts. She's clearly over done her make up for a walk in the park and it makes her look unflattering from every angle. I almost feel sorry for her. And oops, she's got some of that bright red lipstick on her teeth too. I almost stifle my laugh but she notices that I'm unable to control myself from laughing out loud. "Are you laughing at me bitch?"

How many times is she going to call me bitch? And with that face, I don't think she's calling me a name so fitting with who & what she is.

I get in front of her face. "My name is Abby, and don't you make the mistake of calling me anything else but that!" Her blue eyes bulge out in shock and then her face crinkles with anger. She grabs my hair and I regret momentarily not putting my hair in a ponytail. I kick my leg at her; she's provoked me enough to summon the old Abby of high school, who gave it back as good as she got, to the likes of Betty and Emily, who have been kind recipients of these kicks. My blood is boiling at this point and she's still pulling my hair. I dig my fingers deep into her neck to get her to loosen her grip on my hair. Then I start punching her face. Of course she's yelling that Tyler loves her and he can't stand me at all. People notice the catfight we're in and someone holds me and pulls me away from Cindy. I can see her crying and the scratches I've left on her. She sneers back. The guy holding me lets me go after he senses I've settled my score with her. I turn around, pleased with the outcome and begin to walk away. Who's the bitch now?

My steps are slow walking back to the apartment. Did I feel good punching her and giving her what was due? Yes! Did I feel good about me turning into a complete bitch? No. I reach home, eager to step into the shower again and feel the warm water cleanse away my guilt and anger. I see my body covered in scratches and my hair's all messed up again. My head is throbbing with pain. I step out and change into fresh clothes. I make myself an instant out of the box Mac & cheese meal; I didn't have the energy to prepare any lavish meals and neither was I inclined to. I had lost my appetite and felt like I could sleep all day. I take a seat on the couch and watch reruns of 'I Love Lucy' and my bowl of comfort food. I find myself laughing over Lucille Ball's famous antics, she's hilarious. For a short time, I forget all that's happened and dig into my bowl, grateful for the bowl of warm, gooey and cheesy goodness. I hear the door open and see Ty come through. I haven't seen him since last night, presumably because he was with Cindy? I give him the benefit of doubt but it makes me uncomfortable given the timing of her morning visit at the park.

"What are you doing baby." He asks visibly concerned.

"Just eating." I say in an attempt to ignore him. I could see guilt written all over his face.

"Sit, I'll serve you." I say and go over to the kitchen to bring him dinner. He nods, grateful that I didn't question him about where he was the previous night. We sit together watching 'I love Lucy' and unknowingly, we ended up laughing together in each other's company. Ty holds my hands and for a moment, I felt like it was just like the old times. I was hanging around in a pair of super short cropped denim shorts and a long white tee with no bra underneath. He knew it and I could see his eyes burn with desire. He gets close to me on the couch and whispers that he is sorry the way he treated me last night.

"You are beautiful Abby." He says and then kisses me cheek with the same tenderness of the Ty I knew and loved before.

My heart delights at this renewal in him, is he the same guy I loved? He continues to touch me tenderly, kissing each of my fingers. My body responds to his touch and this time he makes love to me. He whispers 'I love you' in my ears over and over again. I felt like everything was getting back to normal again. We made love all night and fell asleep holding onto each other. Perhaps all's going to be okay.

I know Ty loved me in his own way; I wasn't eager to justify his previous actions or infidelity just because he was singing a different tune now, but perhaps given a chance, he'd prove me wrong? I had hoped for that. I wake up the next day and Ty has already left for work. I make myself a quick sandwich and get around to my chores at home. I sing while I clean, that's how happy I felt. I hear a knock at my door and open to see Dad greet me with a wide smile. I'm so happy to see him! He gives me a big hug but I could smell alcohol in his breath; old habits die hard apparently.

"Hello Dad!"

"Hello Sweetheart!"

"What are you doing here?" I ask eyeing him curiously, surprised by his impromptu visit.

"Can't I visit my daughter?" he says, all smiles.

"Sure Dad, you just surprised me, that's all. You should've called; I would've made you some lunch. I can cook a decent meal now" I say with a beaming smile.

"Well Abby, I just wanted to see for myself that you're doing okay."

"Please sit Dad. Would you like some coffee?"

"No Abby, I just wanted to drop by and see you."

He hugs me again. I love my Dad. I'm delighted to see him; it's been 4-5 months since I've seen him.

"Have you talked to Megan?" he asks as he stands up to leave.

"No Dad, I haven't."

"Call her, Abby."

"Okay sure." I say, wondering if something was up with Meg.

"Is he treating you right Abby?"

"Yes Dad." I say, giving him a big hug and smile. I could never bring myself to tell Dad how Ty treated me; besides last night showed signs of improvement.

"You tell me if he treats my baby bad."

"Okay Daddy." I say with glee and he gives me a peck on my cheek. He says 'Bye' and leaves. I pick up from where I left with my chores and finish cleaning up and get some prep work done for dinner.

It's early evening and Tyler walks in slamming the door behind him.

"Abby, where are you?"

"I'm in the kitchen." I say as I quickly wash my hands to go give him a hug.

Instead, I see a scowl etched on his face. Something was wrong.

He holds me with the full force of his strength and I'm afraid he's going to throw me on the floor.

"What's wrong? What wrong?" I ask my eyes wide in terror.

"You beat up Cindy." He says angrily with eyes staring down at me.

When I hear this, it's like suddenly every trace of fear disappeared. How dare he defend that girl, the very one he cheated on me with. I'm suddenly towering in strength though my petite frame manages all the physical strength to hold him by his collar.

"She started fighting with me first and why do you care Tyler? Why do you care more about her than me? Answer that for me Tyler," I say my face red with rage. I cannot believe his audacity. He slapped my face so hard that I fell down to the floor and hit my head on the corner of the kitchen cupboard.

"Abby I'm so sorry! Didn't mean to hit you, believe me baby."

He tries to touch my arm.

"Don't touch me! Go to that slut Cindy. You seem to like her a lot better than me."

"I don't want to be with that bitch Abby!"

"Then what do you want Tyler? Because I'm really confused right now! You're angry with me because I defended myself from Cindy's attack on me in a public place? You say you care about me but your actions say something else. Do you even hear yourself? Instead of asking me if I was okay, you have the gall to defend the same girl you cheated on me with?! I don't trust you Ty; you say one thing and do another. I don't want to see you Ty, get away from me!" I feel like my face is on fire with anger, I've never felt so enraged before. I walk to the bedroom and slam the door and lock it.

The next morning, when I step around the house, Ty has already left for work, as is routine. I feel nauseas and feverish. I puke at least a couple of times since I've woken up. I may be coming down with something. May be an upset tummy? Perhaps that out-of-the-box instant Mac & cheese isn't going down too well. I lay down on the bed in the hope it'd be okay in a few hours. I feel a full-blown fever coming over me so I wrap myself in two blankets and fall asleep. Later, Ty walks into the bedroom and sits on the bed. He touches his fingers on my face and feels the heat.

"Abby what's wrong with you?" Ty asks with concern.

"I don't feel too good."

"Have you eaten?"

"No, I'm not hungry." I say as I curl up in bed.

"You have to eat Abby." He goes to open a can of chicken noodles and some crackers.

I devour the noodles and soup hungrily, surprised that I wasn't throwing up anymore. I felt nauseas again the next morning and Tyler takes off from work and takes me to the doctor, which I initially resisted. At the clinic, I'm told to take a couple of tests and we're to wait for the results before being prescribed any further medication. Ty is suddenly behaving like he's walking on eggshells and I'm both amused and surprised by the amount of care he's shown me over the last two days. He takes the day after the appointment also off so that he can be with me at home. Two days later, Ty is back to work, I convinced him that I can manage just fine. I was feeling better and my appetite was returning. The test results arrive and I go to pick it up and wait to hear from the doctor. I'm seated at the doctor's office, tapping my feet nervously, just wanting to get out of the clinic. To my surprise, he says I'm pregnant! I can hardly believe what he's just said. I'm ecstatic! This is the best news I've received in a long time. Though not fully prepared for the responsibility of a baby, I'm over the moon with delight. I can do this. But it may not be the best time for Ty, he's not even ready to marry, forget about fatherhood. I'd have to break this news gently to him. I don't want him to get wound up over it and make it another fighting match between us. Will he be happy when he hears the news? Or will he be angry? It was time to find out. I call Tyler and tell him to pick me up from the doctor's office. He sounds worried and I assure him there's nothing serious. He hurries and meets me outside the clinic in ten-fifteen minutes. He holds my hand. I can see concern on his face "So what did the doctor say baby?"

"Tyler, could we eat somewhere." I say, to deviate and break this news in a more relaxed environment.

"Yea, let's go to Jack in the Box."

It's my favorite place. We drive and get there in a short time. We take our seat at our favorite corner table, I make a quick order. I see Tyler peering into his menu card, wanting to try out something different. I look over at him, taking in the man he is, "He said, Tell me what's wrong baby?"

"The doctor told me this morning that I'm pregnant."

"What! Are you sure?" he says as his eyes widen in shock.

"Yes I'm not one of your whores Tyler."

"Don't start Abby, you know I'm not ready to be a Dad." He says protesting.

"Well that's funny, because you sure don't care about that when you're having sex."

He looked back at me with a pained face, distraught with worry. It felt like I'd hit him with a curveball he didn't see coming. I knew this was going to be difficult for him but he had to make peace with it and do what needs to be done.

Over the course of the next few months, we didn't say much to each other. I had a bad case of morning sickness which meant most days; my mornings were spent being in bed. Tyler wouldn't return home for nights together and I thought maybe he's cheating on me again. At this point, I cared more about the baby than I cared about him, he was free to live his life as deemed fit. I was now in my seventh month and Megan threw me a baby shower, a wholly unnecessary ritual given how few people liked me or were close to me. Ty's Mom Anna continued to be cold despite knowing that I was having Ty's baby. If a baby's birth cannot soften a woman's heart, nothing can. I had lost hope of resurrecting my relationship with her. Ty's dad received the news warmly though he knew of Anna's dislike for me. As expected, no one turns up for the party. It's the thought that counts, right? Megan said.

"Sorry Abby that no one came." Megan continued, touching my belly.

I smile back, just grateful that she was here. I had missed her so much.

"God Abby, your belly is so small. Remember that I was huge. My belly looked like I was having twins."

We laugh out loud and give each other a big hug. Megan was over the moon when she heard she was going to be an aunt. What she didn't know however was Ty's lack of enthusiasm for this baby and this pregnancy. He's been largely absent and comes home late most nights from work. If he was around, he'd barely talk but he'd make sure I ate properly. I was so lonely and I had no one to share all my anxieties and worries with. Meg was a consolation throughout.

"Abby are you eating? You're so tiny."

"I try to eat, but every time I eat something, I vomit." I say, rubbing my tummy.

"Well, you don't have to endure that too long now. You're going to have the baby soon."

"Yeah! I can't wait." I say, visibly excited by the prospect of having a baby in my arms in a few weeks' time. Megan had bought some supplies for the baby's arrival – some baby clothes, bottles and blankets. She even knitted a small sweater with Ty and my initials on it as a gift. I loved her for it. She helps me clean up even though no one turned up for the party and decides it was time to head back home to little Kyle, who's now almost a year and half old. She gives me a kiss and hugs me tight, reminding me to take care of myself. Just a few minutes after she leaves, Ty walks in through the door, smelling of alcohol. He's drunk but seems to have maintained his composure. He looks around expecting to see people and gifts all over but instead finds it empty.

"Where are all the gifts?" he asks as he pauses for me to speak.

"No one came to the shower." I say, dejected. I just didn't want to talk to him when he was drunk, it may just lead to an unnecessary fight. I look away to avoid making eye contact. I was lonely and scared of becoming a mother. All I wanted was for a normal family, like the one Kate had, like Megan had. I felt like I was fighting a losing battle even before the baby was born. I couldn't even tell Ty anything, we'd become strangers though we lived under the same roof. My train of thought breaks when Ty comes close to me and lifts my chin to fix his gaze on me. I look up, nervously to gauge how he's feeling. He looks at me and pulls a strand of my hair and puts it behind my ears. I look into his lovely green eyes looking for love. He says he's going to go shopping tomorrow to buy things for our baby. That's the first time he's said 'our baby'. I'm relieved and overcome with emotion at his warmth. He takes me to bed, covers me with a blanket and cuddles with me in his arms. We fall asleep and everything feels okay again.

True to his word, he bought a crib, a dresser and diapers along with a few other bath products for the baby the next day. He even put up the crib which took a bit of time to put together. I knew he was tired after work but he patiently put everything in place and for the first time in months, I felt like perhaps, he could be a good father to our child.

Chapter 22

It's March and the baby is due anytime now. I stroll around the house in my early morning daze with a cup of warm milk in my hands. I look out the window and see the grey blue sky laced with dark clouds pregnant with rain. It's been cold yet humid, a weird mix of weather that wasn't suiting me. I was yearning for sunshine and warmth. Ty has already left for work and I'm glad to have time alone to myself and the life I'm carrying within me. I go to the kitchen to fix myself some breakfast when a pain stabs me in my lower abdomen. It was so intense that it took my breath away. I ignored it because throughout my third trimester, I've had these pains come and go. I start to make a peanut butter & jelly sandwich, my favorite and take a bite into it. Then the second stab of pain. It's more intense than the previous one. I knew this meant I'd have to rush to the hospital right away; there was no time to waste. The last thing I wanted is to deliver in the hallway of my apartment building! I quickly make a call to Tyler but no one's picking up the phone. Frustrated, I make a quick call for a cab. It felt forever for it to get here. By this time the pain is agonizing. The cab driver could see I'm in pain and he helps me in to the cab with my bag and waits for me to tell him which hospital to drive to. The pain is getting worse and I mumble the address. I reach the hospital entrance lounge and breathe a sigh of relief; I'm rolled into emergency care on a wheel chair. The rest of the ordeal is a faint memory and all I remember clearly is lying on a hospital bed, exhausted and waiting for the nurse to bring my baby. A full hour after I'm conscious, a smiling young nurse walks into my room holding a baby in her hands. This is the moment I'd been preparing for the last 9 months. She handed me the baby and said with a smile "Here's your baby Abby, a healthy baby boy weighing about 8 pounds."

I beamed as I finally get to hold him in my hands. He was clutching his tiny hands around my little finger. Tears rolled down my cheek. I was so happy seeing this bundle of joy. He had dark curls like a halo around his head; his skin was pink and he had big eyes, just like Ty. Though it was too early to tell who he looked like or make out his eye color, I could see a lot of Ty in him already. I hope to see those little dimples pop a few months down the lines. I was ecstatic. I requested the nurse to make two phone calls on my behalf, one to Megan and one to Ty.

Megan came first. It was such a relief to see her; she was over the moon, unable to contain her excitement. She rushed in and hugged me tightly and then quickly took the baby in her hands. She was the quintessential Aunt and was already speaking baby language; it was an adorable sight to behold.

She looked at me and said "How are you doing Abby? When did you get here, you should've called me? Where's Ty?"

"I called Ty at work but was unable to reach him. I wanted to call you but couldn't delay getting to the hospital, it all happened so fast. I asked the nurse to make a call for me to Ty and convey the news to him, so he should come anytime now."

"Oh Abby, I'm so happy you got here safe and sound and everything went smoothly. He's adorable Abby, look at his hair; it's just like how your hair was when you were born."

"Really, I didn't know." I ask, surprised at this little revelation.

"I was around when you were born silly. Remember I'm a few years older than you?!" she says with a chuckle.

I look at her and smile away. I was blessed to have a sister like her. She remembers everything.

"His hair may be like me, but he's got Ty's eyes, they're so big and gorgeous" I say, fondly looking at my baby.

Megan nods smiling, playing with his tiny hands and tickling his little feet.

Ty should've been here by now; it's been two hours since the call was made. Megan handed the baby to me and kissed me on my forehead.

"You're going to be an amazing mother Abby, I couldn't be more happy and proud of you for having come this far. I wish you, Ty and your little bundle of joy all the happiness in the world. I'm going to deliver this happy news to Ma and Dad as soon as I get home!" she says with a ear-to-ear grin.

"Thanks Meg wouldn't have been able to do this without you." I say and hold her hands in mine.

"You and baby get some rest now and hopefully Ty will be here soon. I'll get going and I'll bring you some freshly baked goods the next time I see you both" she says, kissing my baby's head.

"See you soon Abby. I love you"

"Thanks for coming. I love you too."

Megan's visit is like my personal dose of sunshine. I needed to see her and needed her with me in the absence of Ty, who still hasn't come to see our baby. It mildly upsets me but I look at our baby's face and forget everything. He was my world now.

It was the next day morning that Ty finally makes an entrance. I'm well rested after I finish breast feeding the baby. I have a poker face expression on seeing Ty, unable to comprehend what took him so long to come and see his own child? Was he still struggling to accept that he'd become a Dad?

"May I come in?" Tyler asked, with an expression of guilt in his eyes. He was holding a beautiful bouquet of flowers in one hand and a few blue balloons in the other which had 'Congratulations' written over it.

"Yes please, come and meet your son. Want to hold him?" I ask, hoping he'd be ecstatic to carry his baby.

"I'm scared to, he's so small. Have you named him yet?" he asks. I knew he was feeling nervous and un-ready for this new role he'd found himself in. I didn't press him.

"No Ty thought we should do that together. He's not just my son, he's our son" He seemed visibly relaxed hearing that. "

"So what should we name him?"

"How about James Tyler Miller, does that sound good to you?" I suggest looking to Ty for approval.

"That sounds good Abby." He said with a smile, looking at the baby.

Ty finally ventures to hold James. I show him how to hold him and now little James Tyler Miller was happily being cradled by his father. My heart is bursting with joy seeing this moment which will forever be etched into my memory and heart.

"He looks like you Abby. He's going to have hazel eyes."

"I don't think so." I say, looking at our son.

"Megan says his eyes look like you and his hair looks me"

"So he's a mix of us both then?" Ty says with a mischievous smile.

"He's beautiful Abby." Ty said as he begins to play with James and plants kisses over his little face and tummy.

"Where were you Tyler? I called you at the office and no one picked up. I went through labor alone and as soon as I got James in my hand, I told the nurse to inform you, which was yesterday. You do realize you missed the birth of our son?"

"I know Abby. Sorry I wasn't there." He says with that same guilt I saw on his face when he came in.

"Yeah! Bet you are." I say, with intended sarcasm.

"I got drunk alright!!" Ty says exasperated.

"You always have excuses Tyler." Saying this, I take the baby from his hands in an effort to protect him from his father's anger and despair.

"Not going to talk about this Abby, see you later." And he walks away and out the door.

And that's how things go down. What did I expect from Ty really? He wasn't ready for this baby, not for fatherhood. I need to give him some time to fully embrace the responsibilities that come with this new role.

In the meantime, I get to raise my little boy with all the love and care I can lavish on him.

"Dad will catch up, right James?" I say looking into my son's eyes. He returns an answer to my question with a heart melting smile. I kiss his little hands, knowing that no one could steal him from me.

We're well into March. Winter had been difficult; the heater worked overtime to keep the air warm inside our apartment. I don't remember the last time I had straight eight hours of sleep; Meg had warned me the first few weeks until the baby falls into a sleep cycle, would be particularly challenging for me to get any rest. And she was right. James would sometimes cry for milk at 2 am and I'd be up feeding him, much to Ty's irritation because his sleep was also being disturbed. He was exhausted by day's end from work and he didn't have the energy to take care of James. The rigors of motherhood, I sigh.

James was now about five months old and is growing up to be a healthy little baby and is beginning to show his own personality. He loves playing with my hair and enjoys watching flocks of starlings' fly, when I take him to the nearby park. He loves the feel of wet grass and giggles whenever anyone makes a face. He'll kiss my face apparently for no reason because he's so affectionate. He was easy with strangers and had no problem flashing his big smile. And yes, as I'd hoped, those dimples that Ty and his side of the family are famous for, James has got them too: deep gorgeous dimples on both cheeks! He has Ty's hazel green eyes as well but the hair stayed curly like mine. His cherubic pink lips also looked a lot like mine than Ty's. He seemed to take the best of both of us. Dad & Ma visited me after I had gotten back from the hospital and again during Christmas. They were thrilled to see James and were happy for me. After all things didn't go as badly as Ma had predicted. I was grateful. Ty's parents visited every two three weeks though I had no help from Anna. Megan visited with her son Kyle and those were totally fun. James had taken a liking to Kyle; Kyle is almost two now and he'd be around James like the protective older brother just like Megan was to me. It was a delight watching these two. Megan helped me out a lot, she gave me time-saving tips, how to clean up dirty baby laundry, bought me books on baby nutrition and regularly shopped for James clothes when she went shopping for Kyle. I felt like I was in heaven except for one problem: Ty had gotten into drinking mode more often than not and as a result, when he came home to us, he was always drunk. I kept James away from Ty when he was drunk and told him to sober up for the sake of our baby. He'd stay sober for a couple of days, promise me he won't drink again and then it's back to square one. There's only so much I can do. I'd give James all the love in double portion that his father was unable to give him right now.

But right now, my attention is on James. "Hi baby boy!" I say picking him up from the floor as he giggles; I put my face to his belly and kiss him and he lets out another little giggle. He means the world to me and I couldn't feel more happy and lucky to be holding him right now in my arms; I could face anything in the world if he's with me. I'll make sure that he'll never go through what I went through. Life throws you lots of curves and bumps, but somehow, we survive.

And survive we did. James is now two and half years old. Though Ty didn't get his act together when it came to being a Dad and was still a long way off from being the ideal parent (as if there was such a thing), he was good at something else. I had our second son, Jason Levi Miller. My second pregnancy was vastly different from the first, I wasn't nervous because things get better the second time around yea? Ty was thankfully present for Jason's birth and though I was prepared to go through this alone, Ty wanted to make up for his absence at James's birth, a guilt that had gnawed him for a long time.

Jason's emerald green eyes were more pronounced and he had dark hair, closely resembling many of Ty's cousins I've known from my earlier encounters with them at parties that are best forgotten. Jason didn't have dimples like James but both of them had big eyes and full lips like their Dad. And they had a beautiful smile, one that's going to break a lot of hearts I reckon when they grow up.

But right now, I was in all my maternal glory, a mom to two gorgeous baby boys. James is excited to have a new baby brother for company and he's protective around him, just like Kyle still is around James. James & Jason are a year and half apart in age. When Megan is visiting, we get to see the three of them during playtime and it's a class act.

We're having Jason's birthday party at Tyler's Mom and Dad's house. I didn't want to be in this house; the memory of that life altering party with Cindy & Ty was still afresh like it happened yesterday. As much as I dreaded going there, the edge was taken off looking at the boys. I dressed Jason in a navy blue knit sweater that Meg had made for him with a baby sized denim pants. He wasn't even aware that it's his birthday! James was dressed in a deep forest green full sleeve baby tee and black baby pants with matching socks and baby booties.

We arrive and I scan the crowd for familiar faces, a few of Ty's cousins. However, it felt like Anna, Ty's Mom had left no stone unturned to invite all the sluts from the block who had their eyes firmly on Ty. I rolled my eyes because I was so over with the drama. If it was me five years ago, I'd reacted differently and probably walked out. But I was a Mom and though I cared about Ty, I wasn't going to baby him when he's a full-grown adult and a father. He needs to know how to behave.

Ty took to the BBQ grill and was helping his cousins with smoking some delicious chicken, basting it with marinade. It smelled divine. My baby boys were received with a lot of "oh he's so cute" "he looks exactly like Ty" and more; they seemed happy soaking in all the attention just like Ty was doing at the grill. He was certainly the ladies man.

"A Penny for your thoughts Abby?"

I hear a voice say and turn around to see Tom.

"Hi! Thomas!" I say, genuinely happy to see him!

"I see you're still with Tyler and had two boys. You really didn't learn your lesson did you?"

I roll my eyes and caution Tom "Don't talk to me Thomas, because Tyler will get angry."

"Don't worry; he's too busy talking to those girls."

Thomas starts helping me with arranging the plates, cups and napkins for the party. As we're doing that, we hear a loud voice from behind. "Get the fuck away from Abby, Thomas." And I look up. Sure enough, it was Tyler; his palms were rolled into a tight fist, ready for a fight.

Tyler pushes me to the side and Thomas gets in front of me.

"You want to fight with me Tyler? Let's do it! But leave Abby out of it! Either you want her or those girls you been talking to!"

"Shut the fuck up Thomas, this is none of your concern."

"You're sure making it my concern."

After a day of hell and two fights later with Tyler, I was exhausted. I got the boys in the car, guilty that Jason's birthday was ruined because of his own Dad. I drive home minus Ty with my babies strapped at the back of the car. Funnily enough, Anna didn't stop me from going, it's as if she was just happy to get rid of me. However, she half expected me to leave Jason there with her so that Ty would bring him later; after all this party was to celebrate Jason's birthday wasn't it? I wasn't having it, none. I picked up a few fancy cupcakes so that Jason could blow the candle and complete his birthday ritual. It was his first birthday and there was no way I was going to have my son not get a piece of cake and eat it; Jason seemed fairly happy, oblivious to the drama of the day and James seemed cool about it, there was no fuss with the boys. By the time I get home, I was exhausted and all I could think of was to put the boys to bed and sleep my head off. Ty didn't return home that night. Dare I say I had gotten used to his absence but James and Jason were my world now and I could care less which slut he roamed around with or where he was at; it was past that point.

The boys fell into a sleep routine as time progressed and I was able to rest after 8pm as that seemed to be their sleep time. I cherished that time of peace & quiet and started reading books again, something I missed doing as a full time Mom. Ty and my intimate life had become lifeless and I could never relax when he came around drunk. My romance novels provided a high that I couldn't get from my personal life at the moment. I knew I couldn't continue like this and planned to get a diploma as soon as the boys got to school going age. I needed to get back to work and a fulltime job because I don't know how long Ty will stick around. I want to give my boys the best and I'm going to try with all my heart and strength to give them that. Life is cyclical; there's a season of rejoicing, a season of sadness. There'd be highs and lows.

It's been a decade since the birth of my first son James. Ty is still around to my surprise, I honestly didn't think we'd last this long though they weren't any real improvements.

The boys look a lot more like their Dad now and a lot less like me, but they've got a part of me in their personalities. They both enjoy being in nature, love trekking and hiking, they especially like studying birds and animals. James is a lot more reflective and gentler while Jason is more verbally expressive and curious. Both of them are good at school, always in the top five of class, something I'm proud of. James is also athletic and enjoys running marathons while Jason enjoys swimming. And predictably, they're popular with the girls. Jason is too young for that, but James is a class favorite but is too shy with girls around. I was happy with the way they were growing up. The three of us would often spend an hour at the park at the end of the day; I'd catch up with all the day's events, what they studied in class and asked them about their dreams, what they wanted. We were a closely knit trio. Ty didn't spend time with the kids as much as I did and their connection hadn't taken off the way they did with me or even Megan, Miles & Kyle. Perhaps, with time, things will improve.

I took that diploma I'd been eyeing and finally landed a decent job. The next month, I'd be celebrating my 6th work anniversary at this company. They were a decent bunch and I was glad to have my time being utilized this way.

It was a long work day. I pick the boys from school and instead of going to the park like we usually do, I drive them to the patisserie to pick up an assortment of cream filled doughnuts and gourmet sandwiches, a treat! The boys beamed in delight and were glad for the surprise. I'd been feeling uneasy the last few days with that familiar knotty feeling rearing its ugly head again; that same feeling of dread and gloom was coming over and this was my way of avoiding it. I get home exhausted but happy seeing the boys squeal with excitement; they don't waste much time to unwrap their goodies from the brown paper bag. I take a shower and change into a baggy trouser and a long top. My hair is up in a messy bun, no makeup, this is mom life but no one's complaining! I join the boys at the table and they're already devouring the last bits of their favorite tuna sandwich. They've saved me a roast chicken sandwich and a 'Dulce de leche' cream filled doughnut, a personal favorite I discovered when I first came across this patisserie, well known for its European style baked goods. I'm taking my third bite of sandwich, smiling at the boys when the phone rings. I walk with the sandwich in my hand, not wanting a phone call to come between me and its delicious goodness.

I pick up.

"Hello?"

"Abby, it's me, Megan. Ma's had a heart attack" she said, her voice distraught.

I drop my sandwich to the floor and the boys look at me knowing something's up.

"I'll be there as soon as I can" I say, too shocked to say anything else. Ma's at the same hospital where I delivered both the boys.

I made a quick call to Ty's office and informed him about it. Thankfully, he was gracious enough to come home early to watch the boys so that I could rush to the hospital.

I turn to James and Jason, both wide eyed, watching my every move. I calmly tell them that Nana is ill and is in the hospital, that I have to visit her and Aunt Meg is already there. Both of them love Ma and her famous cookies that she baked specially for them. James was close to her and has received her affection the most. She loved Jason too but by the time he was growing up, she was beginning to have health problems and visited us far less. I'd take the boys occasionally home to see Dad & Ma and they have fond memories of their time there. So when I tell this news of her taking ill as gently as I can, I see James tear up a bit and ask "Is she going to be alright Mom?"

"Yes, she will, you know how strong she is right?"

I say to pacify him.

"I want to see her Mommy" Jason says and I hold both of their hands and give it a squeeze.

"She's going to be alright. I'll tell Dad to bring you both to the hospital once I go and see her okay?"

They seem okay with that answer. I tell them to finish their food and complete their homework, taking special care to not annoy their Dad with any mischief. They could be a handful.

I pick up the keys and drive to the hospital without wasting much time.

I get to the hospital under fifteen minutes and reach the room number Megan had given me. I've never liked the smell of hospitals.

"How's Ma holding up" I ask, still panting for breath.

"She's asleep, Megan is inside." Miles said, motioning in the direction of the room.

I see Meg and hug her and then sit beside Ma. I ask Megan how all this happened and she told me Ma has been complaining of intermittent chest pain from a few days but never went for a check up to the doctor.

I look at Ma and see how pale and sallow her skin had become. There are tubes all over her, through her nose, an oxygen mask, an I.V. drip, all connected to monitors showing her heart beat. I'm overwhelmed and so is Megan. We hold each other's hand and sob, hoping not to wake her up.

"Abby, I don't think she'll make it" Meg said, caressing Ma's forehead.

"She will Megan, she's strong." I said trying to reassure her, though in my heart I felt otherwise. Perhaps Meg was right. Ma was physically weak these last few years and she's been hanging in there. It'd be a miracle if she makes it through this.

"Not this time Abby" Megan said, confirming the thoughts running through my mind.

The whole family had descended over the hospital. Uncle Mario, Anna and their kids, our other Aunts and Uncles with their children, everyone took turns staying at Ma's side.

Ma was conscious and awake after about four hours. She expressed her desire to talk to Meg and me alone so everyone was ushered out of the room so that I and Megan could be there with her.

"I'm glad to see both my girls here" she said and held our hands with all the strength she could muster. We brought our sitting stools close to Ma's, so that we could hear her speak because her voice was feeble, weak as she was with medication.

"You're my kids and you're the best. I hope you know that I loved you and gave you the best I could even though it may not have seemed that way to you."

Her words hit us like an emotional avalanche and Megan and I lost whatever little control was left in us from crying in front of her.

I tell Ma "Ma you were the best possible Ma we could've got and we love you." Megan nods in agreement, sobbing that she could barely speak.

Ma continued "I want you both to take care of your Dad and to make sure he isn't alone at the time of his death. My time has come but he's going to be around a little longer and he needs you"

I'm crying so bitterly now, realizing how little we've thought about Dad when we got on with our lives. Megan and I look at each other and tell Ma "We promise you Ma, we'll take care of Dad, don't worry about him."

Ma seemed relieved at that and felt pacified. She trusted us and loved us. Looking back, though I had misgivings about her beating me up and her dire warnings, I was grateful because she was watching over Megan and me like a guardian angel with a firm hand. I knew she wanted us to be safe and even though her ways were different, she did the right thing. Right now, my heart was heavy and I see Ma slip back into a sleep. A nurse comes in to usher me and Megan out so that Ma can rest.

She had said her goodbyes to everyone and saw Kyle, James and Jason together. Meg and

I decided that it's best that the boys take a day off from school and spend a whole day with her. It was the right thing to do. The boys were deeply touched by all that she said to them, she was their 'Nana' as they fondly called her.

A week later, she passed away peacefully in her sleep. It was a dull, cold morning when the news of her death reached me. I whispered a silent prayer and called Megan. Her death had closed a long chapter in both of our lives but we remained indebted to her for her love and care.

The funeral arrangements were made; the church was decorated in baby pink and cream roses with ivy greens. It was beautiful. Her casket was a deep mahogany lined with cream satin. Those present for the church service were those who've known Ma for decades, there were even some who've known her from her childhood days. The skies above had mirrored the gloom below; her death had left a void that cannot be filled. Dad cried the most and was inconsolable. Ma was a strong woman, strict as hell, but we all loved her. She was our anchor through the storms of life, unmoving and stable. We took years to fully understand her deep love masked underneath her tough exterior; after Megan and I became Moms we understood why Ma was the way she was. Time brings us insight but the sadness we feel in her absence is making us feel guilty about every moment we complained about her being harsh. How I missed her now, it was too late.

Megan and I dressed in black dresses and veils as is customary. Dad, though weak with the emotional toll of her death, took to the podium in front of the altar and delivered a beautiful eulogy, celebrating Ma's life and her larger than life personality. It had moved everyone to tears. The service was wrapped up quietly without much fanfare and a post funeral reception was arranged at Ma's house.

I see a sea of familiar faces back at Ma's house. I go around making sure everyone's comfortable and is served food. I'm exhausted and stand quietly at the corner of the kitchen, welcoming the few quiet moments. Megan joins me after a few minutes and we hug each other. We glance through the crowd, observing what everyone was doing. Some stood in corners catching up after what seems like a very long time; most are drinking. Pa and Dad are the ones that are staring mindlessly into the void. They knew they'd be alone in this house now and their sadness was heartbreaking. I remembered the promise I and Meg made to Ma and was determined to make sure not just Dad, but Pa was also taken care of.

Tyler was surprisingly supportive through this whole ordeal right from the time Ma was hospitalized to making sure the funeral arrangements were done properly, coordinating with Miles, Megan's husband; an odd sight for both me and Meg because Ty & Miles never really got along that well. Ty proved to be the friend in need is a friend indeed. It managed to lessen the sourness of our now lifeless marriage and I felt hope for the first time in a very, very long time.

That's until I saw him drinking with a few of my cousins. James and Jason never took a liking to the drinking bouts Ty had and had developed an aversion to it. They were watching Ty closely now. Ty turned to see me and the kids watch him like a hawk and then immediately recognized the inappropriateness of his action at a time like this. The old Ty I knew wouldn't have stopped but thankfully he did.

Megan was mourning Ma in her own way. She was awfully quiet and collected through all this. Miles was the sober rock of Gibraltar in the midst of this. He offered to let me stay at their place with the kids or to drive me and the kids' home seeing Ty partially drunk. He knew how things were between Ty and me. He was like the older brother I never had.

"Are you going to be okay Abby? Let me drive you and the kids home; I want you to get there safe and sound" hinting at Ty with his eyes.

"Thanks Miles, the kids are tired but I think I can manage the ride back home. You take Megan and Kyle back home, she's exhausted crying." I said, wrapping my hands around Megan's back.

She looked up at me, her eyes pooled with tears "Take care of yourself Abby," and then we lock ourselves into a long, tight hug.

I pull myself away and look at her, kiss her forehead and rub Kyle's head. I take the boys with me and call out in Ty's direction.

"Ty, we're leaving." He looks in my direction and protests. Of course he doesn't want to leave; I can see the reluctance in his eyes.

"Just wait baby, give me a few minutes" he says to extend the torture of it all.

"Don't want to wait okay!" I say in a high-pitched voice to make sure he hears.

"Alright Abby!" he says as he gets up from his seat and walks towards me.

"We're going alright?" I say firmly.

"Don't yell at me." He retorts.

Ty drops us off at the apartment like he always does. For a moment, I think he'd stay because everyone's exhausted with the flurry of activity leading up to the funeral. He could do with the rest as much as I did and this would've been an opportunity for us to cement what has been an unlikely friendship blossoming in the midst of one of the most emotionally taxing times in my life. But he banished all thoughts of us having any quiet time together at home when he left. I didn't know when I'd see him again and everything fell flat on my face again. I could hear Ma's voice in my head 'You're naïve Abby, you need to toughen up cookie.' I put the boys to bed, shower and change into regular clothes. I pull out a tub of cookie-dough flavored ice-cream and sit in the kitchen thinking about Ma. Somewhere in the middle of the night, after going through half a tub of ice-cream, I fall off to sleep exhausted.

Chapter 23

It's been ten years since Ma passed.

Dad passed away five years ago and Pa was the last man standing. He passed away two years later with a heart attack, just like Ma. Dad was diagnosed with stage 4 cancer of the liver two years after Ma's death. He stopped drinking but it was too late to undo the damage done. Chemotherapy was agonizing for him and he begged the treatments to stop, he had lost all hope to live. Megan and I tried our best to be there for him and make things as comfortable as possible because there wasn't much that could be done at this stage of the disease.

Dad's death had affected me deeply, more deeply than I had anticipated. It's like something inside me died. Megan and I consoled and comforted each other and Dad through the three years Dad was undergoing treatment. Cancer was a slow killer, things didn't end in an instant; it'd prolong it's torture and seeing Dad struggle through it was painful. Dad had left an insurance intended for me and Megan but our conniving Aunt Teresa made sure she didn't let that go without a fight, putting unverified and false claims to inherit the insurance money. She was a gold digger and everyone in the family knew she couldn't be trusted with anything. Megan had already done the paperwork necessary to sort it out and Dad had appointed Meg and me as beneficiaries in the presence of a lawyer, Miles and Pa when he was still alive. We knew she couldn't do anything but she annoyed us nevertheless.

She'd create unnecessary drama at the hospital, much to everyone's shock. Apparently, our cousins and other aunts & uncles didn't know how low she could stoop for a few pennies. She made the days after Dad's death pure hell. Meg and I managed to keep our cool and proceed with making necessary arrangements and gave him a beautiful funeral. Megan gave the eulogy and it was the hardest I'd cried yet. Ty was my pillar of strength through this time and those were a tough couple of years. All good things must come to an end or as I'd say, all not so good things must be put to an end.

I left Ty two years ago. Our non-existent family life had become a liability for both of us and we still had dreams to fulfill. The boys were all grown up and I was satisfied that I'd been able to give them everything they could ever want: good morals, decent standards, good education, manners, and faith. I felt like I did my part. James was now 20 and Jason 18 and a half. They've absorbed the best of what I've given them. James did well throughout school and was determined about getting a college degree. He worked two years at odd jobs as an accountant and a sales officer after finishing school; he was very much inclined towards business and had great financial acumen. Jason on the other hand, loved toying around motorbikes like his Dad. They've had 3 girlfriends by the time they turned 18 and they've both given up on the idea of relationships for the time being. They thought girls were an unnecessary distraction at this point in their lives and for once, I agreed with their wisdom. Ty went on to open his own motorcycle shop just like he dreamed of. We still talked and he gifted me a new house, a beautiful 4 bedroom townhouse. I was delighted by his gesture and the friendship that I always hoped I'd have with him actually happened after we separated. We're good friends and there's no weight of expectations on either of us. For my part, I left the company I worked for a good 15 years after a saving up a healthy bank balance. I had a passion for makeup and hair and wanted to make it a business idea. I trained at beauty school and began a beauty & hair salon named 'Sexy Hair'. I had a 6 member, all female team working under my supervision. It was hard work getting the business started and took time to establish a solid reputation. I worked 16 hours each day and didn't have much time for anything else. One day, overwhelmed and exhausted, I crouched on the floor, crying and feeling alone. In those times, I had felt Ma and Dad's presence comfort me. James was moving away to Iowa for his degree in business and Jason spent a lot of time at his Dad's motorbike shop. I felt lonely but this wasn't the first time.

It's Friday morning and is a beautiful sunny day. I plan to surprise my team at the salon with coffee & muffins from a new, fancy coffee shop called 'Starbucks'. I've heard great reviews about the place and the outlet has just newly opened in town.

I dress myself in a body-hugging charcoal grey pencil skirt and a black fitted blouse. Despite my age, I look fairly okay and fit. I work out at the local gym four times a week and it shows! I wear black eyeliner, put on some mascara and some muted red lipstick for that bold yet chic look. After I need to look the part of a salon owner!

I feel confident looking at myself in the mirror. This was no longer the Abby who was bullied, beaten, victimized, played around with or taken lightly. I've come a long way.

I spray some Victoria's secret perfume, a heady vanilla scent which happens to be my favorite. And then strap on my heels, take my handbag and walk out the door, ready to conquer the world.

I feel the morning air caress my face with warmth as I get into the car and drive, in anticipation to 'Starbucks' to see if they finally live up to the hype. I park my black Honda and step out to see a long que outside; damn the coffee must be good I say to myself with a chuckle. I join the que and it takes forever to finally get my order of 6 mocha lattes, 1 regular coffee and 7 blueberry muffins. The girl at the counter serves up my first 6 lattes in a coffee holder stand and hands me a bag of muffins. "I'll be back for my coffee; just let me put these in my car." I say and motion to her that I'd be right back. She gives me a smile in acknowledgement and I walk back slowly to the car, so as to not drop anything. That's when someone walks straight into me.

Ouch! The hot lattes have spilled over to my blouse and skirt.

"Fuck that's hot" I say loudly, still feeling the hot sensation of the coffee over me. I'm so annoyed right now. "Can't you watch where you going?" I say, short of hopping mad, continuing my rant.

The man responds, "So sorry, I really didn't see you."

"Well, next time watch where you're going!"

"Here, let me pay for those coffees."

"They're lattes."

He hands me napkins and tries to use them on my breast.

"I'll do that buddy!" I snap and look up to finally see the reason for ruining my morning.

"I was just trying to help, sorry!"

I look at him, his features vaguely familiar though I'm unable to recognize him. I know him from somewhere.

The man stares in my direction like I was staring at him before as I continue to clean up the coffee when I hear words of utter surprise.

"Abby? Is that you Abby?"

"Yes, it's me." I say and suddenly those blue eyes smile in recognition.

"Abby didn't you recognize me? It's me Rick!"

"Omg!" I say out loudly in surprise.

"Gosh it's been so long!" I say, totally taken aback by this fateful meeting.

"I am so sorry Abby that I dropped your lattes, here lets order some more lattes for you."

We walk back to Starbucks and wait patiently for my second order of lattes. I look at him, suddenly shy and nostalgic. It's been long, he's become older, wiser, has a mustache but that mischievous grin hasn't left him. He was dressed in a black suit and I stare at him, delighted at changes he's been through.

"So Abby are you married?" he asked, he sure didn't waste much time. "No, not really. I mean, I have two boys but I never married the father of my kids." I replied, not looking into his eyes.

"How about you?" I asked

"No got divorced." He said, looking down.

We both hear the girl at the counter say,

"Your order is ready"

I was grateful for her timing as the awkward silence between Rick and me needed an icebreaker.

"It's ready. Well, it was nice seeing you Rick."

"Let me help you to your car to be safe. We don't want to drop those lattes again."

"You're the one that bumped in to me, remember?" We both laugh.

He walks me to my car.

"I'll buy you a new blouse."

"It's okay Rick you don't have to."

So we put the lattes in my car safely. We were blushing like teenagers who had just met their school crush. We were grown up adults for heaven's sakes!

"Well Rick I'm really late." And I hurry to get back into my car when he asks,

"Abby would you be available to have dinner with me on Saturday? If you're not too busy that is?"

"Sorry I'm actually busy this Saturday." I didn't want to tell him the girls at work are taking me out for my birthday that weekend.

"How about next Saturday?" I ask, looking for a confirmation.

"I think I could manage that! Give me your phone number and I'll give you mine so we could catch up sometime?" He says with a twinkle in his eyes.

We exchanged numbers and I drove off, smiling at this odd meeting.

I walk into my salon and all the girls turn to look at my messed-up blouse and skirt. It looks like I've peed in my skirt but I smell like coffee!

"What in the world happened to you?" said one of them while another chuckled and said,

"You smell like coffee or is that your new fragrance?"

I roll my eyes as they laugh.

I say "Let's get this meeting started."

"Hey! My latte is cold really!" Cynthia chimes in, pouting. She's a really beautiful and talented girl who's working in my team.

"Cynthia, I'm really sorry but it wasn't my fault!" I say holding my hands out in a way to indicate I was helpless.

"Abby you're still coming with us on Saturday for your birthday, right?" she asks.

"Yes Cynthia!"

She smirks. "Forty is a great number Abby."

"Yeah it means we're getting old. This is going to be a long day."

"So tell me what happened that got you so late?"

"Let's not talk about it now. Mrs. Williams is coming for a color, haircut and styling and you also know she's temperamental and mean. I just don't know why she wants me all the time." I say, my brows knit together in irritation.

"Because Abby you're the best and the boss."

"Cynthia you're being of no help when you say that" I say chiding her.

And is on cue, Mrs. Williams arrives. I'm so not looking forward to her Diva like demands right now. "Where is Abby? All I want is Abby to style my hair. Don't tell me she's not here." She starts.

"Dear, she'll be right out Mrs. William."

"Hello! Mrs. Williams." I say, managing my best smile.

"Hi Abby." She says extending a handshake.

"What would you like me to do with your hair today?"

"I already told you honey, Want a few highlights, and a haircut, but don't chop off much hair honey."

All I could think is that she doesn't have that much hair, and she basically wants a miracle. That was the longest two hours of my life. She told me to not cut off too much hair like fifty times. I wanted to scream but I had to be patient.

"You're leaving the highlights too long."

I rolled my eyes. When I finally finish, she's pleased with the result and I let out a sigh. The rest of the day passed without much drama. It's seven o'clock and I'm beat. My feet aches and I'm ready to go home. I lock the shop and decide to pick up some dinner on the way before I head home.

It's Saturday and my birthday. I'm so glad it's my day off.

I'm forty and single, my life pathetically revolved around work. I brush all thoughts of turning another year older and make myself some hot coffee from the espresso machine. My living room has minimal furniture—a four seat dining table set towards the side, a vintage cream couch, an ivory love seat, a recliner, and a coffee table with an old style lamp. I have picture frames with photographs of my sons, it's a photo collage of their childhood- birthdays, them hanging out with Ma and Dad, some with Megan, a lot of them with Kyle. I have also put up a few pictures of wild flowers on the wall adjacent to my balcony. The walls are painted in a deep ivory. I liked things simple.

My phone is ringing and I know it's one of my sons.

"Hello Mom! Happy birthday to you!"

"Thanks James."

"So what are you doing today for your big day?"

"Well Cynthia and a few coworkers are taking me out, you know just girls."

"Be careful Mom."

"I will son, okay got to go, love you."

"Love you too."

I have a big goofy grin on my face as I relish the sound of my son's voice. I finish my first cup of coffee and head to take a second cup when the next phone call comes. It's Jason.

He's arranged for me to receive a bouquet of flowers and I want to cuddle him up for his thoughtfulness, but he was working far away with his dad at the bike shop.

He inquires about my plans for the day like James did earlier and cautions me to not stay out too late. They both were very protective of me and I assured Jason that I was going to be just fine. I hang up the call, feeling pleased as a punch about both my boys and stop to look at their photos on my wall. They've grown to be such beautiful, big, strong young men! How time flies.

It's still morning and with nothing much to do, I lounge around in yoga pants and a long tee, my favorite home clothes to wear. I settle down on to my couch and switch on the television and try to see if there's something funny on there. I hate watching the news so that's not an option.

I hear a knock at the door and open to see Tyler standing there with a bouquet of dozen red roses.

"Happy birthday Abby, could I come in?"

"Sure, thanks for the flowers!"

It's always hard to see Tyler; it just makes some part of my heart ache. Even though it's been a few years since we separated, it's been hard. But we're both over it, hopefully. "Want some coffee?" I ask.

"Sure!"

While I'm in the kitchen making coffee, I take a peek at him. I really miss him, we just couldn't be together.

"So Jason tells me you're going out?"

"Yeah the girls taking me out."

He tenses up like he wants to tell something.

"Be careful Abby! There are a lot of assholes out there."

"Don't worry Ty, I'll be fine."

"Thanks for the coffee." He quips.

And I smile at him. "Thanks for the flowers."

"You're welcome. He hugs me tight. Happy birthday Abby."

"Thanks."

And with that Tyler leaves. Well that was awkward. After having so much coffee, I drive to Jack in the Box for my favorite tacos and pack a few extra for lunch. I've to get ready for the evening but it's not something I'm looking forward to. Clubbing and party just wasn't my style. I never seem to get a kick out the touchy kinda dancing people do at clubs. I don't like strange men touching me here and there either. So the whole point of going to party was lost on me but I didn't want to turn down the girls invite because they planned it with a lot of excitement.

I get ready for the evening after taking a quick nap. Those tacos were delicious. I look into the mirror; and start putting on some evening appropriate make up. I do a smoky eye look with some silver-grey shadow and nude pink lips. I straighten my hair and add a matching pair of grey-brown smoky quartz earrings. I wear an age appropriate LBD with black heels and pick up a steel grey metallic clutch to round off my look. I dab on a bit of perfume when I hear Cynthia's car horn. I go out and see Cynthia waiting for me; she's dressed in a little red number and has paired it with black boots; her makeup is chic. No red dress with red lips for this girl! Instead she's worn a soft pink nude lip gloss and kept her eye makeup simple. She's a lot taller than me and has a divinely voluptuous figure which the dress highlights with its low front V-neck. Her brown eyes glisten with joy as she sees me. She gives me a big hug and wishes me 'Happy Birthday' before we drive off.

We are in the club and order a few cocktails to get the party started. Some of the girls from the team are already dancing to the tunes the DJ is belting out on the dance floor. I see women and men huddled in little corners, necking, kissing and cuddling under the dim lights; it's like a mini make out session…! I glance over to Cynthia who is now gyrating to a song with a guy she's just met. She didn't lose any time getting hot and heavy. Was I jealous? Maybe? After all I had lost the ability to give my body to just about any guy. I look away and see a couple very close to my table almost making out. I don't know if I should take this as a compliment or what but the guy necking this woman keeps glancing at me and tongues her and then smiles at me...?! He starts to remove her shoes and kisses her toes, her ankles, and makes his way up to her thighs, its one hot kiss after the other and that occasional glance at me. DAMN. I looked at him a little closely or at least what I could see in such poor lighting. He was blonde haired, blue eyed and had tattoos all over his arms and back. He caught me eyeing him and whispered looking in my direction, "You're next" as he continued to make out with his girlfriend or whoever she was. "Yea right" I said, rolling my eyes again. He really seems to enjoy kissing a woman's toe or he has a foot fetish because he's back kissing her feet. It grosses me out and I immediately regret coming out here. No one's asked me to even dance yet, it's like my forehead reads 'Boring' or something! I would've been happier at home reading a book or cooking a dinner from scratch. Cynthia now covered in someone else's sweat and saliva after dancing and kissing for a good hour, comes over to my seat, feeling pity for me. She calls the bartender to get us a couple of shots. She notices the blonde guy and his girlfriend; their foot fest was still on.

Cynthia says, "Fuck! That's Hot."

"No it's not; he's been at her foot for a good forty minutes" I say....

Cynthia's eyes widened "forty minutes? Eeew"

I just laugh because I was put off by it. Cynthia then looks at someone behind me and says, "Hey Abby there's a guy watching you,"

So, like an idiot I immediately turn around.

I see a tall, dark, handsome man walking my way. Cynthia kicks my leg like I've hit the jackpot! I've never been in a situation like this before so I'm tongue tied even before he's had a chance to say anything. He's a sight to behold, masculine and a complete charmer.

"Can I have a dance with you?" He asks with a wink.

"Sure, why not" I say. I see him grin with delight. At this point, I've lost count of how many shots I've had with Cynthia but I'm feel fairly bold.

We dance together for a couple of songs and he buys me a drink. He introduces himself to me as we sit on the bar stool, having a drink. His name is Hunter Hendrix. He has a small printing company. He offers to take us up, including my girls out for a real dinner at Denny's. The girls are excited and are eyeing him like he's Swiss candy. We have a great meal together. At the end of dinner as everyone was going back home, he predictably asked for my number. I give him a wrong number on purpose because really, I don't want to date a guy like him. He told me he goes out a lot and that's a problem. I've been there done that! I like permanence and stability; he simply didn't cut it for me. Hunter is open about his wanting to find random girls every week and in my head, I roll my eyes. Guys like him are dime a dozen. Cynthia however takes a liking to him like a bee to honey. On our way back to drop me, she's like, "If you don't like Hunter, could I go out with him?"

I knew she'd ask but still couldn't believe why she'd waste her time with a guy like that. I paused briefly to see her pretty face and then I give up.

"Sure, here it is" and send her his number.

I didn't put up a fight with Cynthia because I know how she was; she liked being around guys and wasn't quite discerning about who she was going around with. Guys naturally gravitate to her sexy vibes and it was easy for her to lead men on. I guess she was the female match to Hunter's personality, two peas in the same pod. Only, I can predict they both weren't looking for any long-term gig, just a short-term fling that may end as soon as it begins.

I step out the car and tell her thank you for the evening and for the ride back home. I wave 'Bye' as she drives off. I turn in the keys to my sweet home, relieved to finally be back in my cozy space. I relive the day, starting with the call from the boys, Ty's visit etc. as I walk into the bedroom and get into the shower. All things done, I must admit it wasn't a bad day for turning forty. I have a lot to be grateful for. I step out the shower and whisper a prayer in gratitude for everything and sleep off like a baby, ready for a hangover tomorrow morning.

Chapter 24

It's Sunday morning, and the aftermath of the 'Big Forty' begins with an enormous headache, a hangover I well saw coming. I had my carton of apple juice on the bedside knowing that I'd wake up like this. I pour myself a glass and savor its taste. It's sunny outside as sunlight streams in through my windows. I try sitting up and soak in the warmth and light coming in. I feel exhausted and nauseas as is typical of all hangovers. I finally drag myself out of bed, my head still hurting and look into the mirror. My hair is a tangled mess and all I have on is a thigh length Victoria's secret night tee and a super cropped pair of vintage denim shorts. I felt like a mess and looked like a mess.

I hear a knock on the door. Oh no! Can't anyone leave me alone? I don't want anyone seeing me like this. I moan like a toddler woken up for school. The knock gets louder and more urgent and I yell

"I'm coming! Can't you wait?"

I open the door annoyed to my last blood cell only to be surprised seeing Ty.

"What are you doing here?"

"Just wanted to see if you were alright Abby."

"Well as you could see, I'm just fine." I say with a smirk.

"Are you by yourself?"

My face reddens when I hear this.

"Why don't you just say it Ty that you suspect I slept with someone or maybe I'm hiding him in my bedroom? Tyler this is none of your business but if you want to know, no one's here! I'm not a slut Tyler! So please leave."

I could tell that he starts to breathe again like he's relieved that I didn't have a man in my room. He really is selfish. Ty really wants me to be alone. He makes my heart hurt.

"Sorry Abby."

"Well now that you're here I'll make you some coffee." I say leading him inside.

My head is pounding and I pop an aspirin to ease the pain. This is a bad hangover but I can't lose my composure in front of Ty. I feel much better after a few minutes, the medication coursing through my veins. I make lunch for Ty – scalloped potatoes and a classic chicken roast.

We talk about James and Jason, what they're up to, how they were doing, especially since Jason was mostly working at the shop with Ty. Ty was genuinely impressed with Jason's aptitude for mechanics and he was confident he was in the right field. Both of us agreed that perhaps he should take a formal course in something related to automobiles and mechanics that would help him excel in this. Ty seemed to be happy with lunch, helping himself to second servings of both dishes. There's no dessert but there were those 'Dulce de leche' cream flavored doughnuts in the fridge. I offer him that and devour what happens to be a life-long favorite of mine. I remember half my trips with the boys after school were either to the park or this patisserie that makes these yummy melt-in-the-mouth desserts.

Ty gets up to leave. I look at him, my heart always having this twinge of pain when I see his beautiful green eyes. He seems more vulnerable and distressed now than before. But his ear-to-ear smile puts all concern to rest. "I have to go Abby, the lunch was delicious, thank you for the lovely time."

"You're welcome." I say, giving him a hug.

I wave at him as he leaves and head back in to lie down on my living room couch. I thought about Ty, James and Jason, my precious three and didn't realize when I fell asleep. It's past 4pm and I hear my phone ring. I pick up on the third ring, mildly disturbed.

"Hello!" I say with a long yawn.

"Hi! Abby it's Rick, did I wake you?"

"Yeah! I was taking a nap."

"Sorry didn't mean to wake you."

"It's alright!"

Then we were silent for a moment.

"Abby what are you doing later?"

"Not much."

"I know we have a date next week, but I would love to take you to dinner."

Another moment of silence.

"Abby! What do you think?"

"Sure Rick, what time?"

"How about six? Give me your address Abby so I could pick you up."

I can't believe I just said yes to a date before a date to Rick! What was I thinking; it's happening all too fast. Did I care? May be not!

My hangover has subsided so I head for a good long shower under cold water, to awaken my skin and senses. I'd been sleeping a solid four hours and if Rick hadn't called, I may have slept my way to dinner time and sit up like an owl through the night. I felt the excitement of a date but I had no idea what it was going to be like. The Rick I knew when I was young was a lot different from the Rick I met a week ago. And so was I. We both had changed so much through time that it's a new experience altogether.

I decide to dress a bit casual but keep it classy: Faded dark denims, a black turtle neck sweater, a pair of black slip on shoes, a pair of thick silver hoops and a silver toned bracelet. It's not like I didn't enjoy dressing up but I always liked keeping things simple; maybe that's why I felt like I was boring in the world of dating. I wear light eye makeup and wear a deep berry shade lipstick. I slick my hair back with some styling spray to keep the baby hairs in place. I feel giddy with excitement as I head downstairs. Was this really happening? I wondered to myself as I hear a knock on my door. I open to see Rick, smiling wide. He looks dapper in his blue Levi's and burgundy sweater. I could smell his cologne standing three feet away; it's musky, decadent and woody. Heavenly! I struggle for words taking in the sensation of seeing him like this.

I say "Hi."

"Wow! Abby you look amazing."

I blush.

"Are you ready?"

"Yes," I say with a shy smile. I don't know how to date or even be with a man. There was only one man and he broke me to pieces.

I push thoughts about Ty aside and go with Rick, fully intending to savor this time out. He takes me to Venice Beach. We eat at one of their little sea-food specialty restaurants. We get a table in the corner. There are lovely tropical flower centerpieces with candles on each table. The lighting is dim and the atmosphere is romantic and cozy with a lovely view of the beach.

The waitress asks what we would like to drink.

"Abby what would you like?"

"Just water and some lemonade thanks."

The waitress rolls her eye at me. What's her problem? And of course, she gives her sexy smile to Rick; who could blame her, he gets lemonade too.

"So Abby tell me why you are still single?"

"Well, I could ask you the same question, can't I?"

Rick grins. "Well, you tell me your story and I'll tell you mine." So Rick starts first.

"Okay here it goes, I got married, and you know Betty Cox."

"OMG! You married her??!!!!!" I say staring at him in disbelief!

"Yes! I did and it was the biggest mistake of my life Abby, real big mistake."

"Did you have children?"

Seeing his beautiful face frown so sadly,

"No Abby, she couldn't have children. We had lot of problems because of that. In a way, it saved the heartache. Divorce is never easy when kids are involved." We sit in silence for a couple minutes. "You know Abby, I was faithful to her in every way I could be but she broke my heart. She went with my best friend, took half of everything I owned."

I saw his pain and knowing what Betty was like firsthand; my heart ached for what he went through. Without thinking I hold his hand. He stares straight in my eyes.

"You know Abby I missed you so much, always wondered what happened to you and where you were" He squeezes my hand.

"I missed you too Rick, a lot of things happened and well, we're here." I say, looking at him with a smile.

"You're still sweet Abby."

We eat our dinner–a seafood platter, some clam chowder and prawn cocktail. It was delicious. He tells me through dinner, that his mother passed away of cancer; that she had never stopped drinking. She drank till the very end despite knowing her doing so could be fatal for her. His father left them when he went to college. Rick now owns a business company. He manufactures computer parts. I ask about his two older brothers Tommy and Scott. He said they're fine. Scott is married and has two kids. Tommy has a girlfriend but hasn't yet married. "So Abby, now tell me your story."

"Okay, I wouldn't know where or how I should start." I take a deep breath trying to articulate my thoughts but Rick notices that I'm struggling for words. He squeezes my hand, assuring me that he's there for me.

I tell him the story. I begin from when I left home and stayed with Kate's family. It's quite a long story and I'm overwhelmed when I stop midway. Rick knows it's been a tough ride; he was there with me during the few years till senior year. Rick is lost for words after hearing everything. Our conversation has been intense and draining. We both felt like we were in the same boat and that life had come a full circle. It was time to move on. Rick pays the bill and we walk the boardwalk. We hold hands like we used to when we walked to school, it felt oddly satisfying. I felt a lot of peace having shared some of these things with Rick; I haven't had a heart to heart conversation like that with anyone in years. I was grateful for Rick's time and company, knowing that coming on this date was definitely a good idea. We keep walking along the shoreline, with no sense of time. We don't talk; we just hold hands and soak in the sunset, the beautiful sky and the waves that kissed our feet ever so often. It was beautiful, not having to say anything, to have our silence understood. We sit down near the beach, feeling the sand through our toes.

"Abby, tell me what happened next?" Rick whispers, wanting to know the rest.

The sun had set and the sky was lit up with stars, I look up to see them twinkle and sigh. In a low voice, I tell him the rest of the story, up to the point where I open the salon.

Rick takes a deep breath and says, "Wow! Abby and I thought. I had it bad."

I look at him with sad eyes; merely thinking about all that I had gone through, what Rick had gone through, it was enough hell for a lifetime.

Rick asks how Megan is.

"She found her love and happiness with Miles. She has a son Kyle, who's a year and half older to James. Both boys are at college now. She's happy."

He puts his arms around me. We both stare at the vast ocean in front of us and the waves that came ashore. We take our shoes off to feel the cold water wash our feet as the sand grazes against our skin. We hold hands and stand there feeling the waves come one after the other. We look at each other and know that we don't want this night to end.

I can't believe this was our first real date in over two decades and it was beautiful in every way. We had this level of comfort because we had known where we came from, our shared history and a love that had great promise but was cut off by Betty's poisonous hold over him. The drive back to my place felt like a ride through the clouds, I was at peace. We arrive home and Rick pulls open the car door for me and takes my hand, helping me out. We walk to my front door, still entranced by the magical evening we spent together. Rick's smile is so beautiful.

"Thank you, Abby for a wonderful date, it was memorable in so many ways." He says this and leans to kiss me. I don't resist because for once, I know this felt real and I haven't felt like this in a long time with any man. His kiss is so gentle and deep, it makes me melt.

In my head, I'm like Wow! He knows how to kiss. We kissed when we were young; this was way different.

We pull apart, trying to catch our breath. He smiles that gorgeous smile again.

I'm still kinda breathless from the kiss when Rick says,

"Abby I would like to take you out on more dates and spend time with you. Is that okay?"

My face reddens in an obvious blush. Suddenly, I'm coy and say

"I would love to date you Rick. I'll call you tomorrow?"

"Sure, I look forward to that Abby" he says with a wink."

"Me too Rick"

"Goodnight Abby, I should leave now, it's pretty late. You take care"

"Goodnight Rick," I say as he leaves and drives back home.

I take a shower going over the time I spent with Rick. Why did I feel the way I did today with him? I wish it was like this back in the day, perhaps we both would've saved ourselves some serious heartache.

I settle into my bed, dressed in silk pajamas. I felt like a teenager in high school who just met her crush. It was so silly yet endearing. He was endearing seemed so, matured? It's like he's gotten better with age in every way, like good wine. It's barely two hours since he's left and I already miss him.

I used to feel this way with Tyler but that was short lived. I reminisced about this little gorgeous fella who taught me to play marbles and protected me from bullies in school; now he's all grown up into this dashing, strong man.

My phone rings.

"Hello!"

"Sorry Abby! Just can't stop thinking of you, were you asleep?"

"No! Rick, I was thinking about our time together," I say shyly.

We both laugh and end up talking for two hours before we realize that we both have work tomorrow and decide to hang up. He's a sweet talker. I sleep happily, lulled into sweet dreams and memories of Rick.

I wake up the next morning feeling energetic and humming through my morning coffee and breakfast. I didn't realize that a single date with the right person could make such a difference. I was tired of being alone and yearned for someone who understood my broken parts and didn't treat me like damaged goods. Rick made me feel whole again and though we've just started, I already feel so alive and hopeful. I've never felt this way before. I dress for work in a black skirt, a pale dusty pink pull-over sweater, sheer nude panty hose and black heels. I trade my neutral light make up today for a soft pink blush, a peach lip gloss and lots of mascara. I leave my hair open in loose waves and drive to the salon, feeling like a million bucks. I even stop at Starbucks and get myself a latte.

Latte in hand, I walk into the salon, feeling different. Cynthia turned her head as soon as I walk in.

"Wow! Abby you look pretty today. You must have had a great date. Did you guys have great sex because that glow on your face sure looks like you had some fun?"

I choke on my expensive latte as soon as I hear her comment. The coffee went through my nose. God! I wanted to tell her I'm not a slut like her! But I know saying that would be highly offensive and inappropriate. I try to regain some composure and say,

"No, I'm not the type to have sex on first dates, sorry to disappoint Cynthia."

"Oh! Sorry Hon! But you don't ever have sex at all."

I get a couple of tissues and wipe the latte off my face and ask, curious to know whatever happened to Hunter…

"What about your date Cynthia? How did it go?"

I pour myself a cup from the espresso machine at the salon before we open for business.

"Well Hunter and I went to the movies. Oh! God Abby! We were kissing, his hands all over my tits, and then we had to leave. We had hot sex. He's very kinky by the way." She says giving me a wink.

I rolled my eyes. Who does that on a first date? Apparently, she does. May be my first impressions about her were proving to be true. She behaved like a slut and had no shame admitting to it as much. Maybe she confused sex with love? It's twisted.

I truly cared for her because I know she's had an equally, if not more troublesome childhood. She was raped by a family friend who lived next door when she was only thirteen. I was no psychologist but I knew that an incident like that could influence an otherwise healthy attitude towards sex into something that's bordering on lust and confuse that with love and affection. I wanted the best for her and when she went out with guys like Hunter, it was natural for me to be concerned.

We carry on with business, happy to be busy. Later on, in the day, Cynthia received a dozen red roses from Hunter. I was happy for her: all the guys she went out with never gave her anything. Maybe there's a spark between them that will work out after all? I was hopeful.

After a long day, I'm exhausted and dying to take a leisurely bubble bath. I pick up some dinner from Jack-in-the-Box, some yummy fries with cheese and a jumbo Mac. Both totally junk and totally satisfying I think to myself as I devour them in a jiffy. I run the bath and pour some rose perfumed bath and relax into my bath tub with some wine in my hand. This felt like a real treat. I was just about to sleep off in the tub when my phone rings

"Hello." I say, slightly awake.

"Well hello there Abby."

"Hi! Rick."

"Did I call at a bad time?"

"No, it's fine."

We talk for an hour and I still haven't got up from here. The water in the tub is no longer warm enough. But my heart was melting like wax. He made me feel beautiful and wanted. We plan another date and I feel everything is going my way. Even though things were going well with the salon and my relationship with Rick, there's that gnawing fear at the back of my mind about a storm in the distance that's inching closer to me as time passes. I was no longer afraid and was ready to confront things head on; life is never fair, sometimes we have to fight for the things we want, sometimes we have to let go. Life isn't a bed of roses for anyone and it sure as hell doesn't come with guarantees. I believed in 'happily forever after' as a young child but adulthood has banished all thoughts of magical endings. However, I did believe that good things could come together if bad things fell apart, it was just a matter of perspective.

Chapter 25

It's funny how life has its twist and turns when you think that things are progressing smoothly. Life is not a fairy tale because reality always throws off the rose-tinted glasses you're wearing. Rick and I have been seeing each other for three months now. He calls me nearly every day. Every chance we get, we go out on dates but never touches me inappropriately or pressures me to have sex. If there were any touching going on it would be holding hands, kissing, like we would in high school; though it felt silly at times, it felt pretty amazing most of the time to indulge in our childlike affection for each other. Rick asks me to take off from work this weekend. Of course, I say yes, but at the same time, I'm nervous at the prospect of spending a whole weekend with him. I mean, we'd gotten close and this was a natural thing. I've been intimate only with one man and that was Ty. So obviously, this was going to be my first time with someone else other than Ty. Rick called to let me know of the plan of Sunday. I'm already a ball of nerves and it's only Tuesday! I try to keep calm and keep myself busy with work as to avoid thinking about it. Rick has been real sweet; I knew he wouldn't hurt me and I trusted him completely. It's Thursday and I'm running late to get to the salon. Rick and I spoke for more than three hours last night and as a result, I woke up late. Did I regret it? Nope! I was happy that I had a reason to run late for work, having been a punctual time clock for the last several years. It was oddly satisfying.

I park my car and rush out of the car, trying to take out my keys, handbag in one hand, phone in another when I stop dead in my tracks. Tyler and Rick are standing in front of the salon holding coffee for me; I did not see this coming. I wanted to introduce them properly; this is going to be super awkward. I try to contain my anxiety and walk towards them coolly. Ty looks furious while Rick couldn't be more bothered about the guy standing next to him. Rick knows the person Ty who was my partner all these years; he just hasn't seen Ty in person. I think I have no choice but to roll with this.

I finally open the salon and invite both of them in. Ty hands me the cup of coffee he's holding for me and asks with a scowl on his face.

"Who is this guy Abby?"

I roll my eyes at him,

"Tyler this is Rick, Rick this is Tyler."

Rick reaches out his hand to shake and Ty just pushes it aside like a petulant child; he slams the door behind him and says, "I'll talk to you later Abby!" Ty leaves like one of those summer storms that hit you out of nowhere and suddenly it's all and back to normal. That was intense.

Rick says, "Sorry Abby, you haven't told him about us yet?"

"No, I haven't, and now you know why."

His fingers tilt my chin. He stares at me and I at him; he leans in to give me a gentle kiss.

"You're so beautiful. Can't wait to have you for the whole weekend, Abby. I'm not scared of Tyler so don't worry! He had you once, he blew it. Talk to you later baby."

Kissing him I walk him to his car. For some reason I feel Ty is still around, hidden in some corner to see what I was doing with Rick or who he was. Why did he just turn up with coffee in hand? He's never brought me coffee or breakfast to the salon before so why start now?

This is the first guy he's ever seen me with, maybe that's why he's acting so weird. He's truly selfish. I understood his insecurities about the situation but he needs to let go of me just like I have let go of him. The boys are the reason for our friendship and there's nothing more to it. As parents we had our responsibility to them and always present a united front in terms of providing them support.

He's broken my heart all along, cheating with women I knew nothing of and I've caught him in the act; he's not going to start dictating how I get to live my life or who I go out with.

I walk back to the salon cautiously wondering if Ty will pop in again. I heave a sigh of relief when I don't see him; instead I'm welcomed by Cynthia who's giving me a naughty smile and a wink. She eyes the two Starbucks lattes placed on my work desk and says "You didn't have to buy me a latte Abby?"

"Well I didn't!" I say with a smile.

She stares at me all confused.

"Then why do you have two?" she asked.

"Good question Cynthia! Rick and Tyler were at my door with Starbucks coffee."

"You're kidding?"

"I kid you not."

"Wow! Abby, I wish I was there to see the live action! So what happened?"

"Tyler was furious because of Rick being there. Testosterone and men, ugh!" I say rolling my eyes.

"Wow! Abby, you went from having no man and suddenly you have two. Oh! Girl that's pretty awesome, yeah!"

"You would say that!" I say with a chuckle.

"What are you going to do?"

"I don't know." I said, mildly irritated. These were two men who were and still are an important part of my life. One, the father to my children and the second, a love that never had its chance before but now has.

I am really trying to keep my wits about me and motion her to get started with work. I close the salon at 6, a little earlier than the usual 7pm because I was just too tired. It was an eventful morning and all I wanted to do was relax with a long bath, some good dinner and may be even some music.

When I arrive home, I'm half expecting to see Ty but there he was, in all his glory. I sigh. This was going to be a long evening.

I walk up to my front door and get the keys to the house, glancing at him I ask.

"What do you want Tyler? I'm very tired."

"Yeah! I bet you are acting like a whore!"

"If this is the reason you're here, I'd rather you go home. I don't go to your house calling you a man whore, you don't get to tell me what to do anymore."

"Who is he Abby?"

"It's none of your business Ty."

"Everything about you is my business Abby. Tell me."

"He's a friend from school when we were young. So go home Tyler, now you know!"

Tyler turns to face me squarely and grabs my shoulders tight. I could feel his breath on me. I can feel the air around us crackle with sparks and he just forces a kiss on me. I feel the passion in it but I don't kiss him back. When he senses my resistance, he pulls away. His face is tense and he seems visibly annoyed my lack of reciprocation.

"You will always be mine, Abby, always. Don't ever forget that."

I stand there in total shock. What is wrong with him? I'm in countdown mode already. Tomorrow is Friday and I'd be with Rick from tomorrow evening until Sunday. He hasn't told me about the plan yet keeping much of the weekend date a surprise. But we were going to finally make love to each other; I felt butterflies in my tummy and couldn't contain my excitement.

Cynthia is going to give me a makeover of sorts to get me ready. She's on the way to my place with some stuff from the salon. I can't be bothered to cook so we agree on ordering a pizza. She also picks up some wine. When she gets here, I've got some music on, the classics – 'Whip it' by Devo, 'Groove is in the heart' by Deee-lite, 'Stoney end' a Barbara Streisand favorite and finally 'Show me the meaning of being lonely' by Backstreet Boys. We were dancing and singing on the top of our lungs, it seemed like a girl's pajama party and was so much fun! We finally get down to the real deal. She sets me up with some lovely highlights and gives me a much needed blow dry. It looks fantastic and I'm very pleased with the result. Cynthia does her work exceptionally well and it's why she was on my team.

"Thank you, Cynthia." I say as I can't take my eyes off my hair.

She gives me a few beauty tips for the just bitten lips and tousled hair kinda look women die to have.

I smile in delight.

"You're beautiful Abby. He will be so hot for you."

She hugs me tight and winks at me.

"See you tomorrow at work Abby."

I walk her to the door and she leaves. All I could do is stare at myself in the mirror and smile. It took me a lifetime to feel this way.

I feel good, I look good; this has been a major confident booster.

It's Friday and I really do want to get the work done soon before I can ride off into the sunset with Rick for the weekend. I've been nervous about this all week long and finally the day is here. However, of all days, today was turning out to be the busiest because we had new clients coming in. Some of them aren't happy campers and they are a dime a dozen like Mrs. Williams. Then there was one in particular who didn't like how much I cut her hair and refused to pay; I was forced to give her a discount.

Phew, it's been quite a day and Cynthia nods in agreement.

"Let's have some coffee girls" I say as I slouch into my desk chair. One of the girls, orders in some cupcakes with delicious frosting, the perfect ending to an otherwise nerve-wracking day. "Awesome, just what I need–some more calories." I say as I bite into my second cupcake, it had a frosting that tasted like lemon meringue pie, heavenly…!

We close the salon at six sharp.

I see everyone off and hurry to my car. Rick and I decided that I'll drive to his place than him coming to pick me up. I stored his address on the GPS. I've a small travel bag packed and in the backseat that has my clothes & toiletries for the weekend stay at Rick's place.

I drive to his place playing music in the car, soft romantic acoustic tunes to calm my nerves. I drive through Montecito Heights; the sun was getting low and his place was, unsurprisingly up the hill, close to the park we used to go when I stayed with Ma. It seems like ages ago that I've driven around here and it still had a rustic beauty about it. This was the first time I was seeing his house.

It was a little after half past six when I finally arrive. I navigate my car to park behind Rick's car in the driveway. I step out and take in the little details of the house before me. The house was a classic fixer upper, farmhouse chic style kinda structure that was painted a pale baby blue with white window frames and a white fence; there were cream, white and baby blue roses to mirror the colors of the house out in the front garden. It had an old style charm to it, straight from an old Hollywood movie even. I loved the rustic vibe around this place. Rick waves to me and walks toward me. He's wearing a white t-shirt with faded jeans; his light brown hair is a tad messy and he has some leather slippers on. He seemed a lot muscular in a tee because I could see his arms, unlike when he's wearing a business suit. Ty was beefed up in a very hunky way but Rick was more athletic, lean but strong. He looked gorgeous and so relaxed; I couldn't take my eyes off him. Rick could see me like no one else could and made me feel like he had eyes only for me even in a room full of people; he knew how to make me feel special and treated me like a princess. The three months we've been together has been nothing less than a dream. His touch is just tender and he knows just the right words to make it better.

I give him a big hug as he leans in. There's a big grin on his face as he takes the bag from my hand and puts his arms around my waist.

He knows I'm nervous. "This way." He says leading me to the front door. He opens door and I step inside to this gorgeous blue and white themed living room. There were lit candles, two white lamp shades and a blue couch set; there's a table for two and a large window from where one could see the city lights below. The view was incredible from here, utterly magical!

Rick holds me from the back and kisses me near the nape of my neck and rubs his nose into my cheeks and then plants more kisses. He's so soft and gentle and I let down my guard. "This is amazing Rick." I say, drinking in the view of the sun setting over the hills and city lighting up below us.

"That's the reason I bought this house. I fell for the view and I wouldn't trade this for anything in the world. I knew you'd love it here Abby" he said, looking into my eyes. "Do you want to sit out on the balcony? It opens up to the full view and you could feel the breeze on your face" He says knowing that I loved that feeling of the wind. I nod shyly.

He leads my hand to the balcony that opens up to this view which is partially hidden by the window and the wall between the balcony and the living room. There are two folding chairs and a small round table with little white string lights around the railing.

"This truly is incredible Rick, it's like being at a hillside resort" I say with a chuckle.

"Well, why don't we have dinner out here, would be a shame to miss this view" he quips as he gets inside to bring a bottle of fine wine, a cheese platter and some old photographs from school. He puts some old school jazz to set the mood for the evening. The fire place roars into life, enveloping the living area in its light and warmth, a beautiful contrast to the twilight sky outside. He has pictures of us from school! I blush in embarrassment as I browse through it; there's one of him and me in baseball uniform, another in PE, a third still from grade six. Gawd, I roll my eyes as we both giggle over memories we had of school.

Turns out, Rick's a pretty good cook too; he's made me steak, baked potato and green salad. I was famished after surviving the time post lunch on two cupcakes, I had wiped my plate clean and Rick was pleased that I enjoyed his cooking as much. After dinner we catch a movie–Rocky. I'd seen all the movies in the series so that's another thing we had in common. We picked through a box of assorted gourmet dark chocolates he'd bought for me. It paired beautifully with wine and we were two glasses and four chocolates in. I signaled I couldn't eat more chocolate though I would want them later and winked at him. I was never the type to wink, ever! I knew Meg did when she was younger and so did Ty, but not me. Was it the wine, was it the love, was it the chocolates, I don't know what it was, but I was feeling brazen in a good way. Rick was happy to oblige with my request and put my chocolates away.

He was sitting close to me now on the couch and started to play with my hair. He removed the hair pin that was holding my hair in a messy bun, delighting in the way my hair fell over my shoulders. He starts kissing me slowly, softly and whispers how much he wants me and how beautiful I was. I was feeling all sorts of things: I could feel the blood rush to my cheeks and down, my stomach was all butterflies and I could feel goose bumps on my skin.

Unable to go slow or exercise patience any longer, we start to go all over each other; it's pure passion and it's exhilarating in the best way possible. I'd been lonely for so long and I reckon he's missed having a companion like I did. He lifts me in his arms and takes me to the bedroom and puts me down gracefully on his large bed.

We tear at each other's clothes, savoring each other's presence–physically, emotionally, on every level. This felt and was true intimacy. There's only the light of the fireplace cascading through the door of the bedroom and a few lit candles. The moonlight is streaming through the open bedroom window on the other side. It's beautiful being in this moment as he tightens his grip around my waist, drunk on each other's love. Our breathing is slowing down as we rise and come down together in this warmth and passion. "I always loved you Abby, ever since you walked into the classroom when we were six." It made me smile and I saw real love in his eyes, I was so lucky to have him.

We kissed and made love for ten more minutes and then rise and come down, rocking our bodies to each other's rhythm. The pleasure is indescribable; we fall into each other's arms, exhausted but hold each other tight. We fall asleep, our bodies and spirit as one.

When I wake up Rick is still sleeping. I tip toe into the shower, reliving the amazing night we just had. It was beautiful in every way I had imagined it to be. I was overwhelmed by the emotion of it all, wondering why it took so long for us to get together.

I step out of the shower expecting him to be awake but he's sleeping like a baby. I quietly slip into his white tee which was strewn over the floor. I inhale his warm cologne and delight in the sensation.

I walk to the kitchen and make some coffee and get some scrambled eggs & bacon going, I turn on the toaster when I feel his hands grab my waist.

"Hi beautiful." he says and kisses my neck. I moan in pleasure, wanting more of him over me. It's hard not to.

We start to kiss. My lips are swollen from last night's kissing but that's alright with me.

"You should have waited for me in the shower, I would have joined you." He says with a chuckle. Rick is holding me so tight as if he was going to lose me or something.

After finishing our breakfast, he's got a grin with mischief written all over it.

"Let's go play ball in the park Abby." He says.

We change into sporty attire; I'm dressed in vintage Levi denim shorts and a black tee while Rick wears a navy-blue tee paired with distressed, faded denim pants. Oh, and a baseball cap, an old one he's had from when he was young. We walk down the hill play baseball with a few people he knows around here. This has been so incredibly refreshing, I haven't played in a while. The last time I played baseball like this was when both the boys were home during high school. We finally get to a much loved spot, the place where I and Rick had spent so much time together: our oak tree. It held so many memories, it was here that Rick and I first forged our friendship, where I received my heart shaped pendant necklace from him which Ma quickly gave away when I left home; it's also where he tried to make out with me the first time. "Did you have fun Abby?" he said, awakening me from my nostalgia.

"Sure did." I say with a big smile.

He starts to kiss my lips then he deepens the kiss and all I wanted to do was run up that hill to his bed. I think great minds think alike because that's exactly what we did; all weekend was sex and sex and some more sex.

The three days flew by quickly but both of us agreed, we had an amazing time and a new level of intimacy between us. And it's getting pretty serious. Sunday evening, I had to drive back home and there was an ache in my heart when I was leaving. He hugged me tightly and promised to plan something soon; I nodded in agreement and drove off with my heart filled with memories of Rick and the weekend.

Chapter 26

I got back home around dinner time on Sunday evening and called to let him Rick know. Monday meant back to work week but Rick made sure to call me and we made plans to meet up more often. We went out on many dates after that, once he hung out the weekend at my place and then I went to his. Most nights I'd get away to Rick's house to the beautiful hills and memories of this much cherished place. At Rick's place, he'd make sure I eat something more nutritious than a bunch of tacos or cheese fries; he'd cook slow cooked roasts and stews which I was beginning to get addicted to. Work was busy but we made time for each other. Rick always told me how much he loved me; sometimes he'd say it, sometimes he'd show it in the care he had for me, sometimes he'd even write in a small poems or scribble something on cards. It was mushy and I couldn't ask for more.

I had known and experienced the fear of having good things fall apart because of storms no one can foresee. I lived in fear of that. Things with Rick had been going beautifully; it's been the most memorable part of my life for the right reasons. I was scared that I could lose him or what we had in a twist of fate like it had happened so many times before.

It was after one of these dates when I drive back home, I see Ty at my place. He said he wanted to say 'Hi' because it'd been awhile since he saw me. I brushed it aside as a courtesy because we shared two sons between us and a decent understanding about our responsibilities about it. But after that, Ty's visits increased frequently and I wondered what he was up to? What did he want from me?

It's Thursday night. Cynthia and I are on our third glass of wine, catching up on a movie I had promised her we'd watch together. There's a tub of rocky road ice-cream in front of us, waiting to be devoured as soon as we finish our wine and fish steak dinner. Rick had managed to kick my preference for junk food though I cheated every once in a while, with a pizza or my favorite tacos. "So Abby how are things with Rick?" she asks, looking in my direction.

"It's really going well. He always tells me he loves me. He is really showing me that I'm worthy of being loved and respected and that I mean a lot to him. I feel the same way about him as well" I say smiling and thinking about Rick.

However, Ty's visits disrupt my delight over Rick momentarily. I think out loud to her

"You know Cynthia, I've never been this happy in my life, it's almost scary. Ty has been visiting me a lot more often and it's beginning to worry me a bit".

Cynthia nods and says.

"He's jealous Abby. Remember he didn't want you."

"How about you and Hunter, things going anywhere?" I ask.

"We have sex a lot Abby. We go out, we see other people. You know."

Now I'm nodding, trying to resist rolling my eyes. "Just as long as you're happy Cynthia."

"You too Abby."

We hug each other and devour our ice-cream like toddlers... it's just so good. She goes home soon after. I'm still drinking more wine when I hear a knock, who could it be at this time?

I had a couple of glasses of wine so I wasn't surprised that when I get up from the couch, I feel dizzy and light headed. Stumbling to open the door, I try in vain to fix my messy hair and look presentable enough for whoever it was.

I open the door and my eyes widen seeing Rick stand there with that mischievous smile of his! "Rick! Hi!" I say and hug him.

"Sorry Abby, I just missed you and you look amazing and drunk!" he quipped saying with a smile.

"Come on in." I say giving him a wink.

All I'm feeling is my cheeks burning and my tummy in knots.

I close the door when he turns towards and grabs me close to him. He kisses me a little roughly, with rising passion. I love it! Rick says, "Loving this side of you baby." He starts to kiss me all over. We make love until we can't keep our eyes open anymore. He sleeps over holding me tight like he never wants to let me go. I wake up the next morning to sweet kisses on my cheeks. Rick is lying in bed awake, tracing his fingers over my body. I could get used to this. I look into his blue eyes and say "Good morning". He returns that with a deep kiss. I lay my head on his chest and feel his heartbeat, I feel safe in his arms, something I haven't felt elsewhere. It's a beautiful feeling and I don't want to get up from bed.

He looks at me and says "Okay Abby, would you like me to make you breakfast or take you out?"

"Let's stay in, just want some fruit and coffee." I say, lying in bed lazily.

"Got it baby." He says and jumps from bed with an energy of a young adult... I smile and roll my eyes.

While Rick is making me breakfast, I rush to take a quick shower. I dress up in black yoga pants and a pale pink sweatshirt. I hear a knock at my door when I am walking out of my room past the kitchen; the knock gets louder each time and I motion to Rick that I'll get the door.

When I open it, it's Ty standing there with a flirting grin and those dimples, staring at me from my head to toe. I'm not impressed.

"WHAT DO YOU WANT" I say showing my displeasure to see him.

"Be nice babe." He says with a wicked smile.

I roll my eyes at him when we hear Rick say out loud, "Come on baby, breakfast is served."

I just wanted to go back to bed and throw the blankets over my head.

"I'm busy Tyler can we talk later?"

"Who are you talking to baby?"

I didn't see Rick come from behind me but he laces his hands around my waist and kisses my hair. Ty's face went from a flirtatious grin to an angry, hurt lion that got his ego kicked. It was priceless. Rick stared at him like he was dead meat. Ty looked at me and then back to Rick, frustrated and helpless.

"Talk to you later Abby," he says and turns away.

"Well Abby, he seems to come here anytime he feels like, is it?"

"Come on Rick, let's have breakfast."

Rick closes the door behind me and kisses me roughly again, it's so intense with him.

"Love you baby and I'm jealous. Also, don't want him here whenever he wants." He says.

Frowning, I say, "Rick! Don't worry about him okay! Let's just enjoy our day. Let's eat."

Rick and I went back to his place. I knew Rick was frustrated when it came to Ty and who could blame him. Ty was acting weird. Why?

Don't know. Rick was changing me in a good way. I'd been broken so many times over and over again, only Rick saw and understood that. His love was mending me in a way I had never imagined. He made me feel worthy, loved and wanted and for the first time in my life, I was hopeful that this could last. We were so in love. A week went by since that last episode with Ty and we were getting close to Christmas.

I went shopping with Cynthia to buy gifts for everyone, something for the boys, Rick and even Ty. After shopping we went to my place. Cynthia wanted to drink some wine and watch a movie, that was always her idea of relaxing. She let me pick a movie. I choose 'Urban Cowboy' an all-time favorite of both Cynthia and myself. I didn't enjoy the idea of staggering around drunk so I opt to make some coffee and unwind while Cynthia poured her second glass of wine. "So Abby how is Rick?"

"Everything is great. How is Hunter?" I ask curiously.

"We're still seeing each other. I don't know Abby, he is too handsome for his own good."

Stuffing my face with a freshly baked cinnamon bun and coffee, I nod in agreement.

"He's tall, dark and handsome."

We both, giggle.

"You bitch Abby." She says while I let out a laugh.

"What! I'm just agreeing with you." I say teasingly.

"Abby, you have two gorgeous guys that love you. You're so lucky."

"Doll that's not true." I say holding my hands up protesting that weird notion she's just suggested.

"Really Abby, can't you see it? They both love you. I just hope you never have to choose between them."

"Why would I have to choose? God Cynthia, why would you say that?"

"I'm just saying. Don't get angry Abby. I know you love both of them. You have history with both men."

Now I'm getting angry.

"You're insane Cynthia."

I continued, visibly annoyed.

"You know you should probably fix your life before you analyze my life."

Cynthia frowned. "Sorry Abby that I hit a nerve," and with that girl's night was over.

Cynthia leaves all hurt. I'm upset with myself that I allowed her comment to get to me. I lay in bed awake, with tears rolling down my cheek. What did she mean by saying that? What if she's right? Was that really the truth? I tossed and turned all night, unable to sleep. Deep down it struck a chord but I was refusing to acknowledge it. The rest of the week was uneventful. Christmas Eve is on Saturday and its only Tuesday. Rick is taking me out for dinner tonight and tells me that he's going skiing with his brother Tommy to an upscale ski resort they'd wanted to go for a long time. The boys would be home for Christmas so it works out but I knew we'd miss each other.

Rick knocks at my door. I open the door and he take's my breath away. He's looking dapper in a formal suit in deep charcoal grey matched with a patterned silver-black tie. He'd indicated this was going to be one of those fancy restaurants so I finally dressed up for the occasion, something I haven't done in a while. I wear a black lace knee length dress, a pair of small diamond studs and a matching bracelet; my hair is in a formal bun and my makeup is classic-winged eyeliner, blush, and nude lipstick. Rick looks delighted and tells me I look amazing. I felt amazing whenever I was with him irrespective of what I wore. He escorts me like a gentleman to this beautiful and scenic restaurant up in the hill. We sit next to a huge window to see the city lights. It's so romantic: a nice candle in the center of the dark wooden table, the waitress takes orders for our drinks and appetizers.

I can see the waitress flirting with Rick, couldn't blame her; he was eye candy.

I don't have to worry about Rick; he never looks at her. All he sees is me, like I'm the only woman he could ever see. Rick's blue eyes never leave mine. I notice he's nervous and unusually fidgety. It feels like there's something he wants to tell me OMG! Maybe he's leaving me? I'm drinking my wine nervously when the waitress is waiting for me to order the next course. She almost snaps in front of me and I just give her a glance. I order a steak and some salad and Rick orders the same. We eat our meal in surprising silence; it's never been this quiet between us. I'm beginning to get really worried because I can see that the silence between us had become awkward. When we finish our dinner, we share dessert—a delectable chocolate fudge brownie cake but I don't savor it because my head is bursting with worst case scenarios. They clear our table.

Rick holds my hand and then gives me a big smile

"I have something to ask you Abby."

"What is it?" I ask wondering if my worst fears were going to come true.

My heart is taking a beating and then, suddenly he takes my palm in his and kisses me... I feel a sense of relief wash over me, so maybe he's not breaking up after all. "Abby I've loved you since you were six. You were the only girl I ever saw, you are the love I will forever want, you're the one woman of my dreams, I've wanted you to be in my heart forever. You always take my breath away. You're the one that captured my heart Abby! You hold my heart. With that being said, would you please be my wife??" he said with pleading eyes.

I was like OMG!! I was all tears and on cloud 9 when he'd finished speaking. I see him pull out a turquoise blue Tiffany box and held it for me to see. Inside, I see a big princess cut diamond ring that sparkled beautifully. At that moment, it felt like my life was building up to this and every hell I walked through seemed worth it.

"Well baby?" he asks again, his eyes well up with emotion.

I pull him close to me and kiss him and say 'YES'! He's so happy he lifts me off the ground and swings me around before putting me down again and kisses me. He slips the gorgeous ring onto my finger, it fits perfectly.

It couldn't have been more perfect if we tried. "Come on baby, let's get you home to celebrate." He quips with a smile. We hold hands to the car. When we get to Rick's house it's almost close to midnight. It feels like a day scripted off from a fairy tale. Rick had made arrangements with the help from a few friends, at his place to have lit candles and rose petals sprinkled everywhere. When we enter, it looks so beautiful. Rick holds my hand as we walk in.

Rick, holds my waist and twirls me with his hands, starting to dance slowly to the soft music playing in the background. He plants little kisses on my neck and looks into my eyes. "Abby are you happy?"

My tears are just falling.

"Don't cry baby."

Rick wipes my tears with his thumb.

"This is the best Rick. No one has ever come close to doing something like this for me. It's amazing." I say, beaming with happiness.

"Abby, I wanted you to remember this day because you're the one for me. You have my heart always."

We drink champagne and Rick holds me tight all night and we sleep like we were in heaven.

Waking up with rose buds all over my skin and a sexy man next to me is pure bliss. I can't believe I'm engaged. Rick was planning this for weeks and tried to keep it a secret. He didn't let me have a clue about it and I thought he was going to break up with me. I laugh off my silliness. I turn to look at him curled up at my side. He's asleep.

I wondered what my sons will say or how Tyler will react. Is he going to be angry or will he just accept what I and Rick have? I was really tired of being alone. And I couldn't be happier to spend the rest of my life with this man as my husband.

Rick wakes me up from my thoughts. "Good morning beautiful."

Shyly kissing his full lips, this guy could kiss. I loved his kisses.

"Are you happy, baby?" he asks with a wink.

"What do you think sweetie?" I say teasingly.

He starts tickling me and with that we were in bed all morning.

It's the Friday before Christmas Eve. Rick is leaving for a week with his brother. I accompany him to the airport. My heart was heavy because this was to be our first Christmas together after dating, our first as an engaged couple and we'd not get to be together. "I'm going to miss you Rick!" I cry into his arms.

"I know I'll miss you more if that's even possible."

"Oh baby." I say as he cradles me in his chest.

"Love you baby. Enjoy your time with your sons. Stay away from Tyler, Abby!"

"You know he's coming to my place for Christmas, right?"

"Well send him home after dinner."

With a grin he kisses me ever so gently, "I'll call you tonight baby, okay."

I go back to work. I have a full work day and as I drive back, I'm already missing Rick. I think I'm going crazy in love. When I reach the salon, I see Cynthia already getting started. She waves a 'hi' and then hops to me for a quick minute.

"Do you need more coffee, Abby? I know you are already missing Rick." She says trying to comfort me.

"I'm okay" I say looking at her, my heart far away with Rick.

I get on with my day trying not to dwell much on Rick's absence. I was feeling alone and empty without him around; Cynthia could sense that and suggested we go to Denny's for dinner after work, which I gladly take up. A bit of mindless chit-chat and delicious dinner wouldn't hurt. The day passes and we find ourselves devouring our plates of bacon and pancakes, and lots of coffee. We talk about everything under the sun and wrap up the night on a positive note before we head home.

Chapter 27

It's Christmas Eve! I wake up to a phone call. I pick up the phone, half asleep.

"Merry Christmas Abby" I hear Megan say excitedly. I smile, happy to hear her. I know they'd be spending Christmas Eve with Miles's Mom & Dad in the valley.

"Merry Christmas Megan."

"Did you just wake up? Are the boys' home yet? Wish them Merry Christmas from me, will you? I hope to see them soon when I visit with Kyle."

"They're not here yet but they should be home before lunch. I have a lot of cleaning and cooking to do, I'm glad you're the first one I talk to on Christmas Eve. Can't wait to see all of you."

"Love you Abby, you get started with your day, I'll call later."

"Love you Megan, Bye!" I say and hang up.

I drag myself from the bed and look outside. It's a chilly Saturday morning though the sun is peeking through the clouds. I've done all the prep work for Christmas dinner, so that's one thing less to worry about. But I do need to cook up something delicious for the boys and Ty who'd be here soon. Plus, some tidying up around the Christmas tree I've already set up. Perhaps a few more decorative touches here and there; I've done a classic red, green and yellow theme for the tree and the decorations around the house. The Christmas tree lights are little string lights in yellow & red; the gifts are all wrapped in shiny red wrappers tied off with golden bows and the ornaments are all a metallic red, golden and burgundy on the tree. I may have gone a little over the top this time but I was so in the mood for it. So, I created centerpieces of pine cones covered in gold glitter and arranged them with candles in red & gold on mirrored plates; even the furnishings have been changed to match the décor. Though I love my ivory and neutral color scheme, I've always enjoyed the little pops of color during the holidays. The cushions are a soft champagne gold; some with gold sequins and some with beige tone, dyed artificial fur. There are two Christmas wreaths; one on the front door and one near the fireplace decorated with gold ornaments and red ribbons to match the tree's theme.

I take a quick bite of my breakfast; a grilled sandwich with a creamy tuna filling, one of James's favorites from childhood. I fill up on some espresso in a hot flask and get on with cleaning and prepping lunch for the boys. I've settled on doing a full roast chicken with gravy, greens and crispy roast potatoes. The turkey has been soaking up the flavors of the brine and should be the centerpiece of the dinner tonight along with a classic sausage & bread stuffing and creamy mashed potatoes. It's going to be a feast. I picked up some Christmas fruitcake from the store but plan to make some pumpkin pie for dessert. When the boys were growing up, I'd cook up all the traditional goodies typically associated with Christmas, things which I could only dream of as a child.

After about two hours of going to & fro between tidying up the house and doing prep in the kitchen for lunch, I finally finish and settle down on my couch with a cup of hot coffee. I'm physically exhausted but I'm so excited to see the boys. James called to check in and let me know they'd make it on time for lunch.

The phone rings.

"Hello!"

"Hi baby."

It was Rick, gawd did I miss hearing his voice or what.

"Hi! Sweetie Gosh I miss you so much."

"Me too, what are you up to?" I ask.

"Not much, skiing with Tommy and you?"

"Just finished cleaning up and prepping for lunch, was taking a time out to sip on some coffee before I go to take a shower. My sons will be here in two hours."

"Okay baby, looks like you've got your hands full, I'll talk to you later tonight sweetie."

"Sure, will do. I miss you Rick."

"Miss you Abby, more than you ever know. Bye."

I hang up and savor the last few gulps of warm hot liquid coursing through the back of my throat– coffee is my life saver and it's an understatement. I thought about Rick, my heart filled with happiness. I hadn't told the boys or Ty about the engagement though I was hoping to break the news tonight after dinner. Am I expecting drama, oh yes! Ty & drama are synonymous with each other, so that comes with the territory. I know the boys would be supportive of Rick & my relationship; they've grown up seeing how Ty & my relationship deteriorated and they're all too aware of Ty's abusive behavior and drinking problem. Especially James; being the older one, he'd always run to me standing between me and Ty to protect me from being hurt. He was always the sensitive one as a young child and his aversion for drinking came from watching Ty's drunken rants as a child. Jason has always looked up to James as a role model and has stayed away from the bad stuff I thought he'd be vulnerable to, given that Jason has taken so much after Ty when it comes to his temperament. He was a little more ragged around the edges. He was more like a tough guy on the outside while being a softie inside; James on the other hand was more like an old school gentleman, he was quiet strength and the protector, typical of older siblings. Much like how Megan and Miles are; they were both the oldest in the family and Kyle has benefited from their wise & sober approach to life and parenting unlike me and Ty.

I take a quick shower and freshen up. I wear a deep burgundy turtle neck, knit sweater and black slacks. I wear a pair of gold drop earrings that had cushion cut rubies; it was one of my favorites and was perfect for the occasion. I couldn't bother with any other jewelry since I had this gorgeous diamond ring sparkle on my left hand. I don't wear makeup at home but my chapped lips were pleading for a good dollop of tinted lip balm, I pick a cherry flavored one to suit the mood. I slap on some moisturizer and tie my hair in a messy bun and get lunch ready, knowing the boys would be here anytime now.

Forty minutes later, I hear a car park in the driveway. I know it's them and hurry to open the door. They wave "Hi Mom" as they pick up their bags from the back. James rushes toward me and picks me up in a big hug, Jason joins in next. We're huddled in a hug for at least a minute. I pull away to take in the sight of them, I beam looking at my beautiful boys. How I've missed them. They pick up their stuff and walk in; I didn't see Ty waiting his turn. He walks up to me and stands real close, a little too close for comfort. I think of giving him a quick hug and finishing this silly formality when he leans in and kisses me, catching me off guard. He smirks as he pulls away and my face reddens in anger. It's not the first time I've been struck by his audacity to behave with me as if I was some commodity he could use at will. I follow him in, not wanting to make a scene; after all they've just gotten here. There's enough time over the weekend for Ty related dramas. I roll my eyes.

"Nice tree Mom." James says, standing next to the tree and looking at the ornaments.

There's a special box of ornaments that we've been keeping since the boys were small. They are ornaments that have been gifted or were personally inscribed with names or pictures of us.

Jason is looking at one that has a picture of both the boys when they were four and two & half. He's grinning ear to ear and playfully knocks James in the shoulder.

He looks at me with his toothy grin "I can't believe you still have this Mom."

"You know I'm the sentimental type. There's no way I'm throwing anything with your faces on it," I say with a laugh. They giggle and roll their eyes; they had to take something after their Mom too, it wouldn't be fair otherwise, I say to myself with a chuckle.

"Don't you think you've gone a bit overboard this time Mom?" James says, continuing to admire the décor around the house.

"Well, it's Christmas, stop being a Grinch now will ya? I say teasingly looking at James. He gives out a hearty laugh and puts his hands up to motion he's given up. Lunch done, we agree that a nap would be nice before we get on with preps for the big dinner. An hour of rest later, I find the boys and Ty indulge in a game of monopoly. I look at them and smile, it looks like a picture-perfect Christmas; my boys are together with their father and we're under the same roof. They've managed to repair their relationship over the course of several years and Ty has tried to be a good father, though I wish he came to his senses sooner. Right now, however, a stranger walking in wouldn't be able to guess Ty and I had separated or that there was an undercurrent of tension running between us like a dormant volcano. An explosion was imminent but I was trying to delay it for some other time. I wanted to soak in these precious moments of peace and quiet with my children and their father. It looked picture perfect but the reality was anything but rosy.

I start to walk to the kitchen when James looks up.

"I'm coming to help you in the kitchen Mom," he says and excuses himself from the game; Jason lets out a disgruntled sigh.

James enjoys home cooking like I do and doesn't eat much out; he helps me out with peeling the potatoes for the mash and is a complete natural around the kitchen. Jason is the more adventurous one, trying out exotic cuisines and sometimes even take-outs. He'd taken a liking to Mexican and Italian food; on his last visit home, he was all about Asian style pork and sticky rice. I remember a Korean style BBQ that was a particular favorite with him. He'd always encourage me to try out new dishes but appreciated the classics just as much, especially when I or Ty cooked it.

James notices the ring on my hand when we work in the kitchen and gives me a curious smile with raised eyebrows but doesn't question it. He knows I'd tell him when I'm ready and this was not supposed to be a tell-all in the kitchen kinda thing. It was a family announcement and I wanted to give it due respect and divulge more details later if anyone was interested to know more (which I doubted!). I planned to tell everyone about this after we were through dinner, so that there are no dramas to ruin the dinner we've slogged to make. This is where I especially appreciated James's sensitivity; he never rushed anything and gave people the space they needed, a firm believer of 'live and let live'. I was grateful for that.

It's evening and I get ready for dinner and slip into a black knit dress with little gold and pink flowers embroidered on it. I touch up on a bit of balm and leave my hair open, which is now in soft waves from staying up in a bun for most part of the day. I go downstairs and James being the ever-gracious gentleman helps me set up the table and cutlery. Ty and Jason are setting up gifts under the tree while we get dinner set out. I save my beloved silverware set for Christmas and place it carefully, happy that I got it polished just in time. It's sparkling under the lights and everything looks beautiful and magical, just the way it should be. I wish Rick was here, I wanted him to be part of this, however knowing that Ty is unaware of our engagement, I guess things were better like this for the time being. Just thinking of Ty's reaction was beginning to make me nervous. I push all thoughts of it aside and call out to Jason and Ty to come for dinner.

We finally gather around and take our seats, eager to dig in. James raises a toast to the evening and Ty, being the expert carver, dissects slices of the roast turkey and serves generous portions onto our plates. We laugh, talk and relish the food, catching up on everything that's happened. Jason helps me serve slices of spiced pumpkin pie onto dessert plates, need I say, that's his favorite after fresh blueberry cheesecake pie. And as expected, he goes in for a second serving much to the pleasure of my maternal pampering instinct and James's playful grin.

Ty has been well behaved for most part of dinner, smiling a lot more than usual at me; I'm not sure how to read that but I brush it off. Maybe he's just happy to here, enjoying Christmas with our sons.

So far so good, everything goes without a glitch. James helps me take back the dishes to the kitchen and Ty helps with the dishes. It's when I'm washing the dishes that Ty suddenly grabs my left hand covered in soap, with wide eyes that look more shocked than surprised.

Oops, the cat is out the bag I guess. I look up at him, my stomach doing a somersault.

"What the hell Abby! What's up with this ring? What the fuck is this Abby?!!" he thunders.

"This is none of your business Ty, so leave me alone. But if you must know Ty, Rick asked me to marry him."

"Over my dead body!"

He's furious; his clenched jaws and palms rolled into a tight fist gives away his seething anger. Talk about a volcanic explosion.

Oddly enough, my heart aches for him. I know he's hurting.

He gets very close to my ear, close enough for me to smell his musky cologne and minty breath.

"You'll never be his because you're mine Abby. That dude is never going to get his hands on you."

I roll my eyes at Ty; he's unaware of how many times over Rick has had me and I've relished it every time.

I try to stay composed, but not calm because I'm baffled with Ty's reaction.

"What's wrong with you Ty? Our ship has sailed a long time ago and not only did it sail, it sunk like the Titanic. How dare you be so selfish? All I ever wanted was to love and be loved, something you obviously couldn't do."

I didn't see this coming but tears were rolling down my cheeks. James walks in to the kitchen, hearing the commotion, unable to make out what's going on.

Ty continues, ignoring James's presence.

"Abby, we need to talk when the boys go back to my place."

"We are talking." I say, in frustration.

"No, we're not!" Ty replies, feeling helpless.

"I want you to leave Ty, right now."

"This isn't over Abby." Ty says and then turns to walk away.

He pushes James aside on the way out of the kitchen. Jason joins his brother waiting for me outside the kitchen, unsure of what just happened.

I tell them the news I'd been waiting to tell them; I knew Ty's reaction would cause drama but didn't see it play out like this. As expected, the boys were happy for me but I see Jason's face etched with worry and may be sympathy for Ty?

He's lived with his Dad the most and if he felt that way, I understood that. I couldn't take offense to that. James knew I was happy, he had sensed it when we worked in the kitchen while getting dinner ready. But right now, his face mirrored his younger brother's concern for their father.

With Ty and the drama over, there's a pall of silence & gloom that comes over the house.

I try to change the atmosphere and the awkward silence that's now radiating between the three of us; I decide to watch a movie with the boys, hoping it'd distract them from what happened. We sit on the couch, with blank faces staring into the television. I was physically present but my mind was thinking about Ty. I could see the boys weren't enjoying this either. James gets up midway through the movie and tells me that he feels they should be at Ty's place.

I suddenly feel like the villain of the drama. The boys leave; they give me reassuring hugs that they wanted whatever was best for me and didn't hold anything against me. My heart is overwhelmed with sadness. This is not how I imagined this evening end.

 I go to bed, feeling emotionally and physically drained. I toss and turn in bed, unable to sleep. I cry and let out a sigh, wondering if things had to always be this way for me. As promised Rick calls me sometime around ten, but I don't pick up. I'm unsure of what I'm supposed to tell him or if I should even tell him of Ty's reaction. It was unsettling. I didn't realize when I fell asleep.

The boys would wake me up with shouts of 'Merry Christmas' on Christmas morning because they'd be eager to open their gifts. It hadn't changed even after they'd grown up and James would even go and make hot chocolate for all of us. Not this time; the house feels dead without their familiar laughter. The presents are under the tree and there's no one here to open them or drag me out of bed. I'm still in bed, half awake and its past nine am. The phone's been ringing off the hook and I couldn't be bothered to pick up. I felt like I was having a hangover, I had a throbbing headache. The boys had planned to visit Ty's parents after the weekend here but they would've left early after last night's argument.

I'm feeling low and beat. I drag myself out of bed and step into the shower, letting the warm water soothe my tired body and mind. I step out the shower and slip into some casual clothes. I was in no mood to even look at myself in the mirror or make myself presentable. Who was I supposed to look pretty for? The walls? I was going from feeling low to being plain annoyed.

I needed coffee, lots of it. I fix myself a lousy breakfast of toast and eggs. If the boys were around, they'd be asking for left over dishes- pancakes made from mashed potatoes and turkey sandwiches from the turkey roast, smothered in mayonnaise. I'm feeling like crap and there was nothing that could lift my mood right now.

I pour myself my third cup of coffee and go over all that's happened, reasoning it out in my head. Ty and I were good parents, we tried to do our best and respect the friendship we had forged over the time after our separation.

At the time I had separated from Ty, it felt like an easy decision because things were literally heading nowhere. I felt lonely in my relationship with him because he seemed like he was never there; his drinking and subsequent abusive tirades was a point of no return for me. I had enough of it and when I let him know that I was leaving him, he didn't protest it.

I moved on. I had dreams and wanted to live my life on my terms, not someone else's. Being with Ty had snuffed out most of my ambitions; the freedom I had after our separation to pursue the things and interests that mattered to me, was emancipating. I thought I'd never find love again after Ty; he was the only man I had truly loved. Sure, I was young and naïve, with a good measure of rebel thrown in. Ma had warned me about Ty even then and I refused. The refusal to heed her warning had turned into a deep regret that I endured for a good part of my life until I made the decision that things couldn't continue the way it did.

Until I met Rick again, I was resigned to my boring single life. Though I was working hard at the salon, life was slowly becoming meaningless. The boys had their own lives to live and it would've been selfish of me to expect any one of them hanging around me, to stay close to me. This was their time to explore and make their place in the world.

Meeting Rick again felt like fate had given us another chance. I never felt what it was to be truly loved and cherished; Rick had taught me that and his love healed the broken parts of me that I thought were beyond repair. He made me feel alive again and was everything I had ever hoped a man to be. I'd be a fool to say 'no' to a future with him. But I saw pain in Ty's eyes when he found out about Rick and me. I wasn't willing to admit it to myself but I remembered Cynthia's ominous comment. She had said that I couldn't see Ty's love and that she hoped I'd never be in a position to pick between Rick & Ty. Rick and Ty were as different as chalk and cheese, like the earth and sky.

Rick was sweet, he always was even as a kid; it was what made him attractive to so many girls in school and made Betty Cox insanely possessive. He was like honey that'd attract bees by the dozen. I'm not one bit surprised that Rick turned out to be the gentleman and lover he is today.

Ty was the complete opposite. He thought he could get away with every mistake he made because of his charm and good looks; he didn't care then, he didn't care now. He cheated on me when we lived together barely three months into our relationship. He started out being the bad boy and remained a bad boy even ten years into our marriage. Only when the boys had grown and I had separated did he start to mend his ways or even try. A little too late I'd say because the damage was done. Yes, I ached for him at times, wishing he'd started mending his ways earlier, wondering why he didn't cherish me or what I did for him and the family when he had the chance to.

My mind goes back and forth between Rick and Ty and finally settles on the pain I'd seen in Ty's eyes yesterday.

I need to shake this off. I change into joggers, a tee and a sweater and head out for a walk. Perhaps the fresh air outside might bring some clarity and peace. I always enjoyed spending time in nature, it was therapeutic.

As I walk a little from my house, I think to myself; I want my happiness to be a win-win for everyone, where all involved are good with the decisions I make and the final outcome that comes as a result. When I left Ty, he didn't care and he didn't stop me from leaving. He'd given up without even trying. The boys knew I deserved better and they made peace with that far more quickly than I had imagined. That decision was a win. Ty and I went on to focus on our dreams and accomplish what we had set out to do. And with that, a chapter of my life was behind me. I had moved on and found happiness with Rick; so why is Ty being a complete ass when he can just be okay with it and let it be. Doesn't he want to see me happy?

Suddenly the sound of a Harley Davidson motorbike interrupts my thoughts. I don't look to turn back and continue walking, hoping against hope it's not who I think it is.

Sure enough, I hear my name loud and clear.

"Abby, wait up."

I turn around, roll my eyes and glare at him.

"Why me? Why? And why now?!! What do you want Ty? Are you stalking me now?" I say flustered.

"Get on babe."

"No thank you! I want to be alone."

"Get on the bike."

"We need to talk Abby! Just hear me out, then I'll leave you alone okay?"

I get on his bike reluctantly, preparing myself mentally for another showdown. I want this over with. We go to my townhouse. I try not to stare at Tyler because he looks surprisingly beautiful; I've never seen him this healthy looking in a long time. He's wearing the black sweater I gifted him for Christmas a week earlier because I didn't want it to become awkward when the kids are around. A white tee is peeking through the sweater collar. His hair is a mess, it always is. And those green eyes are as beautiful as they were the first time I saw him. We reach home. He takes the sweater off. His muscles & tattoos are showing through; he clears his throat to speak but no words come out. I catch myself biting my bottom lip and turn away walking to the kitchen. "I'll make some coffee."

"Make us some leftovers."

After we enjoy some turkey sandwiches and packing a few extra for the boys, we seem to have reached some semblance of calm. It's when I'm downing my second cup of coffee that I look up at him again to see him staring at me. I get nervous but roll my eyes. "Well! Tyler are you going to talk or are we having a staring contest?"

"This is tough for me Abby."

"OMG! Spit it out or leave Ty."

I move to sit on the couch from the dining table, waiting for Tyler to say whatever he has to say. Then he starts to speak. I could see he is struggling for words. I try to stay calm, unsure of what's going to come out.

"Abby please just let me say everything then you could say whatever you want to say okay? Abby, I've been going for AA meetings the last three years. I don't drink anymore or go out; there's no woman in my life. When you left, I missed you so much; I cried so much for you, and I'm so sorry that I hurt you. There are no excuses for the way I treated you. I was just scared to love you Abby, because I knew you deserved better than me. I knew that since I first laid my eyes on you, that you were precious in every way; that I wasn't a man then who was worthy of you."

It hurt hearing him say these things, things I've never known or could've remotely guessed he was feeling. I was breaking down in front of him, unable to stop my tears from rolling down. He doesn't stop talking though, and then the next few words he speaks, surprises me, I wasn't prepared for this…

"I realized how I truly loved you, I can't live without you Abby! Believe me, I tried, but I'm a selfish man when it comes to you."

I shake my head in disbelief; I cannot believe what I'm hearing. All those emotions were now turning into a rising wave of anger.

"All I want is two days with you."

I roll my eyes, this cannot be happening.

"You don't have to tell your boyfriend and if you still feel the same for him and want to marry him, I'll walk away, promise. Abby say something?"

All I could come up with is, "Why now Tyler? Did you get insecure because you saw me getting on with life and being with someone else? Is that it?"

"I had to clean up my life so I could show you every day how special you really are. I didn't know you were going to fall for that prick."

"DON'T YOU DARE CALL HIM THAT! Rick showed me how I am supposed to be treated; he treated me like a queen, like a woman, not like some piece of shit Tyler."

"You love me still Abby! I can see it in your beautiful hazel eyes babe."

"Yeah! Sure, you do!" I look at him with an odd mix of anger and sadness. Emotions are running high.

Pacing back and forth, I find myself sobbing. My thoughts are everywhere.

"Why are you doing this Ty, why?" I cry out.

Then he starts to cry and wraps his big arms around me; all we do is hold each other. It was like years of bottled up anger and emotions had come off.

He pulls away from me and looks into my eyes.

"Abby, I'll call you later in the evening. Give us two days, that's all I ask. I promise you won't regret it."

I felt relieved letting out all the pent-up emotions of so many years. It felt like something had been set free. Ty makes plans to take me to Big Bear Lake for two days. He tells me to get ready by five am the next morning.

Rick had called me shortly after Ty had left. He sounded pissed with good reason that I hadn't picked up his calls the previous day and this morning. I tried to pacify him saying that I'd gotten busy with the boys. There was no way to tell him that I'm going to be with Ty for two days and needed to make an excuse. So after we talk a bit, I tell him that I plan to take the boys to Megan's place for two days and I'll be back later in the week. He thought that was a good idea. I absolutely hated lying to Rick or anyone for that matter, and I had no idea if what I was doing was right or not.

The heart is a strange thing. There was no reason logically speaking to have agreed to Ty's request when he didn't bother listening to me even once; it was nonsensical that I should extend to him the kindness that I never received from him despite being his partner and the mother to his children. But then my foolish heart wanted to give him a chance, to see if there was anything at all left between Ty and me.

Did it make sense, no. Did it feel right, yes; because all he asked me was for two days. 48

hrs, that's it.... I've lived with him for longer than that.

This will be the last chance we'll ever have to be together. Ty had rented a gray Honda for comfort and it was snowing. I sat throughout the drive, looking outside, contemplating what this trip would bring me. I loved Big Bear, having been there once before for a camping trip when the boys were very young. Ty tells me he's rented his friend's cabin. We get there close to noontime.

The cabin has a great view of the lake and looks like a winter wonderland right now. It's a beautiful sight. The interior of the cabin is simple, but luxurious and cozy; the furnishings were in super soft velvet and quality leather, finished in dark earthy colors with a rustic design and feel.

We settle down in the living room. Ty lights up the fireplace and I get us some coffee from the espresso machine.

Ty speaks first. "Abby, I just want to ask you not to think about him just for two days. Please, this is my chance to fight for you."

I curl up my toes hearing this; it isn't as simple as he's making it out to be. I look out at the vast expanse of the frozen lake in pensive silence.

"Stop thinking about it, just relax babe."

I give him a smile, sensing sincerity in his voice. My heart ached with sadness because of the dilemma I was in. Rick's love healed me slowly in ways I hadn't expected, but Ty was the one who broke me. Did the one who broke me have the power in his love to heal me once and for all? This probably will be the only time we'll be together and I don't have an answer to all my questions.

"Why is there sadness on your face Abby?"

"I'm fine." I say as I struggle with all the thoughts whirling in my head. There was no peace.

He lifts my palm and gently kisses it. His eyes are full of pain. I bite my lower lip and my body starts to quiver in cold; tears I've tried to hold back are slipping down my cheeks. The sky outside turns grey, mirroring the storm inside me; my body felt like it had fever, but my heart felt like a hundred-pound block of ice sat on it. Whoever I end up choosing, I'd have to put a stone on my heart and say 'no' to one. This was tearing me apart in ways I hadn't anticipated.

Ty, sensed my discomfort and looked into my eyes; he didn't say anything but held me in an embrace. I could feel the warmth of his body envelope me like a blanket on a cold day; my forehead suddenly feels wet and a drop of water rolls down my head. I look up and see Ty in tears. We look into each other's eyes, mourning the time we've been apart, mourning the times we could have got it right but didn't, mourning the chances we didn't take to make this work. Ty holds my face with both his hands and begins to kiss every inch of my face; his words were being conveyed in the affection and love he was showering on me in this very moment. I felt everything he felt–his pain had become my pain, and mine his.

I pull away, suddenly aware of what we were doing. I wasn't ready for this. I needed time. I caress his face gently and tell him.

"It's been a long drive Ty, I need to lay down a bit. It's just been overwhelming."

"I understand Abby, I'll take a nap out here. Why don't you go inside and get some rest."

I finish my cup of coffee and lay, looking towards the scenery outside. I know how this will play out. We all are going to get hurt and for once I don't want to think about the mess of my life. I went without having no man in my life for a while now I have to choose between two. Who would have seen that coming? Not me, that's for sure. Somewhere in between these musings to myself, I fall asleep.

I don't know how long I've been asleep, but when I finally wake up, I see the sky outside gone from grey to black and see stars twinkling in the distance. I turn on the other side and part of me jumps when I see Ty watching me from a chair in the corner of the room.

I manage to sit up, still groggy from sleep. "How long have I been asleep?"

"Six hours." Ty says.

I can sense sadness in his eyes.

"OMG! Sorry." I hear myself say. Six hours, was I a dead log?!

"It's okay Abby! I made dinner for us." He says with a faint smile.

"You made dinner. Wow!" I say, pleasantly surprised. I knew he could cook, but he's never cooked for me. This would be a first.

"Abby, I do know how to cook." He says with a mischievous smile.

"Come, join me."

"I'll be right out. Give me a few minutes," as I see him out the room.

I'm in dire need of a long hot soak but this was no time for it. I take a quick shower and dress into a deep dusty pink woolen knit dress and a black slack underneath. I leave my hair open and wear no makeup; I was in no mood for dress up. I walk to the living room and see candles lit everywhere. I can smell the cinnamon and sugar melt over an apple pie being baked. Ty has got the rest of the dinner on the table. He's made chicken pot pie, some green salad and hot chocolate. "Just thought you'd like some comfort food."

I nod in acknowledgement.

"All of this looks amazing Ty." I say, looking over the spread.

"Wait till you taste it." He says with delight.

"Thank you, Tyler."

"I would do anything for you Abby, please have some before it gets cold."

I nod and help myself to generous portions of the Chicken pot pie. It's pretty delicious. We finish eating and I help him clean up. He then serves me apple pie with lots of whipped cream, topped with cherries.

"Wow! That looks good." I say, looking at my dessert with child-like eyes.

"Only for you babe." He says with smug satisfaction.

Tyler just watches me eat and boy it's delicious Ty doesn't touch his dessert.

"Let's go watch TV." He suggests motioning to the couch.

"Okay." I say, nodding in acknowledgement.

We sit on one of the couches. He brings his dessert with him. He doesn't switch on the TV; instead he turns to face me. I could see desire in his slanted green eyes as it glistens in the light of the crackling fireplace. We stare at each other; I'm feeling suddenly nervous.

He suddenly digs his hand into the whipped cream part of his dessert and spreads it on my lips; he licks it with his tongue hungrily and gently kisses me. I'm surprised by his sudden passion and tenderness. Then he starts to spread more cream on my neck and lavishes kisses on my face, making his way down my neck to lick off the cream. That's all it took. I don't know what had come over me; whether it was the cozy, lonely cabin, or his kisses or the passion I'm feeling burst through his pores. Our hands were all over each other's bodies; we just couldn't stop, it was like we had walked thirty years in a barren desert and had found an oasis in each other. We were drinking deep of each other's love. It was intense, unlike anything I'd felt with Rick. I felt safe with Rick but with Ty, I felt like this is where I belonged, it felt like home. It felt right. Every touch, every breath we inhaled off from each other's mouth, every kiss our lips fought to make felt right.

Ty lifts me up from the couch in his strong arms and takes me to the bedroom and places me gently on the bed. He continues to kiss my face, my hands, my ears and whispered "I want you so badly Abby. Let me show you how much I love you."

What he said was music to my ears and how he made me feel, was beyond words. This is all I ever wanted all my life, for him to love me. I was home. And for the first time in years, I finally felt peace in my heart; there were no nagging doubts, no fears, and no questions that needed answering. I found what I was looking for in a place I hadn't expected. We love each other until we could no more. He nestles me in his arms and my head rests on his chest, feeling his heart beat. We fall asleep, holding on to each other for the rest of the night.

The next morning, I wake up to see Ty making breakfast for us. He's got a wide grin on his face and he holds out his hand to me and pulls me close. He kisses my nose and then my lips and says "Good morning Abby".

I smile back, "Morning Ty."

I settle into a recliner chair, taking in the view of the lake and start to think about Rick.

What was I going to tell him? That I cheated on him with my ex despite being engaged to him?

I was beginning to feel guilty; this wasn't going to end well. The reality is that I love both of them. Telling me to choose between them is the toughest thing I have done yet; it feels horrible and I cannot see Rick getting hurt just as much as I cannot see Ty getting hurt.

I start tearing up, oblivious to Ty's presence. He's staring at me, well knowing what was going through my mind. "What did I tell you Abby? Stop thinking, this is my time to show you how much I love you, how much you mean to me. Abby will you not even give me a chance?" He says with pleading eyes.

He pulls a strand of hair and tucks it behind my ear and wipes my tears away with his fingers.

"You've always been mine Abby! I know you never stopped loving me."

"I am engaged Ty. You think he'll take this well? He was there for me when you weren't Ty!"

"Stop feeling guilty Abby! This isn't helping."

"I can't help it. I'm going to end up hurting him even though I don't want to. I don't want to see anyone get hurt because of me. Not you. Not him. Nobody. This is hard for me Ty."

Tyler looks hurt. He put his hands through my hair and pulls me to him. His kisses are rough and his passion all consuming. He makes love to me like never before; I'm amazed that the intensity of our emotions doesn't seem to decrease, but only increase, like we're feeding off each other's love. Rick is at the back of my mind, pricking me like a thorn. Tyler and I have the best two days of our life: we shop, have dinner, hold hands and walk in the snow, even throw snowballs at each other like small kids. I was falling in love with him all over again.

Chapter 28

It's crystal clear how guilty I feel as we head back. I sit in the car with the same pensive silence I had when we were heading to Big Bear, but this time was for a completely different reason. The skies were dark and grey; it was pouring cats and dogs and the drive was painfully slow. The weather mirrored the mood between Ty and me. I didn't want to say anything and I sensed Ty struggling to speak; he was never good with words. Reality was knocking us down hard.

We stop midway at the side of the road because of poor visibility. We're sitting in the car; the sound of the windscreen wiper, the thunder and raindrops are the only sounds we hear.

Tyler holds my hand as he speaks first.

"Don't let him touch you Abby."

"Are you for real Ty?" I ask, annoyed.

"Just until you decide who you want."

"You have a nerve making demands on me Ty. You know you're being selfish like you always have been. All you care about is yourself."

"You have to choose Abby, and hoping to God you chose me baby. I promise you won't have any regrets."

"This is not easy for me and you damn well know this. I hate to hurt someone I really care about."

"I'm giving you a week Abby."

"Don't tell me what to do!" I say furiously as tears begin to fall.

"My heart is aching and pained beyond words can tell. Can't you see that? I really don't wish this on anyone, not even my enemy, so just stop ordering me around. You won't call the shots this time around Ty. I'll decide when I'm good and ready." I say looking away from Ty, facing forward.

"Old habits don't change. You're feisty as hell and I'm loving it."

"I guess not."

The rain finally stops and we drive back. I just wanted to be away from Ty physically and put some space between us; I'm unable to think straight. I cannot imagine how hurt Rick is going to be when he hears of all that has happened. One week he's not with me and I couldn't control myself; that's what he's going to think when it really isn't that way. I have no excuses; I feel the guilt in full force. When I get home, nothing feels the same.

I cannot deny that Rick made me feel wanted, like I was worth fighting for. He treated me like a queen, not with mere words, but with actions and he was ready to commit to a future together and no doubt he'd be a great dad to James & Jason.

Now I've broken his heart when all he did was try to put my broken self together, patiently and with great love and tenderness. I was with Ty for a good part of my life and he's never been as considerate and kind as he was in the last 48 hours with me. But I've known Rick since I was a kid, he was like the rock of Gibraltar; he was still the sweet boy I had first met when we were just six. I've dated him as an adult three decades later and he's proved to be a reliable friend, a sweet lover and is an overall nice guy. It's Rick's consistency versus Ty's willingness to change, this wasn't even comparable. I had felt home with Ty in the last two days in a way like never before; there was something. The peace I felt with him meant what he was showing and saying was true. Oh I don't know!

This feels terrible and I'm sick to my stomach.

Rick is coming home tomorrow; he thinks I was with Megan and the boys when I was with Ty. How is he going to take this? Despite having someone like Betty for a wife, he didn't cheat once when he was married to her. He was decent in every way a guy could be or should be something that set him apart from Ty. Anyone who's known me personally knows that I'm not the cheating type because if I was, it'd clearly be double standards and the sheer hypocrisy of it grosses me out. I know the news of me being with Ty will be devastating for him; if he only knew the hell I'm walking through right now. Will he give me a chance to explain myself? Will he walk out on me? Will I lose his friendship?

This is pure torture. I pace back and forth across my living room, in a vain attempt to calm my nerves; I head out for a jog because those usually restore some semblance of sanity. When I get back from a five-mile jog, my body is exhausted. But my mind and heart feel like a pail of burning coals have been heaped on them: the punishment of sin or the guilt of wrong doing.

I feel a migraine coming on and drag myself to bed, too tired to even stand up. Physically, I could be in bed all day but mentally, I was restless like the waves of the ocean crashing against the shore. I've to wake up early to pick Rick up from the airport. I set an alarm and sleep off oblivious to when day turned to night and night to morning.

I've been asleep a good 13 hours when the alarm rings. It's 6 am and the sun is beginning to rise; the sky looks clear, bathed in the hues of dawn. I take a shower and quickly dress. I need to be at the airport by 7.30am. My face is puffy from sleep and crying; thankfully the headache is gone.

I'm waiting at the airport, coffee in hand. Rick's flight is delayed by 30 minutes so I decide to pick up a sandwich for breakfast. I'm nervous, anxious and fidgety; Rick will know something is wrong right away when he sees me. He's always been good at reading me even though I try to hide my emotions. His flight has arrived according to the announcement so I head back to the waiting area in front of the arrivals section. And sure enough I see Rick, beaming his gorgeous smile and waving at me. He runs towards me and wraps me in a big hug. He lavishes kisses on me and inside my heart is breaking with heaviness. We get into the car and I drive, staring ahead trying not to show how miserable I'm feeling.

"I missed you so much Abby! So how's your sister? Did you guys have fun?"

"She's fine Rick, did you get any rest?"

"You look kinda tired Abby, are you okay?" he asks, caressing my head.

"Rick I'm fine. When we go home, we need to talk about something."

"Could we talk later? Because all I want to do is make love to my soon to be wife." He says with a wide grin.

OMG! This is going to be harder than I thought.

I love him so much and right now I'm feeling sick with guilt. And it's eating me alive.

"Abby you are so beautiful." He says, trying to make me feel better. He knows something is up but he's waiting for me to do the talking.

I park the car in front of his house. Once inside, I urge him to freshen up and make some much needed coffee. For what I'm about to do, I might need that extra kick from caffeine because I'm not sure if I have it in me to do this. There's no easy way to do this but tell the truth that I betrayed him.

Rick walks into the kitchen, wet hair and all; he's purposefully not worn his shirt. Instead he's slipped into a comfy pair of sweatpants and slippers. He looks gorgeous and has a beautiful grin on his face. I stare at him in both admiration and in horror of what I'm about to do.

"Baby you like what you see?" He grins, taking a deep breath.

"What's wrong Abby, tell me? You could tell me anything, you know that, right? Did something happen when I was gone?" he asks, his face creasing with worry.

I'm the one struggling for words now, how the tables turn.

"What is it Abby?" he asks and I can sense impatience in him.

"I slept with Tyler." I blurt out. There, it's out. But I haven't breathed a sigh of relief; because I'm looking at Rick now who's standing in a state of shock and pain. I couldn't even go and hug him to console him because I'm the one responsible for his pain this time.

I start to cry, feeling the full burden and guilt of what I did.

"I'm sorry Rick, it just happened."

His expression is one of disappointment and hurt.

"What do you mean, it just happened!"

"Don't ask me because I'm confused." I say, sobbing.

More tears escape. My lips tremble. He stares at me with disbelief at first, then he yells at me.

"Why? Abby why? Did he force you to sleep with him? Or you went willing? Answer me Abby!"

I'm shaking and sobbing inconsolably with my head hung in shame. I answer in a whisper "I went willing."

"Why would you shatter my heart for a man that broke yours in so many pieces Abby? He didn't even want you until I came in to the picture. Mark my words Abby; he will ruin your heart. You're like a possession for him that he's unwilling to give anyone, it isn't about love for him, it's about control. Are you delusional enough to believe a guy who has cheated on you and treated you like you weren't even a priority in his life? Is that what you want? Because you deserve better and you damn well know that! With this, Rick starts to sob. I've never seen him cry.

"I still love you Abby! Just make my broken heart go away. Please, don't go back to him. He will mess with your heart then cheat as soon as he has a hold on you. He'll do the same thing over and over again and get away with it; this time you won't be able to pick up the broken pieces of your broken heart."

Rick was right: how I could even trust Tyler? What was the basis of it, the last 48 hours?

"Rick, I'm going home."

He doesn't answer, and I don't blame him. I'm so embarrassed and overwhelmed. I whisper sorry and walk to the door with tears running down my cheeks.

Rick immediately takes a hold of my shoulder and presses his lips roughly on my neck.

"What we have isn't over Abby! You have to choose who you want. I hate what happened; but you're worth the fight. I'll talk to you tomorrow Abby. Take your time, think of the pros and cons."

With Rick's words echoing in my ears, I walk to my car and get in. I drive home, thinking about what he said. I feel empty and miserable; I'd do anything to escape this. Once I get home, I open a bottle of wine and get drunk to stop these thoughts from consuming my existence. I end up sleeping on the couch and wake up when I feel the warmth of the sun caressing my face. It was morning. Barely have I got up from the couch that I hear a loud knock on the door.

I take a step forward and feel the full effect of my hangover; I feel nauseas and want to vomit so I run instead to the bathroom. The knocking on the door has stopped and I drag myself to the living room and collapse into the couch again. I groan in pain because my head is aching like I've been hit with a rock.

I fall asleep again. A few hours later, I feel someone's hand caressing my cheek and moving my hair out of my face.

I'm struggling to open my eyes, but really I'd rather not because where I was in life, sleeping through this phase seemed like a better idea than confronting reality.

"Abby wake up!" I hear a familiar voice whisper.

It's Rick. My tears start flowing again. He wipes them away but I can't stop crying. "Abby!" he calls again tenderly.

"What are you doing here?" I ask, embarrassed and ashamed of facing Rick again.

"Cynthia came to your place and you didn't answer, so she called me to check. I hurried to see if you were doing alright?"

"Rick, I don't like myself right now!"

I say with my lips quivering.

"Abby I'm worried about you." He says, holding my hands.

"I'll be okay." I assure him.

"Rick don't worry." I say touching his face.

Rick is hurt and he's worried about me?

"You're supposed to hate me Rick."

"I will never hate you baby."

He starts to caress my face.

"I love you so much baby."

He takes his gray suit coat off. Taking his black silk tie off him, he throws it on the chair.

I must look like hell: sobbing all night, my breath smells like vomit. And Rick wants to make love to me.

Just when he's walking toward me, I see Tyler walk in with angry fists.

"DON'T TOUCH HER SHE'S MINE!!" he thunders.

Rick Hits Tyler in the jaw. "Fuck you, she's not yours."

Getting up as fast as I could from my couch, I yell, "Stop it! Stop it!"

Well, they didn't listen. Beating each other, Tyler pushes Rick. They are beating one another. I tried to break it up. They had blood all over their faces. I get between them and end up getting punched right in my eyes. I take a fall, knocked out of my senses.

I lay on the bed, unaware of how I got there; I hear voices in the background.

"Okay baby."

"Don't call her that!"

"Get out Tyler, let her decide. Until then, get the fuck out of here, so I could take care of her."

I wake up, feeling sufficiently energetic enough to say "PLEASE both get out! Get out!"

I say it more harshly than I intended, but I'm hurt and confused.

"I want you both out! Like right now." I shout.

They both stare at me with shock.

"Get out now! Right now!"

They both walk out and leave me alone. I take a shower and slip into sweats and a tee. My eye is swollen from the hit I took and I'm sitting here on my couch, dabbing a warm compress to reduce the swelling. I make myself some coffee and take my cup to the living room when I hear a knock on the door. Not again, I say, rolling my eyes. I open the door to see Cynthia.

" Hey, heard you were fighting with two handsome dudes."

"Yeah right." I say, letting her come in.

Cynthia smirks. "I brought some food: hamburgers onion rings, some cheese fries & milkshakes!"

I lift my eyebrows in surprise.

"So are you hungry?" she asks with a smile.

I nod.

"Well! I was so worried about you Abby! What's going on?"

"Let's eat first, and then talk." I say, getting plates from the kitchen.

"Sounds good to me. And you are going to tell me about that bruised eye."

"Just eat Cynthia, stop talking for a bit, so I could eat!"

"Abby you love both men; it's understandable, you have history with them, I mean, I don't blame you. Those guys are gorgeous and they both are fighting for you, because they truly love you. So the big question is who would win your heart? You know you have to choose Abby"

"I know! Don't know how to do this without hurting one of them or both."

I have to go to the salon today; I have four VIP client appointments which need to be taken care of. I take a shower and stare at myself in the mirror; there's a black eye with bruises that shows no signs of improvement. I expertly put a thick layer of concealer to hide the area as best as I can and follow it up with foundation and powder. It doesn't look as bad but it still does look punched in. I dab on some lipstick and forego the usual eye makeup I do.

I wear a pair of faded dark denims, a powder blue sweater, earrings and sunglasses; I grab my purse and head out of the house, feeling a little put together. I drive to the salon, trying to blank out everything.

I'm not feeling up for work at the salon, but I was running a business that needs tending like a young sapling. I've painstakingly put in the work to nurture it and I wasn't going to ruin it now.

I get to work without wasting much time and my first client is only sixty years old. Her name is Gina. I smile as I style her hair, hearing her out as she bemoans over her boyfriend. I resist the urge to roll my eyes but focus on her hair.

"Abby my boyfriend wants to live together and not get married." She says as she stares at me in the mirror.

I look up, and she continues.

"Been with this man for ten years and he still doesn't want to marry me."

"I don't know what to say Gina, maybe he's not the marrying type." I say, putting the last finishing touches on her hair.

"Don't know either honey, but my hair looks great!" she says, satisfied with my work.

"You're beautiful Gina." I reply, giving her a tired smile.

I get a kick out of seeing happy customers because I want every woman to walk out of here feeling beautiful and gorgeous.

I'm in the office going over the money that needs to be deposited in the bank tomorrow.

It's almost closing time and everyone has left.

"Hey! Could I come in?" Rick says, as he peeks in through the office door.

"Yes!" I say, pleasantly surprised seeing him.

I see a dozen red roses in his hand.

"These are for you." He says handing them out to me.

"Thanks Rick, they're lovely." I say with a smile. I was glad to see him.

"I also wanted to know if you are okay. Wow! You got a black eye." He says, looking at my now weary eyes; that make up didn't do its job well.

"Yes I do." I say with a grimace.

"Sorry Abby, didn't want things to get that bad." He says apologetically.

"Well Rick, it did. And it's not your fault; you're not to blame."

"Let's have some dinner Abby?"

"Just dinner okay? I am kind of hungry." I respond, happy to take up the offer given that I haven't eaten anything since morning.

We go to one of his favorite restaurants, a place known to have the work crowd; mostly people with full time jobs working in corporate and having businesses. People are a lot more formally dressed around here.

The place lives up to its hype, the food is amazing.

I finish the last bits of my dessert, a slice of carrot cake with cream cheese frosting.

Rick pays the bill and walks me to the car.

"Thanks Rick for the roses and dinner, it was wonderful." I say, grateful for the time I had with him.

"It's my pleasure Abby. Talk to you tomorrow?"

He leans in and kisses my cheek.

I get in the car, exhaustion beginning to creep in. I can't wait to get back home and sleep off.

I haven't done my laundry in days, so I sort them out and put them in the machine when I hear my phone ring.

I see it's Ty. I let out a sigh. They talk about giving me time to think and then do not spare a minute to leave me in peace.

"Hello!" I say, not sounding very enthusiastic.

"Hi babe." Ty says.

"What do you need Tyler? Because I'm busy."

"You weren't busy for that dude going to dinner."

"He has a name Ty." I say, mildly frustrated when I realize, that he's probably stalking me now.

"Are you following me?" I ask out loud.

"Yes I am. I take care of what's mine." He responds with a smugness in his voice.

"Please Tyler, can I have one day of peace without drama!" I shout. I'm frustrated and want to kick my hands and feet in the air. He's got his grip on me in a way that's making me feel suffocated.

"I'm sorry Abby, believe me I'm sorry for everything, I won't bother you again, but by the end of this week, I want an answer." He says as if hearing this somehow pacifies me.

And he had the nerve to hang up on me before I could say another word. What the….?! Who does he think he is?

I hate him right now doing this. He's just being the same selfish man I knew him to be and I had no idea why I was playing into this.

I feel helpless as mind races from Rick to Ty back and forth. It isn't helpful because I know at the end of it, my decision will hurt all three or one, but someone's going to have to live with that hurt forever. I wince with pain at the thought of the ordeal that lies ahead of me, choosing between them is the worst possible thing I could've been asked to do.

The next five days of the week were a blur. I woke up 5 am every day and went for a run, just to clear my head. It rained for two days toward the end of the week and I still ran, in the hope that the rain would cleanse me of the guilt I was trapped in.

The clarity I was hoping for finally came. I had made my choice. It didn't quite make any logical sense given that the heart is sometimes known to make the most irrational choices; like it has a mind of its own but I couldn't escape its truth. I did love Ty more than Rick. He was the father to my two beautiful boys and all my life I had pined for his love. True he's hurt me and broken me in more ways than one; but he was the love of my life. I remember the few weeks we went without talking because he had decided to break up with me after finding out that I was a virgin, that I wanted to save myself for someone special. He left because he thought he wasn't special enough or worthy of me but to me he was everything. He came back on a rainy day to the factory where I was working, I was walking hopelessly back home resigned to my fate to be lonely and loveless. That's when he called out my name and rushed to my side in the rain. I knew he was the one for me even before that but something about that moment had sealed it in an unbreakable way. I loved him so much and gave him the power to break me, love does that. It's the ones we love the most that often break us and also redeem us. Ty was my home, this is where I belonged.

I know there was no easy way to say this to Rick; I had already broken his heart by saying I'd cheated on him. Now I was going to tell him that I'm choosing Ty over him. I pick up the phone and call Rick to inform him that I've made a decision and that I want us to meet at his place. The time with Rick has been like a dream but I'm not the one to be in this dream with him. He's healed me in ways I couldn't believe was possible and taught me to love myself first before I gave my heart to another. His friendship and sweetness were my pillar of strength that kept me going when Ty hadn't found the courage to let me know of his love. I feel disgusted with myself and with the cruelty of what I'm about to do. My heart aches for Rick because I can feel how painful this will be for him and yet I was helpless. There was only one man I could choose to be with.

I'm at Rick's house. The man who's been my best friend, whose sweetness has always made me smile, I was going to break his heart. We hug each other at the door and he leads me by my hand to the couch. We sit at the couch, he's facing me and I'm looking down, nervously playing with my fingers. My chest is beginning to hurt. "So Abby, have you made your decision?"

My tears give me away; my hands start shaking.

"Yes Rick, I'm going to try with Tyler."

Now my lips are shivering. My stomach feels like I'm free falling.

Rick absorbs what I say, pauses for a minute and then speaks.

"Do you know? I loved you since you were six. Did you know that Abby? I still have that ornament you made me at Christmas time when we were six? Did you know that? I would have made you so happy! I would have showed you how much I love you every day of your life."

His blue eyes are welling up with tears and I start to weep.

"I am sorry Rick, so sorry." I sob.

Then he continues to say,

"I will always love you Abby. You're the one that made me feel alive, you made me happy. Don't ever forget how beautiful you are inside and out. I will ask for a favor Abby: just stay with me tonight. Let me love you so you'll never forget how a man should love you."

I stayed. Don't know if it was right or wrong, but I didn't protest. I had already hurt him so much that it was hurting me. It was bittersweet; sad, poignant and wonderful at the same time. I've never been kissed as much as he kissed me tonight, his tenderness melts my heart and his tears mingled with mine as we held on to each other, savoring the final few hours of our sweet time together. He was heartbroken and my heart lay in pieces. I look into his blue eyes, grateful for the memories of the time I've had with him. We finally lay exhausted in each other's arms and fell asleep. Somewhere in the middle of the sleep, I heard someone say, as though in a dream. "You'll always be my girl. It's really and utterly hard to let you go. Only by the will of God will I survive this agonizing pain I feel for you Abby."

I fall asleep again, holding on to those sweet words. I feel kisses on my forehead, my cheeks and my lips. My eyes were heavy with sleep so I couldn't open to see who it was. It all felt like a dream I was having. □

Chapter 29

I wake up on Rick's bed. He left leaving a note on the bedside table for me to read.

It read like this.

"My beautiful Abby, by the time you read this letter I will be gone for the day. Stay as long as you need to. Don't know how to live without you Abby! Or what to say because every word I write hurts my aching heart or maybe should've just stayed and fought for you harder. I just want you to be happy. I am not a selfish man Abby. Wishing at this moment that I could be selfish because right now, feeling my heart is excruciating the life out of me. Don't cry anymore baby, it's not your fault that your heart belongs to someone else. Sorry, can't even say his name. He's a lucky man Abby, wishing I was in his shoes right now, I would kidnap you to Vegas and marry you so fast your pretty little head would spin. That's my regret Abby, not marrying you from the start. I just want to say this, if he treat's you wrong or can't appreciate what a beautiful woman you are, you come find me. I'll be waiting with open arms. You're holding my heart Abby, and as long as you have it you also could squeeze the life out of it until it bleeds. No one else can't fill my heart ever again just you Abby! If you ever change your mind find me, I will always be waiting my love. Don't change that heart of yours: that shyness, that innocence. I loved so much, okay baby. Go be happy. I wish you well. Can't say this doesn't hurt like hell, because it does. Well, you know how I feel. You really didn't tell me you love me ever, because your heart is with him, Remember, be treated as a queen. I'll miss you biting your bottom lip when you get nervous, and when you blush you really are adorable. You are by far more woman I ever met in my life. Be happy Abby, life is short don't waste any more time. If anyone deserves to be happy it's you Abby, Bye My True Love.

ALWAYS IN MY HEART

LOVE YOU,

RICK

I read the note and lay on his pillow, inhaling his scent, sobbing and holding on to the beautiful memories he's left me with. He loved me so much that he knew saying good bye for both of us would be like walking on coals of fire. Instead he chose to leave so that we don't have to face this ending in this manner. Rick is and always be an amazing man and friend. I feel blessed to have known him. He had so much to offer a woman and I pray he'd find someone worthy of his love and affection. I get up, use the restroom, and pack some of the stuff I've had left in his place from our time together. On top of the fireplace he has a shelf full of pictures when we were in school and when we got back together.

I weep inconsolably going around the house, cleaning up a little. Then I realize that what I thought I heard in a dream was not in a dream, it was the words Rick spoke to me. He said his goodbye to me when I was asleep.

The kisses I felt on my forehead, cheeks and lips were his. I'm crying, standing there next to the pile of pictures he's had since we were kids. I slip the beautiful engagement ring off of my finger and place it atop the photographs. I feel like a piece of my heart had been taken out when I did that. I was torn to shreds and I cannot imagine what he was feeling at that moment. I couldn't explain the pain or the numbness I was beginning to feel after I removed the ring. That ring held a lot of beautiful dreams of our future together, dreams that were now gone.

I had to leave this place because I was unable to breathe. I step out of Rick's home locking the door behind me, saying 'goodbye' to this beautiful home and the beautiful memories I've had with him. I drove back home in deathly silence, feeling a piece of rock was in place of my heart. I was numb with pain and feeling empty. I had hurt the only best friend I ever had.

I get back home and head straight to my kitchen and drink up a bottle of wine. I was drunk with sorrow so now it was time to be drunk with wine. I sing tunelessly "I Will Survive" by Gloria Gaynor out loud; it was the best woman song ever. I'm pretty sure if anyone sane was to see me singing and giggling out of drunken stupor, they'd find it pretty amusing. I'm hysterical midway through my drinking session and hate myself for breaking Rick's heart into pieces.

I'm crying now, drunk and numb when I hear a knock on my door. My body is aching but I drag myself to the door to open it.

I see Ty standing and staring at me and all I could think is how attractive he is. I can be so vain when I'm drunk….and I laugh to myself, because I was so pathetic.

"Abby are you okay? Are you drunk?" he asks, his face looking concerned.

I collapse to my knees, hands covering my face.

"I did it Tyler," I say with uncontrollable sobbing.

"Did what Abby?"

He's desperate to know. He puts me on his lap. Sobbing uncontrollably in his chest, he holds me so tight.

"Did what! Babe?"

"I hurt Rick so badly. I didn't mean to do it! He's gone. I chose you Tyler. I love you so much!"

Tyler starts weeping.

"You won't regret it, Abby, I promise."

Tyler took care of me that night, and every night after that. It wasn't like I was on a honeymoon. Truth be told, it took me awhile to get over Rick and what I'd done to him. Ty was patient with me, something I haven't seen in him before. He gave me time to heal and loved me enough; we had both learned to love the hard way. We both knew what it was to lose and we struggled admitting to ourselves how much we loved each other. No one gets it right the first time around and may be, things get better the second time around. It's true what they say, that time heals all wounds. Ty loved me in his own unique way. We learned to forgive and make room for our imperfections and flaws, no one was perfect. James & Jason's happiness knew no bounds when they found out that we were back together. Being together with these three precious people is now all that mattered to me. I was no longer picking after the broken pieces of my heart.

I was healed, whole and most importantly, home.

☐

Epilogue

Ten Years later Tyler and Abby are still together, now in their fifties. They text one another like teenagers. Who would have thought? The last ten years they never left each other's side. Yes, they went to work, always calling each other. They couldn't keep their hands off one another even now. So in love, their hearts were like pieces of a jigsaw puzzle that fit perfectly only when they were together. Tyler and Abby sold their individual houses and bought one big house; it was their world. Tyler stayed true to his word: he never made Abby sad or shed any tears. He loved her and he was faithful, giving her love, passion, everything in his heart and everything life had to offer. He treated her like a queen. They both got married right away. That was the happiest day of their life. Waking up every morning with a kiss and coffee, remember, Abby loved the simple life. Abby never saw Rick again, she just wished he found his happiness. She wished the best for him. Cynthia her best friend finally married Hunter and had two beautiful girls. Abby's sons James and Jason gave them two granddaughters. James has a six-year-old girl Kayla. She has blue eyes, dark brown curly hair and fair skin. She's beautiful and looks a lot like her mother. Jason is now Dad to a three-year-old, who he named Madison; she had the trademark Ty eyes, those slanted green emerald eyes and also has her grandpa's famous dimple. Abby was happy for her sons that they found the loves of their lives.

Life is a journey. Abby always felt there were angels around her. There will always be up and downs. There will always be love and loss, that's what makes people strong in the end. Not everything will be perfect. There will be many mistakes. This world will always be a challenge. What we do about it will be up to us. Megan was happy with her life. Abby and Megan always stayed in touch and their bond had only grown strong over the years. Megan and Abby had learned about life the hard way, that life is what people make of it. Though Abby was broken, beaten and shattered for the most part of her life, the cracks in her heart had allowed the light and beauty of her soul to shine through. She eventually forgave Maria for the wounds she'd inflicted on her as a young child. Abby also finally forgave herself for all the times she thought she should end her life. Life is tough and rough around the edges; it will amaze you, break you, test you, comfort you and mold you in ways you can never imagine. Each one has a purpose and a lesson to learn in this life and endurance is a big part of it. Love, faith and hope will always be the foundation on which lives will be built; it's the only things that will survive through the storms of life.

Abby's heart was finally at peace both with herself and the world outside. She had overcome many obstacles throughout her life and now she was ready to savor the fruit of her labor and struggle.

Paul is now a Dad; he had a rough life but now he has a son and a daughter. Paul and his wife are settled in Florida. Uncle Mario had a heart attack but he's recovering well.

Abby once met Josh at the market. He was married to Emily and had five children but still seemed sad.

Tyler and Abby walk hand in hand wherever they went. They laughed, kissed and talked like they had just fallen in love; and in many ways, it was like they had found each other again. They never looked back, only forward. Life seemed wonderful and no one would've guessed they'd be together three decades later. Abby had no regrets about the choice she made. There were no more broken pieces.

Other Books by Martha Perez

In The Dark

These Eyes Have Seen

Novels

Broken Pieces

Broken Heart
Broken Dreams,

www.marthaperez.info

www.brokenpieces.rocks

https://www.facebook.com/marthasbooks

https://twitter.com/MarthaPerezBook

https://www.goodreads.com/author/show/15162126.Martha_Perez/blog

https://www.instagram.com/marthaperez5020

About the Author

Martha was born and raised in Los Angeles, CA. She now lives in West Covina, CA with her dog, Sugar Bear. She has a son, a daughter and two granddaughters. Her hobbies include reading, writing, exercise and long walks.

www.ingramcontent.com/pod-product-compliance
Lightning Source LLC
Chambersburg PA
CBHW030100170426
43198CB00009B/434